Rewiring The
BRAIN

REWIRING THE
BRAIN

LIVING WITHOUT STRESS AND ANXIETY THROUGH
THE POWER OF CONSCIOUSNESS

RAJNISH ROY

Copyright © 2007 by Rajnish Roy.

Library of Congress Control Number:		2007904895
ISBN:	Hardcover	978-1-4257-5975-9
	Softcover	978-1-4257-5969-8

All rights reserved. No part of this book may be reproduced or transmitted in any form or by any means, electronic or mechanical, including photocopying, recording, or by any information storage and retrieval system, without permission in writing from the copyright owner.

This book was printed in the United States of America.

To order additional copies of this book, contact:
Xlibris Corporation
1-888-795-4274
www.Xlibris.com
Orders@Xlibris.com
39251

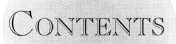

Contents

Chapter 1: The Predicament of Stress 15
- The Predicament of Stress 16
- The Lure of Beliefs 18
- The Inescapable Self 19
- Our Brain: A Divided House 20
- Search for a Lasting Solution 23
- Access to the Power of Consciousness 25
- The Traditional Meditation 28
- Awareness Meditation 29
- The Possibility of Rewiring the Brain 30
- Limits of Traditional Meditation 32

Chapter 2: Memory: The Prime Mover 35
- The Functional Modes of Memory 37
- The Categories of Memory 38
- Impulses of Dynamic Images 40
- The Edifice of Self on the Pillars of Memory 44
- A Conditioning Factor 46
- The Associative Nature 47
- The Pros and Cons of the Associative Quality 48
- A Catalyst of Stress 49
- Symbiosis With Intelligence 51
- The Virtues of Self-observation 53

Chapter 3: Thought: The Errand Boy 55
- Images and Verbal Symbols 56
- An Intelligent Order 59

- The Errand Boy..61
- An Element of Reflex and Rigidity 64
- Cognition and Creative Intelligence 66
- The Limits of Thought..69
- The Perception of Reality 71
- Symbiosis With Emotions and Feelings 74
- The Role of Thought in Stress 76
- A Culprit and Benefactor 76

Chapter 4: Emotions and Feelings...78
- Distinction Between Emotion and Feeling............................79
- Biological and Psychological Desires 81
- Conflict Between Emotion and Thought 82
- Evolutionary Schism..83
- The Creative Force Behind Relationships 86
- Evolutionary Tools for Preserving Life 88
- Intelligence and Emotions. 90
- Role in Stress and Depression..93
- Background Emotions and Feelings 95
- Anxieties and Worries..97
- Background Anxieties and Worries...99
- Shaping Human Destiny 100

Chapter 5: Consciousness 103
- The Question of Consciousness...104
- An Entity Without Thought and Memory 107
- The Conscious and Unconscious Mind 109
- Cognition and Consciousness 112
- The Mother of all Feelings 113
- The Global Quality of Consciousness 114
- Memory and Consciousness 116
- The Question of Self and Consciousness.............................117
- The Binding Problem 120
- Enhanced Access to Consciousness 124

Chapter 6: Expansion of Inner Awareness.. 128
- Widening the Horizon of Awareness 130
- The Limits of Positive Thinking..131
- Awareness Meditation 133
- Diffusion of Intelligence 134
- The Traditions of Yoga—Benefits and Pitfalls....................135
- Precautions in Meditation..139

- The Journey Within 141
- The Techniques of Awareness Meditation 141
- Physical Aspects 142
- The Mental Process 146
- The Hyperactive Brain 147
- Practical Guidelines 149
- Some Safeguards 151

Chapter 7: Benefits of Awareness Meditation 155
- An Instrument of Inner Inquiry 156
- The Ancient Origin 158
- The Benefits of Meditation 160
- Stress and Vitamin Deficiencies 162
- Stress and Accelerated Aging 163
- Impact on Illnesses 166
- The Neurology of Meditation 167
- The Advantages of Awareness Meditation 169
- The Myth of Individualism 170
- Aristotelian Catharsis 171
- The Futility of Punching a Pillow 172
- Meditative Catharsis 173
- The Illusion of Dualism 176
- Purgation of Emotive Afflictions 176

Chapter 8: Rewiring the Brain 179
- A Gateway to the Unconscious 181
- Blocking the Sensory Traffic 182
- The Gatekeeper 185
- Strengthening the Brain's Relay Station 188
- Rewiring the Brain 189
- A New Order in the Brain 191
- Enhancement of Innate Intelligence 194
- Tackling Emotive Preponderance 195
- The Dangers of Mood-Enhancing Drugs 197
- Children and Meditation 199
- Adverse Effects of Meditation 201
- Evolutionary Destiny 204

Chapter 9: A Second Brain and Anxieties 208
- The Second Brain 209
- A Nerve Plexus and Meditation 211
- Diffusing Fear and Nervousness 214

- Search for a Neural Basis 215
- Tackling Stress and Anxieties 218
- Empirical Corroborations 222
- Antidepressant Role of the Vagus Nerve 225
- The Nebulous Matter of Heart 228

Chapter 10: Sleep, Theta Brain Waves, and Meditation 231
- Sleep Deficiency and Mortality Hazard 232
- Evolutionary Payoff 233
- The Sleep Cycles 234
- Sleep and Meditation 235
- Theta Rhythm and Memory 237
- Learning and Attention 239
- Theta Rhythm and Holistic Perception 241
- Theta Rhythm and Meditation 242
- The Stuff of Dream 244
- Meditation and Dreams 247

Index 251

DEDICATION

To NIRMALA,

without whose inspiration and untiring support

this book would never have been written.

Preface

Though at one level, stress is the running thread of this book, its scope is much wider. The larger focus is to *forge acquaintance* with one's *self* by understanding its constructs of feelings, thoughts, memories, and why one behaves the way one does. It is an exploratory journey in our inner world, where the roots of our aspirations, ambitions, pride, and prejudice lie. We go through myriads of joys and sorrows in the long course of life, but hardly have the patience to pause and ponder over the reasons that make them.

Does it matter? Yes, much more than perhaps one realizes.

Stress should not be seen as an isolated issue. It betrays the quality of individual *self* in its ceaseless action of living. We have one and only life—the most precious thing we happen to possess, and it is but natural that we struggle hard to do our utmost to make it a wonderful experience. Stress, in its overt or covert forms, works as a persistent factor that undermines the spontaneity, joy, and beauty of life.

In this competitive and complex world, one faces countless factors of stress that are unavoidable and immutable, including illness, accident, or death. There are some other factors that can be altered through efforts, which play a more decisive role in life. These are individual attitude, mental tendencies, and ways one interacts with external world. There is much truth in the saying, "Life is 10 percent what happens to you and 90 percent how you react to it."

An objective understanding of these individual factors means that half the battle of tackling stress is won. Hence, the book seeks to help the reader face and understand the workings of inner self and its intricacies without resorting to psychological escape or suppression.

Yet an objective understanding is only the first step. It does not resolutely change our mental habits and conditionings that are hardwired in the brain. The negative emotions that fuel stress and anxiety have unyielding force, often not amenable to reason. Similarly, drills of positive thinking and self-hypnotism through beliefs and ideologies accrue only temporary solace and euphoria that wears off sooner than expected.

This suggests the need to go beyond the remedies prevalent now and look for fundamentally new avenues for solution. In such effort, this book explores the possibility of using *the power of consciousness to rewire the brain* and tackle stress and emotional afflictions in a lasting manner. Let me add that this approach does not involve any religious or mystical beliefs.

It is an irrefutable fact that consciousness embodies our unique sense of self and its complex architecture. Moreover, all our mental processes like feelings, memories, and thoughts are not only rooted in consciousness but sustained by it. It is logical that harnessing the power of consciousness, the primordial source of all mental phenomena, will unfold unique possibilities to tackle negative emotions and anxieties that rob us of the charm and joy of the miracle of life.

A theoretical debate is being waged relentlessly among experts on the mysteries and elusive nature of consciousness. However, not much research is done on the practical use of the power of consciousness for tackling the human predicament of stress and anxiety. In my view, it holds amazing prospects of practical benefits for humanity, with implications for its future evolution. A person can have an increased access to the power of consciousness through its intrinsic property of inner (nonverbal) awareness that is devoid of activities of thought and memories.

PREFACE

This book outlines certain ways to access the power of consciousness, which entail benefits such as enhancement of memory, mental power, and learning ability. Besides alleviating stress and anxiety, it brings about emotional equilibrium and slows down the aging process. The practical methods and benefits are outlined in a scientific spirit and correlated with research by neuroscientists, psychologists, and medical institutes.

The methods of using *nonverbal awareness* demand stronger commitment and sustained efforts, but the reward is worth the time and patience. The book does not offer shortcuts or peripheral solutions, because none exists. Neither does it offer self-hypnosis and gratifying beliefs that are concealed in prescriptive actions and mental drills.

* * *

My deep gratitude is due to several well-known philosophers and neuroscientists whose writings influenced me. Prominent among the great thinkers are Jiddu Krishnamurti, David Bohm, and Swami Vivekananda. Among the scientists, the brilliant works of Carl Sagan, Antonio Damasio, Francis Crick, and Bernard J. Baars helped me understand, in some measure, the workings of the human brain. I am also very grateful to other scientists and experts whose names and research have been mentioned to corroborate some aspects of the theme of this book. However, any inaccuracies or mistakes in the book are entirely my own shortcomings.

Let me also express my gratitude to those who directly helped me in this venture. First, I owe immense debt to Nirmala Roy, who fervently and persistently counseled me to take up the task of writing. This book would not have materialized without her constant encouragement and positive appraisals. I am indebted to Andrew Smith and Sandra Smith, who readily accepted the arduous task of reading the manuscript and offering many insightful suggestions that enhanced the clarity of the book. I am grateful to Pramod Kumar Mehta for his valuable suggestions. My thanks to Patrick Costelo and Tiffany Arranguez for their feedback and support in giving the final shape to the book.

I thank Renu and Leena for their analytic comments, which helped in crystallizing some of my ideas. I cannot forget the invaluable contribution by Amit in creating the illustrations that have enhanced the comprehensibility of the book

Chapter 1

Introduction: The Predicament of Stress

The modern mind is in complete disarray. Knowledge has stretched itself to the point where neither the world nor our intelligence can find any foot-hold. It is a fact that we are suffering from nihilism.
—Albert Camus

In the long course of the evolution of life, the human species is endowed with a formidable and complex brain with enormous memory and thinking power that helped it subjugate practically all other forms of life on this planet. Many varieties of flora and fauna are decimated and made extinct by man, which earned him the dubious distinction of being the greatest predator of all. Humankind has won the evolutionary battle of competition for survival against other animals and creatures. Unfortunately, the paradigm of competition has turned upon us like the proverbial genie, and now we are fated to compete among ourselves! The world is plagued with cut-throat competition at every step in our lives, and its devastating consequences are manifest everywhere.

Of course, on one side, the paradigm of competition has worked as a driving force behind the enormous progress made by humankind in the economic and technological spheres. It has been instrumental in creating immense wealth and material comforts that are unprecedented. On the other hand, the culture of competition has its excesses and perilous consequences. Rampant commercialism and stress are the two pernicious products of the competitive ethos of the modern age. In turn, commercialism has created the evil of unbridled consumerism, which is surreptitiously dragging humanity toward environmental disasters, like global warming threatening the very existence of life on this planet. The ecosystem of this tiny planet is placed under such tremendous pressure that its capacity for sustaining life is on the brink of collapse. Again, the commercial interests of nations have failed in addressing the environmental problems and ignoring the welfare and rights of future generations.

An objective perception beyond the dazzle of the modern luxuries would reveal that we are in a much dire situation than our ancestors were some millennia ago in terms of mental peace and health. Even if that is brushed aside as a romantic illusion of a bygone era, it is certain that we are moving slowly but surely toward a suicidal crisis, given the colossal problems of environmental degradation, weapons of mass destruction, terrorism, and spread of diseases like AIDS, obesity, and diabetes. On top of that, we have stress as the biggest killer in modern times.

The evolutionists tell us that many species on this planet became extinct on their own by hitting the dead ends of their evolutionary progression. Hopefully, it should not happen that while impulsively sharing the same fate, we get snared in the dazzling dead end of technologies and commercialism. It reminds us of Albert Einstein's quote, "It has become appallingly obvious that our technology has exceeded our humanity."

THE PREDICAMENT OF STRESS

In the earlier stage of evolution, competition among different species was quite simple at the physical level. But now among human beings, it is more complex and increasingly on a psychological plane. It is no wonder that mental stress and depression have become very painful and devastating afflictions of our time. Much worse than that, stress is a silent killer that keeps corroding the mind and body slowly and surreptitiously. The fiercely competitive world that we have built has abundant uncertainties and insecurity of mind. Such insecurity is often not apparent, but gets manifested as persistent anxieties and psychological fears that wreak havoc in our lives.

Besides being an accelerating factor for aging, stress is a cause of illnesses like high blood pressure, heart attack, and gastrointestinal disorders. It is considered a risk factor in cancer and diabetes. Scientists have found that stress and persistent anxiety can weaken the immune system that protects us against diseases. Stress also distorts thinking and undermines the ability of clear perception and planning. Given these facts, it is no exaggeration to call stress the mother of many illnesses.

As defined by psychologists, stress is an unpleasant state of emotional and physiological arousal experienced by people in situations perceived as painful and fearful. During stress, the heart beats rapidly, blood pressure goes up, breathing becomes shorter and faster, and muscle tension rises. One also experiences a dry mouth and perspiration. Incessant anxieties and worries that have become so common and pervasive in our lives are the manifestations of stress. Fear, largely psychological, is the underlying factor behind stress.

We feel stress when we are under pressure at work and have deadlines to meet or a difficult boss to face. People feel acute stress due to the loss of a job, death of a loved one, problems in interpersonal relationship, or serious illness. Daily hassles like getting stuck in traffic, commuting to work, and noisy neighborhood are some of the causes of routine stress. Persistent or habitual stress can arise from psychological factors such as low self-esteem, traumatic past experience, and imaginary fears of some situations or individuals.

Of course, it is not possible to prevent the external causes of stress like the death of a relative, accident, or illness. There are several such factors that are beyond the control of a person. So how do we address the problems of stress and anxiety? Do we take that as a natural predicament and carry on with passive acceptance? Obviously, that is not a right thing to do. There is a lot we can do to not only reduce but eliminate stress and anxiety, and thus transform our lives. We can, if determined, live life much more *intelligently*. This book aims to explore that.

Notwithstanding the inescapable causes from the external world, a scope certainly exists within everyone's reach for living without anxiety and stress. For that, one has to realize the crucial fact that our attitude and habits are largely responsible for a large bulk of stress in our life. In other words, most of our mental mortifications are of our own making and hence within our own control. Even the stress factors arising from the external realities, though unavoidable, would not inflict so much agony and trouble as we usually experience if we change our ways of tackling them. Yes, it is easier said than done.

We have to realize the fact that the most crucial and central part of the realities of world is *our own self*. The entity of self is nothing but a construct of our own feelings, thoughts, memories, aspirations as well as our pride and prejudices. There is no escape whatsoever from facing them and understanding them if we wish to have lasting solutions of our problems of stress and anxiety. It is not such a daunting task as we normally tend to believe. This book focuses on some innovative methods that encompass the inner workings of our self and rewire the brain to remold our attitude and habitual perceptions.

THE LURE OF BELIEFS

There are countless books on management of stress encompassing positive thinking, psychological counseling, and religious guidance. These books prescribe drills of how to conduct oneself and actions to be pursued with determination. Some writers assure their readers that within every one of them there is an unexplored treasure of extraordinary abilities and potentials for all that one wishes to achieve. Some profess that we are ultimately a divine spirit or soul representing an essence of God. Others promise the same utopian escape from the mundane self, but in a more fashionable garb of scientific idiom stating that we possess *quantum self* that transcends the humdrum of thoughts, emotions, and our earthly frailties. It is not for the laypersons like us to understand the seemingly eerie world of quantum physics, which is said to represent the ultimate subatomic state of the universe, let alone challenge its application to self as such.

Yet it is an open question whether this vast and varied bulk of attractive literature brings the real and lasting solution we seek to alleviate our predicament of stress. One can, of course, create or borrow beliefs and wishful ideas to insulate oneself from the inexorable realities of life, but one cannot go on like that for long and be truly happy. How long, under the weight of such beliefs, can we suppress and hide our sorrows, painful thoughts, and feelings, which are part and parcel of the realities of self? These realities are unforgiving and irrepressible, which sooner or later erupt with vengeance or remain hidden to manipulate our behavior and life from within.

These books initially give us the hope and thrill in the belief of finding the panacea of all our problems, but soon our enthusiasm wears off, and we find ourselves back in square one. At best, such literature provides some temporary benefits and solace. The main reason for its inadequacy is that it feeds the readers largely with beliefs and ideals. Intentionally or otherwise, such literature persuades us to practice self-hypnotism and auto-suggestions through sets of ideas that are supposed to inculcate better behavioral patterns and habits. Such external imposition of beliefs and ideologies, however noble and well meaning, leads to ignoring and suppressing what we actually are. Any attempt to impose a projected ideal of self by negating the actual self is fundamentally flawed.

This book, therefore, does not offer any solace and gratification of beliefs or constructs of thoughts to cover up the ugliness and rough edges of self. In fact, it seeks to caution against such psychological contrivances that some people seek to escape from the unpleasant realities of life. In the same vein of logic, it is advisable to be on guard against the possibility of turning what has been stated in this book into another set of borrowed beliefs and ideas. Healthy skepticism and scrutiny are, no doubt, very rewarding tools. By using them, the reading of this book is intended to be an investigative journey encompassing one's actual life.

THE INESCAPABLE SELF

This book is thematically divided in two parts. The first part is preamble that deals with our inner world of memory, thought, emotions, and feelings. The second is an operative part that focuses on how to tackle stress and anxiety. It outlines certain practical methods that can offer a more effective and lasting solution to the predicament of stress.

One would wonder why we can't avoid the abstract issues of emotions and memory and instead deal straightway with the practical issues of managing stress. I feel that in order to find a lasting solution, it is essential to have some working knowledge of how these mental processes operate. They are not only the ingredients of stress but also the elements that constitute our self as such.

Astonishingly, we remain stranger to *our self* and carry on in an autonomic mode driven by these psychic forces. It reminds of what T. S. Eliot said, "The substratum of our being, to which we rarely penetrate; for our lives are mostly a constant evasion of ourselves." That is the reason why more often we find ourselves against a blind wall. The first part of the book is essentially introductory to forge acquaintance with our self.

I am afraid the story of our inner world goes on a bit further. An endeavour to glean understanding of our emotions, thought, and memory needs to culminate logically in a discussion on the vital core or the *gravitational* centre of self, namely, consciousness. It brings to my mind a comparison with the black hole. The enormous gravity of a black hole binds together and controls the rotation of an entire galaxy of stars, planets, and dark matter. Similarly, consciousness with its underlying force encompasses and governs our self and its integral parts like thoughts, emotions, feelings, and memories.

The question of consciousness is an immense challenge and a conundrum of endless debate among scientists and philosophers. I do not claim to throw new light on it, nor do I aim to do it. Why then talk about it at all? The simple answer is that we cannot escape it, even if we desire, because *we have* consciousness. It is not a strange commodity existing far off in some corner of the world as an object of curiosity and research for experts. It is a reality with which we wrestle day and night whether we like it or not, whether we understand it or not.

Hence we have to make at least some *practical sense* of consciousness in order to know how it governs our behavior. We need to feel its impact and dynamic force, which make what we are in our actions, thoughts, and dreams. For doing so, it is not necessary to understand the full nature of consciousness, which is, in any way, a formidable challenge. However, it is imperative to find out how that mysterious entity is related to the questions of stress and anxiety.

This book is guided by a practical purpose to explore the possibility of using the *power of consciousness* to alleviate and even eliminate the problem of stress. It does not aim to investigate the nature of consciousness and its mysteries. That is better left to the philosophers and scientists who are quite seized with the profound puzzle of consciousness. Though they have not been able to fully unravel its mysteries, a great deal of progress has been achieved.

OUR BRAIN: A DIVIDED HOUSE

I have no doubt that *the thought-based solutions* have inherent limits in dealing with the negative feelings and memories that obstinately fuel stress and anxieties. That is the reason why most of our determinations to correct our ways of thinking and behavior, as counseled in the books on positive thinking and moral guidance, are unsuccessful or short-lived. Our determinations to become better are essentially thought based. Of course, such intentions are tinged with the feelings of enthusiasm and seriousness to become something, but again these are the feelings incited by rational thoughts and no match with the inexorable power of the negative emotions of fear, sorrow, and anger.

Our daily experience testifies that thought is *a weaker force* in comparison to emotions, feelings, and memory. For instance, our rational thoughts tell us that irritation and anger not only distort but make our perceptions downright wrong, leading to complications in life. Yet it is very difficult to restrain a surge of anger. Similarly, we know that many of our worries and anxieties are baseless and uncalled for, and yet our reasoning power is utterly impotent to stave off these *psychic predators*. Reason tells us that it is stupid to remain disturbed with the fear of an arrogant boss. Yet often we remain bogged down in the quagmire of fear and nervousness even though we know that such feelings cripple our intelligence and erode our energy.

Throughout our life, we often bemoan and agonize over such helplessness and vexatious contradictions within us. There may be some neurological reasons why the thought-based actions have very limited impact on emotions and feelings. Let us explore.

Experts tell us that the brain consists of three broad evolutionary segments, namely, the reptilian complex, limbic region, and the neocortex. The reptilian complex is a small nucleic part of the brain that contains some remnants of the oldest phase of our evolution when life existed mainly in the form of reptiles. In the next phase when life evolved as mammals with limbs, the brain developed a new region called the limbic system around the reptilian complex. Our aggressiveness and ritualistic tendencies come mainly from the reptilian complex, while the primary emotions originate from the limbic system (Carl Sagan, *The Dragons of Eden: Speculations on the Evolution of Human Intelligence* [New York: Ballantine Books, 1977], 58).

The implicit (hidden) memories and primary emotions of fear, sorrow, anger, and pleasure are located mainly in these two ancient regions. The neocortex is the third and much-larger segment of the brain, which is evolutionarily a modern acquisition (see fig. 1.1). It is the seat of reason, thinking, long-term memory, working memory, and emotions called social emotions such as compassion, sympathy, pride, wonder, and shame that are typically human.

Our brain is therefore not a single monolithic entity, but an incremental product evolved over a long course of evolution to meet the demands of diverse circumstances. The divide between the ancient and modern regions of the brain accounts for why our thought-based actions exert very little influence on our habits and conditionings of mind that are driven by the primary emotions and memories in the ancient brain.

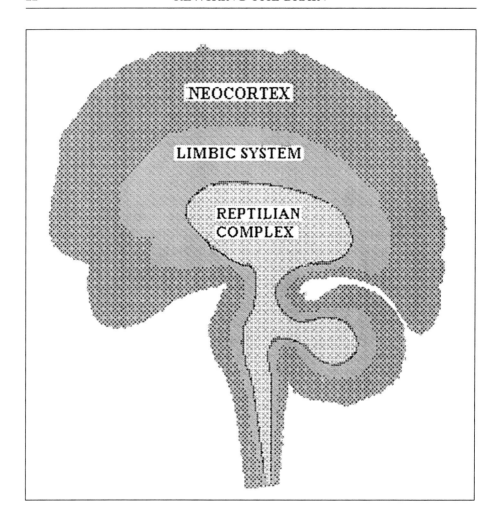

Figure 1.1. Broad evolutionary stages of the brain.

One might argue that the ancient and modern regions of the brain are integrated closely, and the divide hardly matters. Of course, these regions have symbiotic dependence on each other; but it is also a fact that they have their distinctions and territorial supremacies, which are asserted frequently and sometimes forcefully. Notwithstanding such arguments, the impotency of our determinations and reason to prevail over negative emotions and memories is an undeniable fact of life. Hence, beliefs and determinations, which are intrinsically constructs of thoughts, have transient or insignificant impact.

SEARCH FOR A LASTING SOLUTION

So how do we extricate ourselves from this seemingly helpless situation and alleviate stress? An innovative approach has to be found. Logically, it appears that we need to look deeper into our self and find a way to operate at the *subterranean layers* of mind beyond the realm of thought. That sounds not just astounding but impossible, because normally we know only how to operate at the level of thought. We are deeply conditioned to use the route of thought to resolve our problems and achieve our goals. In its absence, we experience a sort of vacuum and seem to sink into darkness, a sort of black hole that dissolves our individual identity. In the state that is devoid of thought, many persons experience a fear of their individuality being obliterated. We are used to the verbal state so much that a nonverbal state sounds terrifying on the face of it.

Of course, the idea to look for a different route than that of thought should not be misconstrued as an advocacy to downgrade or negate thoughts. Anyway, negating thought for a long time is nearly impossible, let alone the fact that it is psychologically unhealthy. Also, one should not forget that with the help of its prolific thinking power, humanity has built great civilizations and made astounding progress in science and technology.

The other alternative then in our search for a solution might be the possibility of using positive feelings to diffuse the negative ones. But that is equally ineffective and often not feasible at all. For instance, when one is hurt or in deep sorrow, no amount of happy feelings, inducted through external means, can wipe out the pain and agony. Moreover, such attempts would constitute suppression of feelings in the same way as seeking diversions to escape sorrow and fear. Unfortunately, such emotions refuse to go away. They remain hidden and manipulate our behavior covertly.

Does it mean that we have nowhere to go for help? Perhaps the last arbiter that can rescue us is the power of consciousness. This owes further explanation. Though the question of consciousness is discussed more comprehensively in a separate chapter, some brief remarks are pertinent here.

As laypersons we have an empirical notion of the conscious mind that includes thoughts, feelings, memory, reasoning power, and linguistic ability, which are experienced explicitly. Further, our explicit sense of self is anchored in it. It is also narrowly referred as *consciousness*. For instance, when one is awake from sleep or anaesthesia, one has regained consciousness. In other words, it represents the theatre of mind wherein the actors of thoughts, feelings, and memory play out their incessant drama in the clear daylight of consciousness.

However, behind the stage in the darkness, there are other more important players, namely, the prompters, directors, and string pullers. These invisible players are our hidden memories, mental conditionings, roots of our emotions and feelings that lie beyond our conscious reach. That is the subterranean world of the unconscious. In the nineteenth century, the well-known psychologists Sigmund Freud and Carl Jung wrote extensively on the powerful influence of the unconscious on human behavior. The modern neuroscientists and psychologists have gone further and dealt more comprehensively with the issues of the unconscious mind.

Obviously, conscious mind and the unconscious (or subconscious) are two divisions of the same larger entity that is referred to as the mysterious consciousness. It is the whole iceberg. The tip being seen is the conscious mind, while the larger subterranean part is the unconscious that is more powerful and governs the former. When I mention consciousness, I mean this wider entity of consciousness. Also, the question of using the power of consciousness refers to that larger entity.

However, one would wonder about how to use the power of consciousness when there seems to be hardly any conscious access to its major chunk, namely, the unconscious.

William James, the great psychologist, whose writings command much respect and authority among modern psychologists until now, has stated in his book *The Varieties of Religious Experience* that a spiritual person has *more access* to his consciousness. Even if one makes allowance for skepticism on the conceptual entity of a spiritual person, William James makes a very notable point implying that a possibility of *more access* to consciousness does exist. In my view, he also implies that more access to consciousness is essential for, rather integral to, emotional equilibrium as well as a deeper understanding of self, which a spiritual person is supposed to signify.

One does not require enlightenment from experts to see the importance of the power of consciousness. We have enough experience and evidence in our daily lives. For instance, when we are confronted with a difficult problem, we apply our power of consciousness to tackle it. In other words, we use the abilities of *attention and understanding*, which are, as acknowledged by experts, the inherent properties of consciousness. When we deal with a given issue in a perfunctory manner, we do not deeply access the power of consciousness, the primordial source of innate intelligence.

Such instances in our daily lives, however, constitute a very limited use of the full resources of consciousness. Even our acts of deep attention in daily life, represent the random and occasional instances of utilizing larger resources of consciousness. We prefer to float on the surface and tend not to operate from the inner depth of consciousness as a *normal and consistent mode*. Our problem of stress owes its existence to the fact that we suffer from overdependence on the machinery of thought, resulting in a diminished access to the power of consciousness.

In neurological terms, the modern human beings have ended up in having a hyperactive neocortex that causes stress and depression by a constant and frantic outpouring of sensory signals to other regions of the brain. In this way, we have subordinated and eclipsed the ancient parts of the brain, where the core of our consciousness and the roots of our intelligence and emotions lie. Though thought is an important part of consciousness, it normally operates peripherally and that too in relatively *a narrow band* of consciousness. This is borne out by the fact that the quality of thought certainly gets enhanced when it flows from the depth of consciousness or with an increased application of intelligence, which is an inherent property of consciousness.

In order to ensure emotional equilibrium and to trace out the roots of our anxieties and stress, we require more access to inner consciousness than what we routinely have. The voice of thought is unfortunately not heard effectively in the subterranean world of emotions, memories, and mental conditionings that are prewired. Consciousness being the foundational structure that sustains and supports all mental processes has the power to diffuse negative emotions and feelings, the ingredients of stress and anxieties.

Humanity at its present juncture needs to restore a balance between the ancient regions of the brain and the modern region. In other words, that would require reducing the hyperactivity of the neocortex. It would call for stronger underpinning of the machinery of thought through an enhanced access to the sentient power of consciousness.

ACCESS TO THE POWER OF CONSCIOUSNESS

That would lead to the following crucial questions: How can we integrate and balance the functions of the different regions of the brain? How can we have more access to consciousness? How can we command the services of inner consciousness to extricate us from the predicament of anxiety and stress?

The answer to this lies in the role of *inner awareness* or *nonverbal consciousness* that can serve as a vital bridge between the conscious and the unconscious parts of the brain. Awareness, like intelligence., is another intrinsic property of consciousness. The inner awareness with its nonverbal power is the only instrument available to the conscious mind to reach closest to the unconscious segment of consciousness. It is in the unconscious where not only the roots of our behavior and self lie but also the mysteries of consciousness.

The sensory or neural signals are a two-way traffic between the conscious and unconscious segments of our brain (see fig. 1.2). The nonverbal consciousness or inner awareness that is devoid of thought and memories is the gateway for the sensory traffic. The sensory outflow from the unconscious and the nonverbal consciousness is experienced at the conscious level as thoughts, feelings, urges, and explicit memories. On the other hand the sensory activities in the conscious mind can either evoke emotions, memories, and desires from the nonverbal consciousness and the unconscious or leave behind impressions there for storage. The role of nonverbal consciousness as a gatekeeper of sensory traffic is discussed with more details in chapter 8, "Rewiring the Brain."

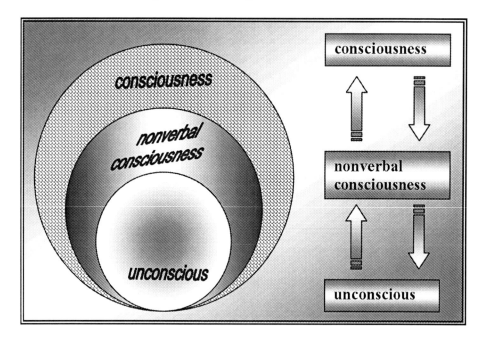

Figure 1.2. Two-way flow of the sensory signals.

One can still argue that the deeper reach of inner awareness does not mean full access to the unconscious mind, which can enable us to manipulate the unconscious as we desire. This is a valid point, but strengthening of inner awareness, which is not different from more access to consciousness, works wonders in the sense that it weakens the autocratic and rigid force of the unconscious over the conscious. Strangely, somehow it empowers the conscious mind to question and resist significantly, though not totally, the arbitrary force of the unconscious that often makes us—our thoughts, memories, and emotions—operate in a slavish and autonomic mode. This autonomic force gets hold of our mind, particularly when we are caught up in stress, anxieties, and worries, and we find ourselves helpless against our own self.

It is a surprising fact that not only our memories and emotions but most of our thoughts tend to be autonomic and habitual. Our common belief that we always think and act under the guidance of our intelligent will power is more often an illusion than we realize. The reflex quality that is inherent in many of our emotional reactions and thoughts is accountable for numerous psychological mortifications as well as problems of societal conflicts, violence, and terrorism. Unfortunately, we hardly question *our self*—a habit of blind faith in our subjective self.

The strengthening of inner consciousness allows the conscious mind to extend further and, in fact, reclaim significantly its intelligent and wise authority over the realm of the unconscious. It ushers in a wise order in the theatre of mind that otherwise allows the actors of thought, emotions, and memories to play out melodramas more wilfully than we relish. It brings in a new experience of liberty—an assertion of a *basic human right* to act freely and more dynamically against the autocratic regime of the unconscious! It will neutralise the negative agents of that regime, namely, anxieties and worries that fuel stress and depression.

How do we strengthen our inner awareness to eliminate stress? That is the theme of this book. It explores some concrete modalities that help establish a healthy balance of our thinking and reasoning abilities vis-à-vis the interplay of memory and emotions. It suggests how consciousness with its inherent property of intelligence can be made to act *nonverbally* as an overall governing force that enlightens our mental activities and behavior without having to resort to externalities of beliefs and ideologies. Such externalities, though fascinating and gratifying, are intrinsically coercive and suppressive.

The main modality for accessing the power of consciousness, which will be elucidated in this book, is *awareness meditation*. It is somewhat different from the traditional varieties of meditation. After persistent endeavours of nearly two decades with an investigative spirit, I have found it to be an amazingly effective instrument that endows marvellous benefits. Before explaining awareness meditation and how it differs from other varieties, let me make some pertinent remarks on the traditional meditation.

THE TRADITIONAL MEDITATION

Nowadays, traditional meditation has found much wider acceptance around the globe. It was reported by the *Time* magazine (August 2003) that nearly 11 million people in the USA alone practice meditation. Similarly in many other countries, people have discovered the virtues of meditation. Many schools and colleges now offer the facilities to their students for practising meditation, and some commercial organizations also extend such facilities to their employees. Many intellectuals and avowed rationalists have embraced it. Of course, any popular following per se cannot be cited as a proof of validity of any discipline. Let us look into why meditation has commanded such a wide popularity.

The main reason behind this is the substantial body of research that has been carried out independently on meditation by many scientists and medical institutes. The profound advancement in science and technology has made it possible to observe the actual neural activities as they occur in the brain. Neurologists and researchers have been able to use highly sensitive scanning devices to observe the changes taking places in different regions of the brain as the meditators progress into deeper meditation. Other studies observed groups of meditators and nonmeditators over a definite period to monitor the biochemical changes such as the level of stress hormones in blood, impact on the immune system, blood pressure, consumption of oxygen, and reduction of heartbeat.

The results of such independent studies, which have been described in the latter part of this book, were found to be mutually corroborative. These studies have unequivocally confirmed not only the antistress benefits of meditation, but also its remarkably positive impact on the immune system, aging, and overall physical and mental health.

Furthermore, some scientists have observed that regular meditation enhances the level of theta wave rhythm of the brain, which is implicated in learning, attentional activity, deep relaxation, and long-term memory encoding. Meditation thus holds substantial prospects for enhancing memory and alleviating the attention deficit disorder (ADD) that is widely prevalent among children and even adults.

One more reason for its acceptance has been the direct and incontrovertible benefits realized by those who practiced meditation seriously, irrespective of whether they knew of the supportive conclusions of the scientific research or not. Any discerning practitioner would also find that the positive impact of meditation is by no means a wishful product of faith or self-hypnotism.

Notwithstanding the well-established discoveries by scientists and medical institutes, some skepticism and preconceived notions still persist among many people due to reasons that are not entirely invalid. First, the vested interests have touted meditation as not only a panacea for all illnesses and problems in life, but also made deceptive claims of supernatural powers. Second, the pervasive ethos of commercialism in our time has infected many teachers to turn Yoga and meditation into a profiteering business. Third, some obscurantist and occult practices have been smuggled in by gurus (teachers) to entice followers and exploit popular fascination for mysticism. Fourth, its strong association with religion in the public mind has also put off some rationalists and skeptics. Lastly, the tradition of unflinching faith and unquestioning obedience to the teacher in Yoga and meditation has stifled the spirit of inquiry and scientific exploration.

AWARENESS MEDITATION

What is awareness meditation? It is an amazingly effective method of enhancing our power of inner awareness, resulting in emotional equilibrium as well as dispassionate understanding of our actions, thoughts, and feelings. Awareness meditation is not a religious practice, nor does it require any spiritual or moral beliefs and ideology. It does not openly or covertly offer self-hypnosis, which is a suppressive and ineffective act. Awareness meditation does not constitute a clever stratagem to escape the realities of mundane self. Rather, its central element is to face our self *directly* to understand the interplay and causative factors of our thoughts, emotions, and feelings.

This meditation has been explained in the second part of the book in a comprehensive manner along with findings from research by neuroscientists and medical experts. Some techniques and practical suggestions are outlined for exploring this unique avenue. Awareness meditation is a more efficacious variant of the traditional meditation. If practiced seriously with insight and objectivity, it is a long-lasting and healthy solution to the predicament of anxiety, stress, and depression that siphons off our mental energy. It acts as a means of strengthening the neural infrastructure of the brain responsible for consciousness. It revolutionises the entire functional environment of the brain by establishing a healthy balance among different regions of the brain. The hyperactivity of the brain that is symptomatic of stress and depression vanishes in an amazing manner.

This method is somewhat difficult compared to the usual meditation and requires more mental alertness and dispassionate action. It is slightly tough in the initial phase, but gradually the mind discovers the joy of unique tranquillity of mind and freedom from stress and looks forward to it. Those who have not gone through it would definitely wonder in disbelief about these claims, but it is advisable to experiment with an open mind before coming to a hasty judgement and dismissal. Let me reiterate that the question of meditation has to be approached in a scientific spirit, putting aside prejudgments and fixed notions.

Readers would notice later that I have extensively drawn on the neurological discoveries by experts and tried to compare their findings with the impact of meditation on different regions of the brain. I have endeavoured to synthesize the relevant aspects of research with actual experiences of meditation.

Let me add a word of caution. It must be borne in mind that though neuroscientists have made extraordinary progress in unravelling the secrets of how different parts of the brain operate, there are still many grey areas in their knowledge, given the fact that the brain is an enormously complex biomechanism. On the other hand, scientists are making new discoveries every other day about the multifunction of different regions of the brain, which render obsolete some aspects of earlier findings. For instance, a great deal of research supported by pharmaceutical industry is being carried out on different processes of memory to find remedies for Alzheimer's disease and illnesses of memory deficiencies. That has thrown up new ideas challenging the old ones. Hence, the present knowledge in neuroscience has to be judged taking into account its evolving scenario.

THE POSSIBILITY OF REWIRING THE BRAIN

While synthesizing some discoveries in neuroscience with impact of meditation on the brain, I have ventured a bit further and put forward a few ideas that would appear to be speculations. Readers would perhaps find that these speculations are useful and based on some supportive facts and logic. Besides, I am convinced these ideas constitute areas of further scientific research that will throw more light on the way meditation can be used to rewire the neural behavior of some parts of the brain responsible for stress and persistent anxieties. These methods hold prospects of being used or refined as therapies for attention deficit as well as enhancement of cognitive performance and memory. In this context, let me briefly cite some instances.

In the tenth chapter, I describe how a person can activate through intense awareness one of the autonomic nerves called vagus in order to establish emotional equilibrium and eliminate stress and depression. Two months after having finished the first draft of that chapter, which included the issue of activation of the vagus nerve, I happened to learn about a new therapy called vagus nerve stimulation (VNS). It is being used by doctors in Europe and USA for treating drug-resistant epilepsy as well as chronic and treatment-resistant depression. I came to know about it through an article on the internet entitled "Vagus Nerve Stimulation: A New Tool for Brain Research and Therapy," written by a team of experts from some prestigious universities and medical institutes in USA. The research coordinator of this team was Dr. Mark S. George, Radiology Department, Medical University of South Carolina.

Let me explain the therapy of vagus nerve stimulation mentioned in that article. An electric pulse generator the size of a pocket watch is inserted surgically like a cardiac pacemaker in the left chest of an epileptic patient and connected with the vagus nerve through a bipolar lead. This implant intermittently stimulates the left vagus nerve with variable electric pulses, which terminates epileptic seizures.

During this therapy, doctors happened to notice mood improvement in the patients, which was not consequent to antiepileptic benefits. Subsequently, several independent studies have clearly established that VNS induced metabolic and functional changes in the limbic structure of the brain resulting in significant antidepressant effects. New studies also indicated tangible benefits against obesity and Alzheimer's disease. VNS was also found to enhance neuro-cognitive performance and improve the quality of sleep.

Medical experts are now looking for a nonsurgical and noninvasive method of stimulating vagus nerve externally. Both the surgery and an implant in the body entail pain and attendant clinical problems, let alone the high cost. They used magnetic devices, but that did not work, and still the search is underway. In this context, the method suggested in this book to activate vagus nerve through application of intense awareness can be a nonsurgical solution.

Awareness meditation as a treatment has some limits that need to be overcome. The awareness route of VNS cannot be perhaps used by a patient during the actual onset of epileptic seizure. Though it might not work as an on-the-spot cure, it can certainly be a preventive measure spread over some months. It takes time and diligent effort, which might be beyond the capacity of some patients. Nonetheless, it can certainly be used by anyone for benefits like emotional stability, improvement of memory, attention and quality of sleep. It can help millions of people facing attention deficit disorders (ADD), obesity, chronic depression, and anxiety disorders. Approximately 18 million Americans suffer from depression, about 1 million of whom have severe treatment-resistant depression. Such statistics in other countries around the globe is equally staggering.

Further, in the last three chapters, some possibilities are outlined for rewiring of the brain and *meditative catharsis* or purging negative emotions vis-à-vis the Aristotelian catharsis. One more method of tackling stress has been outlined later in details, which is indicated briefly here.

Most of us are not aware that we have two brains: one in the head and the second in the guts. The evolutionists tell us that when we were little creatures millions of years ago, we had only a tiny brain, now called a *second brain*. As the living organisms evolved bigger and intricate bodies, they developed the larger and more complex brain in the head, but the second brain is still retained in the guts. Dr. Michael D. Gershon, a professor of anatomy and cell biology at the Columbia-Presbyterian Medical Center in New York, has elucidated this in his famous book *The Enteric Nervous System: A Second Brain*.

According to Dr. Gershon and other independent scientists, the second brain is responsible for the feeling of butterflies in the stomach, nervousness, and can be behind some of our emotional problems. Both these brains, they believe, are still interlinked and need coordination and balance to ensure emotional stability as well as mental and physical health.

Interestingly, both the brains in our body are anatomically interlinked through the vagus nerve. The secrets of these amazing antistress benefits are connected with the fact that the vagus nerve serves as the neural highway for carrying sensory messages, including distress signals between the emotive region of the brain and other vital parts of the body, such as the second brain, heart, and lungs. The sensory traffic that sometimes becomes frantic and chaotic on this neural highway can be regulated and reduced by focusing intense awareness on the vagus nerve—a skill that can be mastered through awareness meditation.

I have indicated in the latter part of the book how activation of the vagus nerve through inner awareness can free us almost instantly from psychological fears, anxieties, and feeling of butterflies in the stomach. I have also put forward how VNS, through awareness route, could be used to balance the brain in the head and the brain in the guts.

LIMITS OF TRADITIONAL MEDITATION

The traditional meditation, though practiced commonly by millions of people, depends more often on repetitive drills and compulsive concentration. It requires a person to recite quietly or vocally some words believed to be sacred (mantra), or to fix one's attention and gaze on some image. The purpose behind that is to put the mind on one track by negating thoughts, memory, and emotions. This calms the mind, and scientists have observed that it reduces the activities in the parietal lobe and frontal lobe of the brain, which function often in frantic and hyperactive mode. The slowdown of their activities brings about a marked reduction of stress and entails several health benefits.

Notwithstanding these benefits, the fact remains that repetitive drills are coercive by nature and amount to compulsive concentration, let alone the fact that it is a highly boring and monotonous task. It is akin to locking up an active child in a room, because it otherwise keeps running around playfully and making noise. Our mind by nature is spontaneous and highly active like the playful child, and one is trying to restrict and confine it to some fixed, repetitive actions. This cannot bring a lasting transformation that can endow one with a capacity to overcome stress without any suppressive action. Such transformation can come about only through the dynamics of innate intelligence. The stress reduction brought about through the repetitive and monotonous drills would be short-lived, necessitating frequent doses of traditional meditation in the day.

There are some more questions on the traditional meditation. In the course of life, we acquire a baggage of negative emotions, habitual tendencies, and mental conditionings through innumerable factors. Most of our anxieties and mental conflicts owe their existence to the psychological factors of our own making. How does the traditional meditation equip us to manage the psychological baggage of self, which otherwise serves as a perennial source of mental conflicts, hurts, and stress?

Further, everyone keeps on encountering situations in daily life that pose emotional challenges and cause stress. These are not necessarily of our own making. We cannot avert the natural causes of stress from the external world, such as death, sickness, a difficult boss, or a breaking relationship. Yet we can certainly minimize our mortifications by realistic approach and clear perceptions. The stress and anxieties resulting from these internal and external causes can be overcome to a greater degree only through attitudinal changes that can be brought about through deeper understanding.

Any one-dimensional meditation based on repetitive drills would be inadequate to address these subtle but crucial stress factors, which are rooted in our attitude and psychological profiles. Negation of mental activities like thought and feelings to avoid stress or pain through any clever stratagem of repetitive drills or beliefs cannot bring a lasting solution. One cannot rule out the possibilities of mental fatigue and pressure on nerves owing to coercive concentration or rigidity of a monotonous discipline.

Unlike the traditional variety, awareness meditation is devised to uproot such attitudinal factors of stress through deeper understanding and access to our innate intelligence. Total relaxation and allowing the mental activities to have their *full play* and *conscious recognition* are the central features of awareness meditation. It also works as a highly effective tool for rewiring our brain to eliminate habitual stress and anxieties.

In the next few chapters we embark on the journey inward to forge a closer acquaintance with *our self.* That is essential before we grapple with the practical issues of tackling stress.

Chapter 2

Memory: The Prime Mover

> *What images are these*
> *That turn dull-eyed away,*
> *Or shift Time's filthy load,*
> *Straighten aged knees,*
> *Hesitate or stay?*
> *What heads shake or nod?*
> —William Butler Yeats

In the arduous pursuit of daily life, we hardly have the time and energy to pause and look inward to figure out the roots of our actions and why we behave the way we do. If we carefully peer into our mind, the following scenario might emerge. Even though our thoughts, feelings and memories are mediated by external and internal stimuli, they seem to work in an autonomic mode, as if having their own willpower. Like some factory workers, they are seized with the frenzy of their work, jostling and cooperating with each other. The end products of their labor are our aspirations and dreams, our pride and prejudice, our anxieties and worries, which get manifested, rather packaged, in the externalities of our behavior and actions. As devoted workers, they service promptly the demands of our body—our desires for joy and comforts, our urges of hunger, thirst, and love.

The modern neurologists also paint a somewhat similar picture of self that is fragmentary and disorienting. They tell us that the brain cells called neurons are the actual workers that manufacture our feelings, emotions, thoughts, and memory. The human brain has billions of neurons that communicate with each other by making synaptic connections. They constantly fire electrochemical signals in synchronized fashion and thus create these mental processes in our brains. In other words, the patterns of neural firings are the actual correlates of our feelings, thoughts, and memory.

In the opinion of some neuroscientists, our subjective experience of self is nothing but the constant interplay of vast neural assemblies in the brain. While observing the neurons with electronic scanning gadgets, they were astonished by the hectic pace of their firing actions, which reminded of a noisy fish market bustling with activities.

It might shock someone's aesthetic sense to find description of the brain activities in such metaphoric idiom of the commercial world. Nowadays, the influence of the world of commercialism is so pervasive and infectious that we tend to describe things in such commercial language. Let that be as it may; but it does make the very significant point that behind the vital world of our thoughts, emotions, and feelings lies the neural infrastructure that is inherently mechanical, material, and driven by electrochemical impulses.

Worse than the commercial jargon, such factual description can rob us of our sense of ownership of the self that is the most precious thing in our life. Our pride and self-respect arise out of our belief of owning an independent and integral self, which is so dear to us that we spend our entire lifetime toiling to defend and preserve it. Our faith in the subjective ownership of self is utterly sacrosanct and inviolable. This faith is based on the belief that our self is a well-integrated homogeneous entity.

Unfortunately, that is not entirely true. At times, we cannot escape the feeling that our inner self is a parallel world of its own, separate and strange. The psychologists like Sigmund Freud and others tell us that the self, which is part of our conscious access and experience, is just the tip of an iceberg. Its larger part is unknown and hidden underneath. That subterranean segment of self, however, is not a dormant and defunct baggage. Rather, it is the heavy machinery that drives our body and mind. We are largely unaware of the forces that make up and manipulate our actions, behavior, and everything that constitutes the entity called self.

It is therefore quite essential to familiarize ourselves with the contents of our inner world in order to deal with the problems of stress and anxiety. This will require careful and patient efforts to learn the art of observing the nature of our memory, thoughts, and feelings. We need to cultivate a detached attitude to understand our motives, aspirations, and worries. Initially it might sound a daunting task, but after some time not only will it become easier but also an interesting and rewarding pursuit. Like any other skill, it requires time to learn. The stress management technique described in the latter part of this book will make it even easier to acquire that skill.

Let us attempt to explore our inner world. In this, we will rely on our direct experience and perceptions of our mental processes. Our quest shall begin first with the subject of memory because it plays the most critical role, both as a supportive infrastructure and catalyst of thought, emotions, feelings and linguistic ability. We will try to understand the nature of memory and how it operates, including the role it plays in anxiety, stress, and depression.

THE FUNCTIONAL MODES OF MEMORY

Memory involves a three-step process of encoding (registering), storing, and retrieving information. Both the actions of encoding and storing information are spontaneous and involuntary. If I happen to see a stranger on my way to the office, an impression of his look is registered in my mind. Most likely it might be erased in a short time as it did not make any deep impact on my mind. If the stranger had twitched his eyebrows to indicate his dislike for my being a foreigner in his land, that impression would have been burnt in my mind as a long-term memory.

We have no control over encoding and retention actions of memory since these are spontaneous processes. In other words, whether we like it not our brain performs these two functional modes of memory. That is the reason why we are more often not conscious of such a memory process taking place. Also, we tend to accumulate involuntarily a great deal of images and impressions in our memory, which work as contributory factors in shaping our individual attitudes and behavior. We gather a significant bulk of our hidden memories on account of these functional characteristics of memory. Such dormant memories are also behind some of our reflexes and instinctive behavior. The involuntary modes of memory were critically important for survival in the course of our evolution.

In contrast to encoding and storing, the retrieval process of memory is voluntary and dependent on a stimulus. One can make a conscious effort to recall previous experiences or information. Also, an external stimulus can provoke a past memory. For instance, witnessing a car accident on the road would evoke past memories of the car accident in which one was involved.

The stimulus can also be internal to body and mind. The empty stomach will bring up images of the food one relishes. Even though our thoughts, feelings, and emotions are dependent on the infrastructure of memory, they also serve as an almost ceaseless stream of varied stimuli for provoking memories. Like the encoding and retention processes, the retrieval mode of memory often gives an impression of being driven on its own, but actually it has internal or external provocations that we are not conscious of. Even a slight exposure in passing that is not registered at the conscious level can stir up a swarm of old memories.

THE CATEGORIES OF MEMORY

Psychologists have categorized memory as short-term memory and long-term memory. They use the term *short-term memory* for our ability to hold information in mind over a brief period of several seconds. For instance, a new telephone number is retained in memory till the time of dialling and forgotten after talking to the person. Psychologists have found out through experiments that the normal retention period of information in short-term memory is around forty seconds, and thereafter one is not able to recall it (see fig. 2.1).

However, if we wish to remember the information like a telephone number for a long time, we do that by repeating it a few times in mind. That is a deliberate effort to place information in the long-term memory. Most animals depend more on short-term memory in life as their capacity of long-term memory is very limited compared to the enormous memory of human beings.

Short-term memory has a variant that is referred to as working memory. In performing a given task in daily life, we are required to remember temporarily some information that is relevant. For instance, while working out a mathematical sum, a student has to remember some figures for a few seconds or even minutes. While entering a grocery shop, a housewife has to remember the items that she needs to buy. Normally after the shopping, she does not remember the list of items and their prices. Similarly, a reader has to remember all sentences in a paragraph to understand the point being made.

Working memory expands as children grow older and declines in adults in old age. That is why old people have to struggle sometimes for words or when recalling information. Working memory is very useful for mental work, for calculations, constructing thoughts and conceptual ideas. For this reason, working memory is perceived as synonymous with intelligence and people having better working memory are judged as more intelligent. In the latter part of this chapter, we will examine the relationship between intelligence and memory.

Memory is also categorized as verbal memory and visual memory. Some people have better verbal memory and easily remember names, dates, and similar information. Accountants, bankers, administrators, and historians are normally known to possess such memory. On the other hand, thinkers, artistes, intellectuals, and philosophers generally have visual memory enabling them to visualize pictures, imageries, and conceptual ideas more easily.

The terminology of *long-term memory* is more flexible and inclusive, which refers to information registered several minutes ago or a few decades ago. The memories of our childhood or what we had talked about with someone a few hours ago can be termed as long-term memory. It also includes skills like learning a language, sport, or driving a car. The long-term memory holds a vast amount of information though some of it will decay and fade out when not renewed and while new stock continues to be added throughout our life. There is no one opinion among experts on how information is turned into long-term memory. Some believe that information is first encoded as short-term memory, and then certain information is processed differently for long-term retention.

Actual neurological process apart, it is our common knowledge that repetition of information and emotional intensity of an experience leave behind lasting memories. Emotions and feelings seem to play a major role compared to thought in causing long-term memories. This is the reason why we remember our sorrows and joys for long time. Similarly, thoughts that carry stronger feelings and emotions also get ingrained as long-term memories. Thoughts that embody logical and less emotional contents have to be repeated for remembering over a long period. The same can be achieved through a deliberate act of concentration to infuse an element of intensity in a given thought.

In sum, emotions and feelings turn into lasting memories commensurate with their intensity. This would also suggest that in its sensual vivacity and dynamism the impulse of memory is closer to emotions and feelings in contrast to thought as a system that is relatively a weaker and diffused phenomenon. This is the reason why emotions and feelings fuelled by memory act as the eye of a storm of depression and anxiety.

Let me add some general information that is relevant. The neurological basis of memory is yet to be fully revealed. Experts have observed that the different types of memory are distributed in discrete regions of the brain. However, they are still seized with the task of identifying the areas as well as understanding different memory functions. They have discovered some overlaps and duplication of memory, which are meant to provide additional support in protecting memory as it is the most crucial infrastructure of the edifice of our self—both the biological and psychic. Such duplication is sometime advantageous. For instance, when one area of the brain is damaged in an accident or by disease, the other region having a similar faculty compensates for the loss to some extent, if not entirely. However, such a benefit is not available in all cases of memory loss.

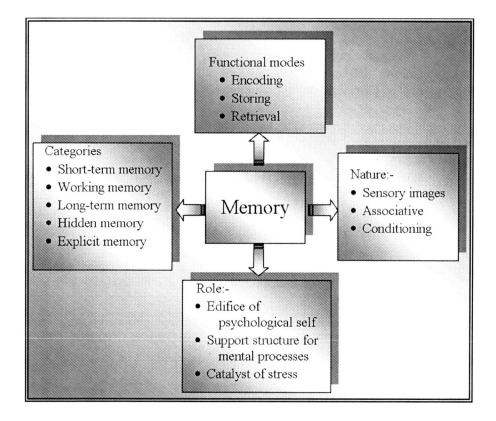

Figure 2.1. Functional modalities of memory. The terms *short-term memory* and *working memory* are overlapping concepts and hence not completely accurate.

IMPULSES OF DYNAMIC IMAGES

Despite the challenges encountered by the neuroscientists, commendable progress is achieved in unravelling the mysteries of memory. The part of the brain called the hippocampus along with its surrounding area in the midbrain is known to be responsible for encoding memory. The advances in technology have made it possible for experts to peer into different regions of the brain and observe their activities with the help of electronic scanning devices. They have observed increased blood flow in the hippocampus during memory encoding. Neuroimaging techniques have revealed that the frontal lobes of the brain are also involved in encoding of memory.

In order to understand the operational nature of memory, it would be useful to know the basic units of memory. The experts in this field tell us that images are the basic units of memory. This is apparent even without the help of the experts if one observes the play of memories with deep attention. Let us understand.

When we see a tree, our eyes first capture the physical images of the tree and transfer them through optical nerves to different regions of the brain. These images represent the color, shape, size of the tree as a whole as well as its leaves, branches, flowers, and fruits. Our nose and olfactory nerves would capture the properties of fragrance of the flowers, leaves, and fruits of the tree. The olfactory qualities are captured and stored as olfactory images in combination with the visual images (see fig. 2.2).

The operation of memory is not a simple, one-dimensional process that relates only to material properties of visual and olfactory nature. The sight of the tree evokes emotions and feelings of joy and happiness with its beauty, flowers, and fruits. It might also evoke feelings of awe, fear, unease, or dislike because of its gigantic or peculiar shape or one's own subjective reasons. These elements of emotions and feelings would also become the integral properties of the visual and olfactory images.

The story does not end here. In fact, a process of cognition is also triggered with the sight of the tree. Our brain tries to find out information such as its name, usefulness, herbal properties, etc. The support of our thought machinery will be enlisted to facilitate the cognition process. The net result would be addition of information to the memories of the tree. It is obvious that the cognitive activities of brain will not be possible without the supportive structure of memory, and the lack of such support would jeopardize the very survival of life.

In sum, it is evident that the images of memory are very dynamic and multidimensional, which include not only ensembles of visual and olfactory sensations but also emotive and informational contents. Also, the defining qualities of these images are vitality, sentience, and subjectivity of experience.

The multiple qualities and contents represent a stark contrast to the memory units of computer, which are mechanical, duplicative, one dimensional, and sterile of emotive and sentient contents. The most crucial difference is that the computer memory does not possess the sensory ownership or subjectivity of experience. In other words, the computer does not feel or experience its memory contents. Experts can devise electromechanical contrivances to mimic and create a virtual but not the actual reality of smell and emotions. That is akin to a motion picture that provides a virtual experience of the real world.

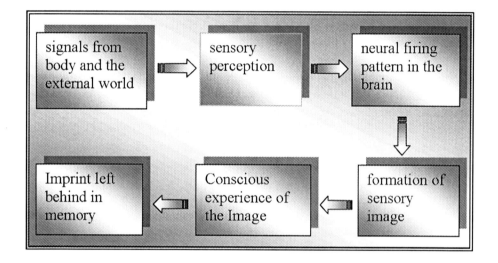

Figure 2.2. Sensory processes and the formation of memories in the brain.

Our memory is thus a world of images. It would be also apparent that our knowledge and storehouse of experiences are nothing but ensembles of dynamic memory images. In fact, our autobiographical self is also nothing but a complex architecture of multiple layers of images. One could argue that the contents of information in the memory could be in the form of thoughts and hence not images. That is not true. If we focus our attention carefully, it would be evident that our thoughts, as the vehicle and custodian of knowledge, are also linear streams of images. Some of the images flowing in the body of the thought can be experienced explicitly during the thought process itself, while the others implicitly in the form of sensations with hidden contents. This matter is discussed further in the next chapter.

A question, however, arises about how the brain stores these images, which in the long course of life would become nearly infinite in number. According to scientists, our sensory experience of a mental image, whether recalled from memory or as a fresh event, is made possible through synchronized actions of brain cells, neurons. The firing patterns of neurons are the actual correlates of the images. From infancy to old age, our accumulation of knowledge and experiences would consist of trillions and trillions of images, while the neurologists tell us that the infrastructure of our brain consists of only about 100 billion neurons, which is grossly inadequate.

This apparent deficiency is, however, tackled in the following manner: The filamentous extension of a nerve called axon has a few thousand dendrites that get connected with other axons for transmitting electrochemical signals. This enhances the capacity of brain infrastructure to a few trillions of synaptic connections. This problem is not yet fully tackled because the entire neural infrastructure of the brain is not available for the operations of memory. Only some regions of the brain are capable of memory functions, which would imply a huge shortfall of neural resources for memory.

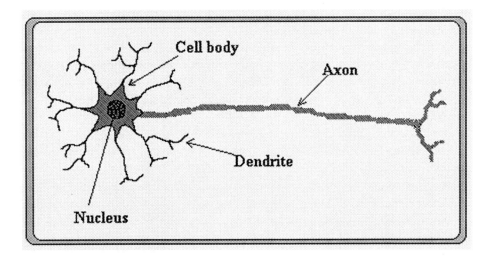

Figure 2.3. Anatomy of a neuron (brain cell). The connection between two dendrites of different neurons is called a synapse that becomes a circuit for transmission of neural signals.

According to neurologists, nature has found a solution by storing not the actual vivid images in the brain, but by retaining only the memory of a dispositional impulse of an image. For the recalling process, this dispositional impulse acting like a switch triggers a particular pattern of neural activities, which represents the actual sensory experience of the image. The neurologists call it a dispositional representation that requires much less memory space compared to a vivid and graphic image having multiple contents (Antonio Damasio, *The Feeling of What Happens: Body and Emotion in the Making of Consciousness* [New York: Harcourt, INC. 1999], 160-1). This also underlines a crucial point that memory of a living organism is a sentient and vital impulse that is integral to consciousness as such and not an insensate and fragmented duplication as in a computer.

The upshot of venturing into the neurological details is to clarify that memory is a dispositional impulse emanating from the unique entity of inner consciousness. The implications of this are quite significant. It would mean that an increased access to consciousness would enhance our ability to tackle obstinate memories during stress and anxieties. This would be relevant when later in the book we discuss a method of strengthening the power of inner awareness.

THE EDIFICE OF SELF ON THE PILLARS OF MEMORY

Let me first briefly clarify my usage of the term *self*. In this book I will divide self in two mutually dependent parts. The first is the biological self consisting of the body proper and its vital organs, including the brain with its sensory apparatus, urges, reflexes, instincts—the hard-core programming necessary for survival. This self would include also the cerebral infrastructure of thinking, emotions, feelings, reasoning, and memory. All these features of the biological self are common to all of us.

The second part is the psychic or psychological self. This broadly includes our individual experiences, attitudes, and conditionings of our mind, which are unique and exclusive to each and every person. It is a complex edifice built on multiple layers of individual experiences, self-images, and perceptions of what we think that makes us distinct from others. The main plank of the psychic self is our autobiographical self that consists of our personal memories, emotional baggage, and experiences since childhood. The psychic self also embodies our pride, prejudices, aspirations, and sense of our accomplishments and failures. It gives us our own individuality that is unique.

We are the main architects of our psychic self. Of course, the external world, the social and cultural factors contribute significantly in shaping it. Yet at the same time, how we interact and cope with the external factors play a much larger role in making us what we are. That is the reason why siblings brought up in the same physical and social environment grow up more often as remarkably different personalities. Earlier psychologists attributed unduly high weight to external environment in shaping human personality, but that turned out to be inaccurate following some further research.

It is evident that unlike the biological self, the psychic self is largely a stuff made of psychological images about our self and our perceptions of other human beings as well as the world at large. Unfortunately, the psychological images hold a vast scope for distorting our perceptions. It is a matter of common experience in life that often there is a significant gap between the host of images we have about ourselves and the reality of what we actually are. Many aspects of our psychic self represent our wishful ideas and subjective notions. That creates a gulf between what we think we can accomplish in life and what we are actually capable of.

Yet the inescapable fact of life is that our brain operates only through images, and we have no other options. The purpose of mentioning this issue is to highlight the subjectivity and shortcomings that are inherent in psychological images. A conscious habit of questioning such images concerning others and ourselves will help immensely in ensuring mature interpersonal relationships and reducing mental conflicts in life.

Since the edifice of psychological self is built on the pillars of memory, the connection between both of them is extremely crucial. In fact, in the absence of memory, psychic self will absolutely collapse, and we will be left with only a truncated biological self making us not much different from other animals. Without memory, all our knowledge and self-images would vanish as these are embodied in the stuff of memory. Besides, it would rob us of our unique self-identity and jeopardize our existence.

The role of the memory in all its different forms—such as genetic memory, hidden memory, short-term and long-term memory—extends far beyond sustaining the psychic self. Our biological self and all our mental processes of thought, emotions, feelings, and imagination depend critically on memory. Even our intelligence and reasoning power will be crippled in the absence of inputs from memory. It is no exaggeration to say that in the absence of memory, sustainability of life would become impossible.

Fortunately, such an extreme scenario of total loss of memory does not occur. Memory loss in practically all cases is partial and not absolute, owing to duplication and distribution of memory functions in several regions of the brain. In the event of loss of explicit memory, the unconscious memory structure remains intact, which regulates and supports the biological self with its basic survival mechanisms of emotions, urges, and reflexes. That ensures a sense of self, even if distorted or eroded by a partial memory loss. Even in the case of vegetative state or coma, where the sense of self is mutilated, the unconscious memory network remains functional.

A CONDITIONING FACTOR

Having briefly touched upon the role of memory in constituting our sense of self, let us look into the practical implications of memory in daily life. Since memory contains subjective experiences, self-biased images, and limited knowledge, it sometimes works negatively as a conditioning factor, particularly when we are required to learn something new or tackle a challenge. We tend to act in a routine manner guided by past knowledge and work culture ingrained in memory. It prevents innovative thinking that requires us to transcend the old mindset and find different ways to tackle the new situation. Many people feel more secure with the known and are inclined to avoid what is unknown and non-traditional. In such instances, memory turns out to be a limiting factor and a constraint on our reason and intelligence. Hence, Albert Einstein said, "The only thing that interferes with my learning is my education."

Our prejudices, superstitions, and beliefs, which are fossilized in memory, work as mental blocks and reflex behavior. In order to become free from that, one has to break the stronghold of memory with the power of inner awareness or consciousness. At the collective level, our traditions—whether social, cultural or religious—are also embodiments of deep-rooted memories that tie us down to fixed ideas and stereotypical actions. This should not be misconstrued as rejection of the traditions and old values that otherwise enrich both our individual lives and societies. This makes it quite evident that memory plays an enormous role in the construct of our self and evolution of human societies.

Memory as a conditioning factor has a much more mischievous role in human relationship at home and in society. When we meet a stranger, his or her impression is formed in mind. If we have to deal with the person more frequently, new images are added, and the old ones undergo subtle changes. The ensemble of these images in our mind expands and becomes complex. Such mental images work as lens through which we look at that person and mould our interactions with him or her.

We have to check the quality and color of the lens to ensure the accuracy of our impressions and judgments. The practical point to be borne in mind is that while dealing with people, we must question and prevent old memories from working as blinkers to bias our understanding and decisions. Such an objective approach would enrich our interpersonal relationship and eliminate the major factors of stress.

Similarly, we have some fixed images of the role we expect from spouse, children, parents, friends, or a colleague at work, and, in turn, they have similar expectations from us. We naturally tend to judge others through the prism of our images and expectations while they do the same for us. The reality of what the other person is and the reasons behind his or her behavior are often overshadowed in our subjective engrossment with our self and one-sided expectations. Our relationship thus becomes a clumsy product, if not ruins, of the clash of psychological images from either side.

Of course, the limitations of memory should not blind us to the equally enormous advantages of memory. Memory plays a highly critical role as both an understructure and a catalyst for practically all mental processes such as thought, emotions, feelings, and even innate intelligence. More significantly, it is memory that endows us with the unique sense of autobiographical self, which in turn creates the primary urge to protect and advance life as such. Our superb linguistic ability would not have been possible in the absence of the memory network.

Besides, memory is the custodian of the knowledge and information that are indispensable tools for our survival. The spectacular scientific and technological achievements of human civilizations are the products of the joint venture between memory and intelligence. It is the enormous memory that gave human beings an edge over other species in the battle for survival.

THE ASSOCIATIVE NATURE

One of the characteristics of memory that is very significant from our practical angle is its associative property. Our daily experience confirms that one image of an object triggers the memories that are connected with it. For instance, when in leisure you remember your old friend, the images of his face, personality, his profession, your past associations, and a host of related memories would gradually spring up in mind.

The flow of images in mind is triggered in different fashions. On some occasions, memory images are evoked one by one but in such a quick succession as to give the impression that a panoramic vista is being unfolded before us. Also, evocation of memories can be sudden, like stirring up a beehive. On the other hand, the triggering of memories can be sometimes slow and gradual in the fashion of a leisurely journey down memory lane.

The associative property of memory also works in another way like a roller coaster. For instance, the word *zoo* would evoke images of wild animals, say, a cheetah. That would bring up images of a cheetah chasing its prey, which you had seen during your African safari. Then perhaps, the scenes would emerge of other wild animals surrounding a water hole against the backdrop of a grassy landscape strewn with bushes. It might further bring alive your experiences of meeting with the native people in the town you had stayed. You might end up even comparing their culture with that prevailing in your country.

All this would turn out to be a long flight on the wings of memory accompanied by associated feelings and thoughts. Only at the end, you would realize how much you had travelled unawares in your imaginative journey. Such outpouring of the stream of images was made possible through the associative nature of memory.

Why does memory have this glue of association? The answer to this is perhaps connected with the functional nature of memory that is dispositional or impulse based. Memory gives the impression of operating like a wave or string of mental impulse having the tendency to be inclusive and get clustered. A more significant reason is the role emotions and feelings play in memory. They are the strongest factors behind encoding and evocation of memories, particularly the long-term memories.

Emotions and feelings by nature tend to bind memory images together, and hence one emotion is responsible for encoding and evoking a bunch or series of memory images. For instance, sorrow of the death of a beloved person or incidents of hurts are large ensembles of interconnected images; so are our ecstasies and joys. Our thoughts play a significant role in memory, but it should be remembered that most of our thoughts are embedded in emotions and feelings, either strong or weak. In addition, emotions and feelings serve as stimuli for generating thoughts.

THE PROS AND CONS OF THE ASSOCIATIVE QUALITY

The associative nature of memory has its advantages and disadvantages. On the positive side, it calls up all related aspects of an issue you are mentally attending to and enables you to take a comprehensive view. For instance, your assessment of a difficult situation and subsequent decision will certainly be more balanced and objective if your memory, with its associative power, brings forth as much information as possible. If the information is stored in a disjointed fashion, our brain would not be able to recall all relevant information, while concentrating on a difficult problem.

On the negative side, this associative nature can be a painful factor in a state of stress or sorrow. For instance, when one tries to forget a mental hurt or fearsome experience, the associative memory will obstinately continue to pour in images of that painful incident. Similarly, when a friend irritates or hurts us for some reason, our memory would start bringing up a whole inventory of negative things involving him. Conversely, when a colleague, who is normally difficult and lukewarm, brings a nice gift, I tend to forget unhappy encounters with him, and in fact, my memory will dig up some positive points concerning him.

Related to this phenomenon is the curious fact that mind recalls memories in partiality to our feelings and desires of what we wish to do in a given situation. Human mind acts like a shrewd advocate who twists arguments selectively in favor or against a legal charge to support the interests of his client. When one morning, we do not wish to do physical exercise, the mind will try to bring up arguments in favour of our desire. The mind would dig out information about the benefits of wine when we wish to drink and ignore the detrimental effects of alcohol.

In conclusion, a pleasant event works as a stimulus for reviving a bunch of happy memories, while an unhappy experience stirs up a swarm of painful images. The associative property of memory is responsible for clustering of positive or negative images. That causes a slanting of our perceptions, and to that extent, it erodes our objectivity by infusing an element of arbitrariness. If we remain conscious of these shortcomings, our mind will learn to recognize and question the mischief that memory plays quite often, particularly in the state of anxiety and stress. The method of expanding the power of consciousness, given in the latter part of the book, makes it easy to perceive such play of memory.

A CATALYST OF STRESS

After the exhaustion of moving around a shopping mall, you might have walked up to a small shop and waited to buy hot popcorn. While the popcorn was being made, your attention might have been caught by what was happening in the popcorn machine. The maize kernels, when heated, swell up and burst open with small explosive sounds. They keep constantly flying off the hot bottom of the machine. The continuous activities of the bursting commotion and flying trajectories of the popcorn would seize your curiosity.

The bursting corn kernels somehow remind of the ceaseless activities of memory in the human brain. One is greatly intrigued by the constant clamour of memory in the mind. If one observes with attention, one finds that images and ideas keep popping up ceaselessly from memory like the bursting maize kernels. Innumerable images start swarming up in mind from the moment we wake up in the morning. Not only throughout the day, but it spills over in our dreams; rather, memory is the prime mover of the phenomenon of dream as well. In sleep, when our reasoning power is either absent or weak, memory takes the advantage and goes berserk. It makes mismatches and weird strings of images and ideas, which accounts for the bizarre nature of dreams.

Why does memory keep popping up tirelessly all the time? The reasons for this were mentioned earlier. The inexhaustible supply of stimuli makes the machinery of memory grind practically all the time. The first source of supply is the external world full of animate and inanimate objects with which we have to interact throughout our lives.

The second source that is more intrusive and unavoidable is the body proper, including the brain with its paraphernalia of sensory activities, urges, and desires. For instance, outside on a hot day, one would remember a glass of lemonade or an ice cream. During a lonely business trip abroad, one remembers one's bosom friend or a small daughter at home. Our natural urges for food, drink, love, and companionship incite memories in order to cause actions or behavior necessary for fulfilment. As stated before, our feelings, emotions and thoughts are also the major factors for evoking memories.

Of course, we welcome and enjoy memories that make us happy. Similarly, we support activities of memories, which are indispensable for our work and fulfilment of our desires. Nonetheless, one gets utterly fed up sometime and yearns for a respite from the endless hordes of drifting memories. In the incidence of stress, the stream of memories gets torrential and wild. In order to rejuvenate itself, our brain needs a break from the ceaseless action of memory.

For the practical purpose of tackling stress and anxieties, it is important to bear in mind the underlying role of memory that is quite crucial. Memory is not only the custodian of worries and anxieties but also a catalyst. It plays a vicious role of a culprit and mischief-maker by prolonging and aggravating worries and anxieties. Memory deepens and acquires strength for itself like a snowball with repetitive actions.

Unpleasant memories become more painful and persistent in proportion to the intensity and frequency of occurrence. When unpleasant memories become unbearable, our mind takes recourse to escape by suppressing and pushing them deeper into the realm of subconscious. We deceive ourselves by describing that as a healing touch of time. Unfortunately, there is no escape from such hidden memories as they continue to operate in a more diabolic manner and even lead to psychological disorders.

One wonders why it is nearly impossible to regulate the activities of memory. Why can't we impose a serene and more rational order on the hectic play of memory, particularly in a state of anxiety and stress? Unfortunately, our thoughtful determinations cannot rescue as they fail to restrain the clattering machinery of memory. The other frustrating fact is that thought seems to behave like a servile bureaucrat against the might of memory.

Emotions and feelings are also equally ineffective tools for imposing a wise control on the play of memories because they themselves fuel memory and act as the eye of the storm of stressful memories. This underlines the need for a new avenue to tackle stress.

SYMBIOSIS WITH INTELLIGENCE

Earlier in this chapter, we discussed how the cognition process is critically dependent on the supportive structure of memory. In the instance cited earlier, the sight of a tree had triggered the cognition process, which, in fact, happens when we come across any unknown object. We try to understand it, its properties and usefulness. For that, the mind has to compare its apparent characteristics in the light of the knowledge available in memory. Even the easiest thing like the green color of leaves may not make a sense unless one has the memory of other distinguishing colors like red, yellow, and blue. The same is true with fragrance and other properties of the tree.

The cognition process is not possible in a vacuum because its product, knowledge, is relative and contextual by nature. Knowledge accrues through a comparative process in the context of the information that is accumulated and stored earlier.

Related to the cognition process are activities like analytical or sustained thinking, calculations, and other mental work that are made possible by the operation of intelligence. But here, a support from the working memory is requisite. Intelligence and memory have mutual dependence. Memory keeps feeding information during a sustained thinking that is essential to understand something or resolve a particular problem. Through its feedback activities, memory works as a catalyst to goad and direct the operation of intelligence and thus helps it achieve an understanding.

The partnership of intelligence and memory has played a central role in sustaining and proliferating life on this planet. In other words, both of them have acted as the most critical forces governing the course of evolution of life. One gets curious to speculate on how this partnership might have come up at the origin of life on this planet.

The evolutionists tell us that in the primordial time, life as such first began to throb in the bodies of single cells. These cells soon began to replicate, but in the course of time, these replicators faced a situation that made them compete among themselves for the limited resources in their ecosystems. Slowly they found it more beneficial to cooperate among them and got united to evolve as multicelled structures. That is how the strange caravan of multicelled life-forms began to move on this earth. The huge lumbering creatures, including human beings, which evolved after the evolutionary grind of more than three billion years, are nothing but the cooperative housing colonies of the replicators! Some evolutionists confide that our sense of self or being one individual is an illusion since our body represents a complex structure that was built in joint cooperation by the replicators for their own benefit and survival, and it continues to be so (Richard Dawkins, *The Selfish Gene* [New York: Oxford University Press, 1989], 19-20, 237).

It is mentioned in the beginning of this chapter that the neurologists portrayed our self as a divided house and, worse, as a mere interplay of the vast neural ensembles in the brain. They told us that our feelings of joys, sorrow, beauty, love, and pride are nothing but firing patterns of neurons (Francis Crick, *The Astonishing Hypothesis: The Scientific Search for the Soul* [New York: Simon & Schuster, 1994], 3, 91). This robs us of our sense of ownership of an integral self.

Our sense of dismay at that does not end here. Now it is the turn of the evolutionists to say that even our belief of owning the biological self as a homogeneous unit is also an illusion. Our bodies continue to be the cooperative colonies of trillions of replicators for their own good. This strange perspective of the evolutionists further compounds our self-doubt and deepens our agony of alienation from our own self.

Be that as it may. At the dawn of evolution of life, what did originate first: intelligence or memory? If it is believed that intelligence cannot operate without thought or memory, then all these three mental phenomena should have originated simultaneously with life. That would mean the life forms of even one or a few cells have had the capacity to think. This would fly in the face of the current scientific belief that grants thinking ability to the higher forms of life, like man, while its rudimentary traces in some primates and mammals. Hence, thought is doubtlessly a recent product of evolution. Also, the millions of species that still do not have even rudiments of thinking power prove that intelligence and memory can function in the absence of thought.

How did then life survive soon after its very creation? At that time, Mother Earth did not yet know how to nurse and comfort its unique baby—the life. Her heart was still burning profusely with enormous lava underneath. The life was born as a self-duplicating cell with an absolute clean slate, having no past experiences to guide. What then guided it to security when the elements on the earth were extremely harsh, ever menacing, and unpredictable? Was it the memory of its first experience, however vaguely felt and defined, and the successive experiences with the passage of time? That would mean the help of memory alone.

That is untenable because memory, being a duplicative process driven by external or internal stimuli, can breed further memory only. On its own without intelligence, memory cannot devise an intelligent and proactive behavior for protecting life, which was so critical at the dawn of evolution. That was possible only through the action of intelligence. Also, life and innate intelligence are synonymous in absolute sense. The hallmark of life has been intelligence at its very core, which is inherent in each and every living cell. Hence intelligence must have originated simultaneously with life as its defining quality. Soon as a next step, memory was built up to augment the functioning of intelligence.

The initial experiences of life in the primordial time were not only required to be remembered but also interpreted to evolve intelligent solutions to ensure food, safety, and adaptation for survival. Memory must have, therefore, played an immensely valuable role in supporting intelligence to carry forward the evolutionary process of life. That is how life as the joint venture of intelligence and memory seems to have flourished on this lonely planet.

THE VIRTUES OF SELF-OBSERVATION

Let us try and glean some practical lessons from what has been discussed in this chapter. Most of the points made earlier are largely the matters of daily experience, and yet we hardly recognize the mischief that memories play so often in the real life situations. During the onset of stress and depression, such mischief assumes a grave dimension and wreaks havoc with an individual.

The important point is that one should try and form a habit of consciously observing how and when the negative side of memory distorts our perceptions and actions. Of course, while recognizing the frequent role of memory as an aggravating agent in stress and depression, we have to note the virtues of memory as well and learn to make good use of them.

The work of memory as an inbuilt bias in our perceptions and decisions has to be understood carefully in daily life. If one cultivates an attitude to observe the complex play of memory, it would enable a person to discover that many of our misunderstandings, mistakes, impetuous actions, and prejudices are, in fact, caused under the influence of subjective impressions in the memory.

Such conscious efforts for objective observation would gradually build up as a virtuous cycle resulting in more mature and empathetic conduct with others. That would bring joy of cordiality and mutual respect at home and workplace. The interpersonal relationship will undergo a positive transformation, enhancing the quality of our life.

Given the fact that self is a complex architecture of multiple layers of past images, it should be borne in mind that the frequent tendency of subjective submergence in one's self is the primary factor behind mental conflicts and agonies. We have to realize that we operate and interact with others through the prism of psychological images. These images have to be questioned and scrutinized to the extent possible. Self-detachment is indeed an invaluable virtue, though a difficult one.

The inner awareness has enormous power of diffusing the onslaught of and consequent sufferings from negative emotions of hurt, sorrow, anxiety, and stress. The result is even better if inner awareness is sharp and unadulterated by memory and thoughts. This issue will be discussed in details later in the book. At this stage, it is important to note that the activities of thought, memory, and emotions erode the quality and objectivity of the power of nonverbal awareness that is an amazing instrument for coping with the problems of stress.

Chapter 3

Thought: the Errand Boy

Thoughts are the shadows of our feelings—always darker, emptier, simpler than they are.

—Friedrich Nietzsche

Memory that we talked about in the previous chapter is a quiet and sneaky operator in the arena of mind in contrast to thought. Memory lies in the subterranean realm of our inner world and has to be evoked and ushered on to the conscious stage for experience, while thought prefers to work in the daylight of conscious mind. Thought represents the tip of the iceberg that is visible, while memory forms the part of its submerged and unknown segment. The significance of thought is, therefore, quite apparent and self-evident, but its absence would be akin to being plunged into a dark vacuum. The empty darkness without the light of thought makes many persons very uncomfortable, and some compare it with a sort of near-death experience.

No wonder Descartes said, "I think therefore I am." Thought is construed as a hard and explicit evidence of our being alive. Though widely prevalent since the days of Descartes, it is a mistaken notion. On the contrary, the fact is that "I don't think, yet I am." Not only in the state of coma or dreamless sleep where the thinking faculty is not operating, but in the perfectly healthy state of the awake mind, thought can be absent when one is immersed in profound inner awareness or trancelike experience. Even during the surge of intense feelings of wonder, joy, sorrow, or anger, thought is absent at the initial stage, though the next moment it joins and takes over the stage of the conscious mind.

In all fairness, however, Descartes' quote was not made in the absolute sense that in the absence of thought, one is dead. It was meant to highlight our daily experience that thought for us is the synonym of our conscious state, our sense of being alive. Hence, *I think therefore I am.* Most of the time, our conscious state is overwhelmed with the omnipresence of thought, though in conjunction with feelings and emotions. It is a moment-to-moment reminder of our life in action. Thought is, no doubt, our lifelong companion and friend in need or otherwise. We get annoyed with it, quarrel with it, hate its intrusive tendency or love its sensual contents and enjoy its smooth and caressing touch. In sum, whether we like it or not, thought is always with us even in our dreams.

For most of us, thought is inseparable from our sense of self or subjective identity. Our feeling of "me" or "I" is perceived as indivisible from our thought. Unfortunately, that lifelong feeling is grossly misplaced in reality, because thought is merely a diffused, small, and relatively weaker segment of our consciousness. It is often pushed around by the stronger forces of emotions and memory. We tend to identify thought falsely with our self or the feeling of me. That is due to the fact that we use it practically all the time in life, and it operates almost ceaselessly by eclipsing our subjective sense of self. During stress and depression, this identification becomes so acute and self-effacing that the objectivity that is needed most at that time becomes an unfortunate casualty.

Therefore, it is quite essential to understand the place of thought in the scheme of our consciousness and distinguish it clearly from our sense of self. Our self-submerged identity with thought needs to be questioned to ensure the objectivity that is crucial for avoiding problems of stress and anxieties. We normally take thought as an objective perception of the external world and our experiences. That is only partially true and sometimes misleading. These lay notions are at the root of many problems in life. Hence, the journey into our inner world has to halt at the door of thought to explore its intricacies and self-engrossing power.

IMAGES AND VERBAL SYMBOLS

Instead of relying on definitions offered by others, let us observe directly our thought process to try and discover its structure. Let us examine one simple instance of a thought: *Tomorrow in the morning, I will go for a walk in the garden nearby*. The first thing that strikes us is that language, which consists of verbal symbols, is the medium or facade of thought. Not only when we express our thoughts vocally, but also when we think quietly, the garb of language is inevitably present all the time. It seems nearly impossible to have a thought process without the simultaneous use of our linguistic ability.

Beside language, the second element constituting thought is the role of images. If we observe closely, it would be evident that linguistic symbols represent images that we mentally experience (see fig. 3.1). We either recall images from our memory or experience them from the external world through direct interaction. The role of images would be evident if we look at the example of thought mentioned earlier, wherein each word has some image content. The words like *garden*, *morning*, or *walk* have images, which can be sensed more clearly. Even verbs and pronouns also possess images of related actions and objects in explicit or implicit forms. However, during the thought process, not all images are experienced in articulate forms because of the rapid flow of thought. If you pause shortly in between or think leisurely, the images in the visual or emotive form can be experienced explicitly.

This raises a curious question as to how other animals *think*. It is believed that some mammals and birds have thinking ability, which is rudimentary in comparison to the complex human ability. Among other species, whales, dolphins, dogs, monkeys, and parrots have relatively better capability to understand human language. It would suggest that when trained, they are able to correlate phonetic symbols with objects and actions. Even without training, the association with human beings enables them to remember and connect some simple sound symbols with gesticulations and objects or actions.

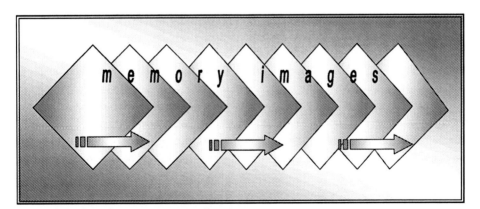

Figure 3.1. A Linear flow of images from memory constituting a thought. These images carry sensory contents of emotive, visual, or olfactory nature and have verbal correlates.

It is reasonable to assume that in the absence of a linguistic skill, the *thinking* process in animals would be highly constrained. Let me clarify this with an instance. Suppose a lion has become hungry. The sensation of hunger in the empty stomach sends signals to the brain, which evokes from memory the images of grazing antelopes. That intensifies the desire for food reviving visual images of the forest where the antelopes roam around. It would also evoke the memories of his last kill: how he had chased it or snatched away a carcass from a cheetah. Thus, the brain of the lion would revive a series of images from his earlier experiences, which would incite him to act and go in search of a prey. As he roams around, he would rely on his memory images to succeed in fulfilling his urge.

The lion seems to rely on visual images to *think out* a strategy to find food or fulfill biological urges. Similarly, other animals would also use memory images for their rudimentary thinking. The images would be visual as well as sensory. The memory of the sensory image of delicious food would guide the lion in choosing his prey. Admittedly, it can be argued that animals rely more on instinct for their action, but it is also a fact that more often instinct is a short-circuited action of hidden or implicit memories.

There is, however, one serious handicap in making extensive use of visual or sensory images without verbal symbols that constitute a thought or language. The constraint is that an image can be evoked only through a stimulus in *the present*. It means only on encountering a leopard, the antelope's brain would be able to evoke the past images of what the predator is capable of, including its hunting tactics. This places an animal at a disadvantage of not being able to anticipate the future and act in advance.

This is perhaps the reason why most of the animals live in *the present* and cannot anticipate the future as explicitly as human beings do. Of course, there are cases of a squirrel storing food for winter and a dog hiding food for tomorrow. But these are a few stray behavioral actions arising from biological urge or instinct and not the foresighted actions based on conscious thought process.

A prolonged thought operation would not be possible with the constraint of evoking images in the present through external or internal stimuli. That is why the ingenious method of verbal representations or phonetic correlates of images was invented in the evolutionary process. The verbal symbols serve as a *constant* and *inexhaustible* source of internal stimuli to sustain the flow of memory images without too much dependence on the external world. This enables prolonged and complex thought operation covering not just present but past and future eventualities. We tend to recognize importance of language merely as a means of communication with other people and are less mindful or even ignorant of the unique and inherently critical role it plays in constituting our thinking ability.

The following instance would explain how mentally suffocating it would be, if we were without a well-developed linguistic ability. The small children are constrained to depend largely on pure images, most of which are devoid of verbal symbols since their vocabulary is far from adequate. They are still in the process of correlating sound symbols with their feelings, biological urges, and numerous objects in the external world. Actually, the growing children face a peculiar predicament, rather, agony of an inability to communicate with others because on one hand their minds are constantly bubbling with numerous images, while on the other they lack matching verbal symbols. Their frequent crying and confused state often represent their dichotomy of a strong urge to communicate and the lack of words for countless images that they accumulate every day.

In contrast, the animals that lack language ability do not face such agonies of communication because they have very limited memory and retain a small number of images unlike our children. A growing child has vast memory compared to animals and hence accumulates countless images. It is a great pity that adults hardly realize the agonies of communication on the part of our tiny tots and often tend to dismiss their crying and confused actions as obstinacy and bad behavior. That, unfortunately, adds to their confusion and suffering.

During our growing process in childhood, we begin to learn and master the skill of selecting and arranging verbal symbols in comprehensive structures. A small child keeps struggling with its innate intelligence to master the dual skill of arranging the mental images in a rational sequence and connecting them with appropriate phonetic correlates. Both these mental processes slowly and imperceptibly get intertwined and become largely indivisible. For humans, therefore, thinking and linguistic processes get merged largely into a single mental activity. There are, of course, exceptions. Throughout our life we often recall images and struggle to find matching words. That is how we fumble for words and continue to learn new words for images, visual or abstract.

In sum, it is clear that memory images and verbal correlates constitute the two indispensable ingredients of thought process that is sustained and well developed as in the case of human beings.

AN INTELLIGENT ORDER

The story of thought does not end with the elements of image and language. Though images and language are indispensable ingredients of thought, a jumble of images with verbal symbols would not constitute a thought. For instance, *In the garden, tomorrow, I, nearby, a walk, will, in morning, go, the, nearby* would not constitute a comprehensible thought. These verbal symbols having images have to be arranged in an intelligible order to make a thought that conveys the sense: *Tomorrow in the morning, I will go for a walk in the garden nearby.*

Who performs the task of arranging such a sensible order? Memory or emotions with their sweeping power of association cannot do that. This task requires a discretionary power, which is our innate intelligence. It can be then concluded that the makeup of thought includes the following three basic elements: (1) images representing objects or experiences, (2) memory, and (3) intelligence (see fig. 3.2). Additionally, a fourth element, namely language, is an essential factor that makes it possible to have a complex and sustained thought process with a remarkable clarity and ease. Language requires an enormous reserve of memory that humans are fortunate to have acquired in the course of evolution.

Further, if you observe carefully, you would realize that the flow of images in your thought is linear like a thread. The thought process appears to bear similarities with the mechanism of a motion film, wherein the still images are projected in a serial order to create a continuum of lifelike action. David Bohm, the distinguished scientist and a colleague of Albert Einstein, had first hinted at this similarity. The still images on the film reel are projected in such rapid succession that adequate time gap is not given to the mind to process them separately, and consequently an illusion of a lifelike picture is created through an overlap of images.

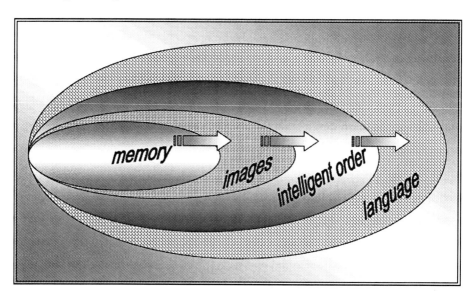

Figure 3.2. The ingredients of thought and its linear movement.

Our thoughts have a similar continuity that is even more dynamic, as our memory images have varied sensual contents. Some more astonishing distinctions are that these lively images are *screened* within the theatre of our mind, and we have the unique experience of subjective identification with them. This mysterious quality of subjectivity or ownership of mental experiences has baffled great scientists, who are still struggling to understand it. A human being always claims and defends "*my* thought, *my* experience or *my* feelings" without ever pausing to wonder at the mysterious qualities of the subjective ownership of our mental processes and sensory experiences. A routine robs us of the charm of life that abounds in the world around us.

The following two characteristics stand out in the nature of thought. First, thought is a linear process, which, by its very nature, imposes limits on the reach and comprehension power of thought as an instrumentality. It acts as if it is blinkered to gauge only a narrow perspective and lacks a wider vision. This is the reason why we have to weave a web of thoughts to get a comprehensive picture of a given situation or problem. Also thought is mechanical, somewhat like the motion film, which is intrinsically arbitrary and inflexible.

These limitations are important to be remembered in our interpersonal relationship and in the context of stress and anxieties that are fueled by thought. The important point to be noted is that thought is a mental entity *in itself* with its virtues and vices. This realization will teach us to be objective and not identify ourselves totally and blindly with our thoughts.

THE ERRAND BOY

It is quite evident that thought was a latecomer in the scheme of evolution. Its origin and sustenance depended on the expansion of consciousness that occurred later. In other words, thought is a product of *extended* consciousness or its conscious window. This is again borne out from the anatomical history of brain development. The extended consciousness is located mainly in the neocortex, the evolutionarily modern part of the brain. The brain stem and midbrain are the ancient parts of brain responsible for the inner (nonverbal) consciousness and primary emotions.

One can speculate that the future evolution of other animals, particularly mammals, might be in the direction of expanding memory and developing some sort of thinking ability closer to that of humans. The future evolution of human species will involve reduction of habitual and involuntary aspects of thought: enhancing a detached approach to thought and relying more on intelligence in the operation of thought. It will also make us aware of the limits of thought. That would reduce self-identification and blind faith in it. Of course, human beings and other forms of life will continue to rely on the time-saving mechanisms of reflex and autonomous actions in the form of biological urges, emotions, and skills-internalized knowledge.

Why did life find it imperative to evolve thinking ability in the course of evolution? Given the importance of thought that is so self-evident in our life, it is not difficult to imagine the reasons. When we look around, it is apparent that human species, with its enormous thinking ability, has left all other forms of life far behind in the game of survival and material welfare. This is an easy perception in the hindsight, but it does not explain why in the first place life found it exigent to create the thinking ability.

One significant reason may be that thought is a dynamic and versatile device to *operate intelligence*. It offers more freedom and choice of action in contrast to behavioral reflex and habitual actions, which are intrinsically autonomic, and inflexible. They are also predictable, and hence a predator can easily anticipate the reflex behavior of its prey and devise a counteraction to kill it. Similarly, in order to defend itself, a prey can anticipate the habitual tactics of a predator.

Though having some advantages, natural reflexes and habitual behavior represent the stereotyped ways of using intelligence in contrast to the ingenuity and pliability of thought. Also, the impulsive and prewired behavior handicaps an organism in adapting quickly to sudden changes in its ecosystem, thereby increasing risks to its survival.

The innate intelligence and the exponential growth of memory in human species were behind the creation of thought. The chances of survival and proliferation of life multiplied by an enhanced use of intelligence through the instrument of thought. The autonomic and stereotyped actions of intelligence in the genetic makeup of life were not adequate to prevail upon the ruthless forces of nature to protect life. These forces required extensive repertoire of intelligent actions and strategies at every step.

Being itself a nonmaterial phenomenon, intelligence needed a material medium to express itself. The apparatus of thought was perhaps the next feasible option for intelligence to manifest and operate at a higher scale. Yet intelligence alone cannot create a thought; it needed an infrastructure of enormous memory, which the human beings have. Unfortunately, other life forms are yet to acquire such prodigious memory, and hence they make do with limited memory images to work out strategies for bare survival. Of course, they also have the nonverbal intelligence built into the biomechanics of urges, reflexes, and emotions.

The connection between memory and thinking power is very strong. The larger the memory, the more robust the thinking ability. In sum, thought appears to be the child born in wedlock of intelligence and prolific memory. What about the role of language, which is indispensable for constituting a thought? We should not forget that language is a byproduct of memory with the helping hand of intelligence.

Nevertheless, the fate of this child was not very enviable. It was destined to work as *an errand boy* for the biological urges and emotions that seek fulfillment but cannot do it adequately on their own. Does it mean that other forms of life lacking thinking ability are unable to fulfill their urges and emotions? They do it, but only at the minimum threshold to sustain and propagate life.

The biological desires, urges, and emotions in human species have assumed highly complex dimensions making their fulfillment an endless and insatiable task. Besides, we have a myriad of psychological desires and feelings in the forms of aspirations, dreams, pride, and prejudices. Our desires for material acquisition and dominance over others are nearly immortal. All this needed someone—an errand boy—to work for their fulfillment. Thought was created to serve that role.

Let us see how the errand boy works in daily life. When lunchtime approaches, the hungry stomach sends a signal through a biochemical process to the brain wherein the feeling for appetite is activated. This region responsible for the feeling of hunger sends a signal to activate the process of thought in the neocortex. Thought, like an errand boy, begins to act. *Which place do I go for lunch? The nearby café has delicious food, but it would be crowded now and the service is slow while I still have a lot of work in the office to finish. The preparation for the meeting in the afternoon has to be accomplished beforehand. Either I choose an eatery where there is a self-service or request my secretary to go and fetch food from a nearby place.*

Some thought is given to selecting the items of food and drink. All this work of the thought machinery results in executing the order of the feeling of hunger. Similar planning and execution are done by thought to meet the demands of other biological urges and desires.

Thought has to attend to the desires at the psychological level such as *I should perform well in the meeting to impress my boss and enhance my image. That will increase my chances of promotion. The other colleagues might try to be smart and present counter arguments to my proposals in the meeting, but I should do better.*

Thought has to work hard to decide a strategy to achieve it. If I were a businessperson, I would wish to outperform my competitors. I aspire to build my commercial venture as the biggest in the country. Some other people would strive to be famous writers, poets, or musicians. All this is not possible without the hard work of the machinery of thought.

It is obvious that our biological urges and psychological desires are primarily made of the strong stuff of feelings and emotions that make the machinery of thought grind day and night. In fact, the emotions and feelings that underpin human aspirations, dreams, pride, and prejudices occupy an imperial position. While thoughts are supposed to fan out as foot soldiers to fulfill our big or small dreams and wage war to destroy or build empires—political or corporate. Feeling is the prime mover, covertly or explicitly, behind the *errands* of thought. The primacy of feelings over thought is unquestionable in the scheme of evolution. It is quite evident that thought was created later as an *action brigade* to serve the orders of feelings and emotions.

It is therefore not surprising that all of us face the dilemma throughout our life over the impotency of thought and its rational ability against the inexorable and often brute force of powerful feelings and emotions. At times our thoughtful decisions to overcome worries and stressful emotions fail to our discomfiture making us feel helpless and miserable. In the latter part of the book, we will explore some effective ways of dealing with that problem by learning to use our innate intelligence to bring about equilibrium of thought and emotions.

AN ELEMENT OF REFLEX AND RIGIDITY

We normally tend to take thought as synonymous with intelligence, but that notion is factually misplaced. Thought per se is never intelligence as such. It is only a vehicle or medium of externalizing and communicating intelligence. Thought is intrinsically neither intelligent nor unintelligent. It merely carries the impulse of intelligence in varying degrees. Yet when we qualify a thought as stupid, it would mean that the thought in question has hardly any contents of intelligence. Similarly, a thought designated as intelligent signifies that it is laden with a good deal of intelligence. Though this issue might sound to be an exercise in hairsplitting, the intention here is to portray the generic nature of thought and distinguish it from innate intelligence.

Apart from thought being a garb of intelligence, we also discussed the role of intelligence in constituting thoughts. It was mentioned that without the action of intelligence, the mental images having visual, emotive and information contents would be evoked from memory merely as a bunch of disparate entities. A question would, however, arise: why don't we clearly experience the effort of our intelligence while performing such tasks?

There appears to be at least two reasons for this. First, our intelligence performs this task so rapidly that we do not notice the effort and instead get an illusion that thought is selecting the words. On the other hand, when we concentrate to construct a sentence, we search for appropriate words. In such instance, the selective effort of intelligence to arrange images can be experienced. It would be incorrect to say that the structure of one thought creates another thought.

The second reason why we are not able to recognize the task of intelligence is the brain mechanism of internalizing the skill learning. For instance, the car driving skill is stored in memory as a set of reflex actions beyond the conscious mind. Similarly the skill of selecting and arranging memory images with verbal symbols also operates as a subconscious action of intelligence.

Let us return to the main issue, namely the element of rigidity and reflex in the operation of thoughts. In addition to skills, our brain also often generates feelings and thoughts in the forms of reflex and internalized action. This accounts for all our habitual and routine thoughts, which we hardly recognize as such. Since we are used to assuming thought as spontaneous manifestations of intelligence, it would surprise us to learn that many of our thoughts are reflex impulses or compulsive replay of internalized behavior. This has serious implications in our practical life.

As we know, the thoughts, feelings and memories arising in the reflex mode often defy our determinations and willpower. That is evident when we look at our experiences of stress and anxiety. We wish to stop the thoughts and emotions of mental hurt or grief, but our rational willpower is unable to prevail upon. Even in daily routine, we find our mind humming all the time with thoughts that also spill over in dreams. The bulk of them are routine and repetitive. On the other hand, the evils of sectarian intolerance and terrorism are largely the products of impulsive and fossilized thoughts. Similarly, our societal divides, prejudices, and superstitions are the manifestations of rigid and reflex thoughts.

Reflex thoughts depend more on memory and less on intelligence. Conversely, when we are occupied in a nonroutine and complex thought process, like responding to a difficult question or writing a serious article, the role of intellect becomes predominant, and memory assumes a subordinate position as a mere supplier of images with or without verbal symbols. Such an intense way of thinking has much less element of reflex.

The great philosopher Jiduu Krishnamurti and Dr. David Bohm attribute reflex and mechanical qualities to all our thoughts (J. Krishnamurti and David Bohm, *The Limits of Thought: Discussions* [London: Routledge, 1999], 45-51). The autonomic operation of our thoughts is much more pervasive than we realize. This explains the element of rigidity and arbitrariness inherent in thought as a system.

Let us speculate a possibility of creating a thinking machine. We discussed in the previous chapter that images are memorized in the brain as what the neuroscientists call dispositional representations *(*sensory impulses). It can be speculated that our routine thoughts as strings of mental images might be memorized in our brain as dispositional representations. Such thought impulses would have fixed patterns of neural firings. Compared to a single memory image, the neural patterns underlying a thought would be more complex and longer.

Does this provide a possibility of creating a thinking machine or robot? A large body of thoughts in the form of integrated units could be memorized in the same manner as the words are presently stored in the computer chips. The optical, audio, and other electromechanical sensors can serve as stimuli for activating specific thought units. One thought unit can also stimulate related units to provide continuum of thought process.

However, the major difficulty that seems insurmountable is to create the *dispositional automation* or sensory impulse that is imbued with the quality of consciousness. It seems that consciousness is the underlying essence of the thought mechanism. The impulse of consciousness is indispensable for endowment of autonomic character to any conceptual thought machine. Additionally, such a machine would require the almost inexhaustible operational stimuli from both the *vital* intelligence and the repertoire of complex emotions that humans have.

COGNITION AND CREATIVE INTELLIGENCE

Let us understand the process of cognition and the role that thought plays in it. When we come across an object, our optical nerves send the visual contents of the object to particular parts of the brain to process. Memory is called upon to supply information to identify the characteristics of the object. Intelligence carries out the task of processing the information and determining the properties such as whether the object is animate or inanimate. This process of accessing and analyzing information leading to understanding and knowledge is called cognition.

The cognition process involves mainly memory and intelligence that normally works through the medium of thought. The thinking process is involved in analyzing and arriving at the final product in the form of an understanding. However, the act of cognition winding through the process of thought becomes a time-consuming action, while many challenges in life do not allow such a long time to react. Mother Nature, being the dynamic force governing the evolution of life, is adept at finding improved and speedier ways of performing tasks. That is the reason why humans and other forms of life continue to struggle ceaselessly to improve themselves.

In order to meet the challenges of life, the mind has evolved an *instant intelligent perception*, which is a way of bypassing thinking process and arriving at immediate understanding. Experts tell us that the right hemisphere of our brain has the ability to grasp instantly the myriad patterns of a complex situation. Instead of tackling just one linear element at a time, the brain grasps in a flash the multiple aspects of a given situation (Carl Sagan, *The Dragons of Eden: Speculations on the Evolution of Human Intelligence* [New York: Ballantine Books, 1977], 177). The right hemisphere specializes in an instant perception in contrast to the left, where the thinking ability operating in the linear mode is located. The methodology called reductionism in science, constituting a step by step approach, is an instance of the linear action of the brain.

Artistic inspirations originate in the right hemisphere. The right hemisphere of the brain of an artist is believed to be relatively more developed, which endows the creative talents of music, painting, and sculpture. Women are often believed to have higher ability than man to operate through the right hemisphere. They seem to be endowed with a greater instinctual depth. This segment of the brain is also responsible for great scientific discoveries and inventions.

Over millennia, people have seen fruits falling down from the trees, but their routine thoughts never found it worth any particular attention. In contrast, Newton's mind was inspired with a creative intelligence, and hence he was intrigued with the apple falling down instead of going up in the sky. In an instant perception, he discovered the profound truth of gravity, the primary force that mysteriously governs the universe. Most of the great scientists like Einstein have attributed their unique achievements to such rare inspirations of creative intelligence.

Let me clarify a point. There is a general notion among people that creative inspiration is something sublime and mysterious while intelligence is a mundane and cool operator. For them, it would sound inappropriate to characterize the instant operation of intelligence as synonymous with artistic and scientific inspiration. In my view, this is an inadequate perception of the nature of intelligence and amounts to downgrading it to a dull entity. Such an impression arises from equating intelligence with thought that operates most of the time in a routine and stereotyped fashion.

Undiluted by thought and memory, the core of innate intelligence is sublime, artistic and truly mysterious like consciousness. Rather, to be more accurate, the generic intelligence and consciousness are one and the same. Intelligence is the defining property of life, and it operates as the prime mover of life in an implicit or explicit manner. On the other hand, the reasoning or thinking mode is just a routine and fragmented operation of intelligence.

It is interesting to try and understand the way the inspirational intelligence works. By the accounts of artists and scientists, the pinnacle of their genius was when thought was tired and resigned to rest. In the case of a scientific or mathematical riddle, the mind struggled hard for days with intense thought process to seek solution. This was followed sometimes by an inspiration or instant insight. It can also happen differently without the preceding phase of intense thinking as if springing from nowhere. However, in such occurrences one thing is quite clear: that thought was not in operation precisely when the artistic or great scientific inspiration manifested itself.

It seems reasonable to conclude that intelligence manifests itself in the *silence of thought* or the *vacuum* between two thoughts. I feel it is true for both the inspirational as well as the routine and slow mode of operation of intelligence. It is useful to reiterate here that thought is utilized as the means of communication by intelligence as it manifests in the vacuum between the thoughts. The silence between thoughts is so amazingly brief and fleeting that we slur it over without clear recognition. What we call as deep concentration is, in fact, an effort we make to dig deep into that vacuum to seek the help of intelligence. Unfortunately, thought is hauntingly around with its usual impatience, like a devoted workman, to carry away the stuff of intelligence.

It would be relevant to consider the nature of intuition in the context of cognition. Intuition is an instant action bypassing the circuitous process of thought and memory. People tend to mystify intuition as something outlandish and defying logic, but that is not true. The intuitive actions and decisions in our daily life are mostly instant reactions of past memories that are hidden. We tend to qualify such reactions as mysterious, because the underlying memories are not accessible to the conscious mind. Secondly, an explicit thought process does not take place at the conscious level. There is no guarantee that such intuitive actions are always right. These might be right or wrong depending on the good luck or bad.

Sometimes, we intuitively like or dislike a stranger or even an acquaintance. Often the reasons behind that are our hidden memories of pleasant or unpleasant experiences of persons having similar physical features or mannerism. These might be prejudices based on old memories, which do not operate at the conscious level. In sum, our routine intuitive behavior is an instant cognitive result of subconscious memories, a sort of short-circuit action. The point to be noted is that such intuitive actions cannot reveal anything beyond the *sum total of past memories*. It also calls for caution and healthy skepticism before relying frequently on intuitive behavior or gut feelings.

It needs to be clarified that the intuition and inspiration experienced by great poets, artists, and scientists fall into a different category. Those are unique phenomena transcending activities of memory and thought. That is an action of intelligence of a higher order springing from the vacuum in the absence of both thought and memory. However, one has to distinguish in each case whether it is a routine impulsive action of memories or a unique intuition of an artist or scientist.

THE LIMITS OF THOUGHT

In the context of stress and anxiety, it is quite essential to understand the limits of thought. Earlier we touched upon the fact that thought is *a string of dynamic images in the linear mode*. If we use an analogy, this linear string of images moves like a beam of light illuminating a narrow band of dark space comprising only a few degrees and not the entire panoramic view of 360 degrees. Of course, we can mentally visualize the complete scene by moving the beam around in full circle. Yet in each focus, we can see only a small patch of the space and at the end we can patch up mentally the full picture of the panorama. The vividness and wholeness of the scenery in your mind will be commensurate with how strong a memory you possess in order to put together the patches of the panorama revealed by the rotating beam of light. Even if you have a powerful memory, the picture would remain still patchy and not perfectly real due to the limits imposed by the narrow beam.

Actually, the working of our thought is quite similar to the analogy of light beam. Thought is in fact a *beam of our consciousness* that helps us to *illuminate* and know the external world. Unfortunately, the picture we grasp is patchy and represents an approximation of the events and objects. Jiduu Krishnamurti defined thought as *basically fragmented* implying that it provides only a fragmented or partial perception of reality (J. Krishnamurti and David Bohm, *The Limits of Thought: Discussions* [London: Routledge, 1999], 56-7).

If we carefully scrutinize our experiences in daily life, the quality of thought, as a fragmented perception, would be more evident. Such examples abound particularly in our interpersonal life at home, or in social life. This is where the limits of thought are manifested in the form of misunderstandings, subjective judgments, and partial perceptions. These lead to psychological conflicts and sorrow, which build up as stress and depression. The painful events in our life like divorce and clashes with friends or colleagues are often accumulations of partial perceptions arising from our habitual and excessive faith in the accuracy of thoughts.

One might argue that all this sounds true, but there is nothing one can do if thought is innately fragmented and inadequate for grasping facts of life. We cannot live tentatively and remain distrustful of our thoughts. That would undermine our confidence in ourselves and erode our decision-making power with negative consequences. Hence, we have to make do with what we have without bothering about such fine distinctions.

This observation is quite valid, but let us go back to the analogy of the beam of light. When it illuminates one small patch of space, we do not take it as a woeful limit, but instead slowly move the beam around to cover the 360-degree view of the panorama. At the end, we put together the illuminated patches and generate a holistic picture in our mind. Of course, it would still remain patchy and approximate. When we have to base our actions or judgments on such a cumulative picture, we do so by taking into account its patchy and approximate qualities, otherwise we are making a mistake. In this instance, we do not get upset or become distrustful of the limits of the light beam. We simply accept the fact, make allowances for the shortcomings, and act accordingly without being indecisive.

Similarly in real life, we have to comprehend the limits of thought in its acts of perceiving or mapping the world—our relationship and our interactions at home, at the office and in society. Then while being aware of the inherent shortcomings of thought as a phenomenon, we will need to make allowances to compensate and ensure that our judgments are as much objective and mature as possible. In sum, our blind faith and subjective submergence in thought have to be questioned and abandoned. Our total confidence in our thoughts and perceptions makes us assume that we are right, while others are not. A degree of healthy skepticism in the perceptive power of thought is very rewarding, and it should not erode our decision power or confidence.

Somehow, deep down in our mind, we are aware of the fragmentary nature of thought, and that is betrayed in our collective and social behavior. In an attempt to overcome the shortcomings of thought, we resort to cooperation and collective actions. The committees, conferences, seminars, and workshops are such instances where we try to gauge the reality of issues by pooling together many individuals and experts. Such joint action is expected to shed more light and provide holistic perceptions of reality akin to the combination of several light beams to illuminate a larger panorama.

THE PERCEPTION OF REALITY

Let me begin with Albert Einstein's quotation, "Reality is merely an illusion, albeit a very persistent one." Earlier, we discussed that the perceptive ability of thought is inherently patchy. Philosophers have gone even one step further and said that however hard we struggle either individually or collectively, we are constitutionally incapable of capturing the actual *reality-out-there*. We can grasp only an approximate reality that is *virtual* to our state of being as humans (see fig. 3.3). They question the actual strength of the light beam of the earlier analogy. It can be dim, bright, or colored, which would affect the quality of illumination and revelation of the picture. Besides, the perception of an object will differ in accordance with the wavelength of the light one is operating. For instance, night-vision instrument will enable us to see what our unaided eyes cannot do.

In order to overcome the limits of our eyes, we use microscopes and telescopes. The vision of the external world will change depending on the specific power of the optical gadgets. The universe will look different if we see it through the x-rays. The image of the table viewed by our naked eye would turn into a large ensemble of dancing atoms, if we look at it through a high-powered electron microscope.

Thus, our vision is a virtual reality *relative* to the viewing gadget. Similar conditions apply to our mental vision obtained through the instrument of thought. Our eye is a gadget for optical perception, while thought is the gadget for *psychic* perception and both have their limits and distortions of the reality-out-there. This would indicate that the external world we see and experience through the optical and psychic visions is a world relative to human perceptions. It is a construct of the human mind with its limited capacities. Notwithstanding our enormous scientific and technological achievements, the world experienced by us represents a totality of relative perceptions of *something out there* that is ultimate and independent of us.

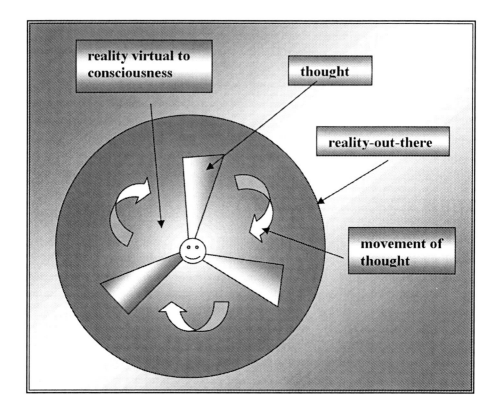

Figure 3.3. The limits of human perception of the *reality-out-there*.

This reminds of the famous dialogue on "Truth and the Nature of Reality" between Albert Einstein, the great scientist, and Rabindranath Tagore, the poet and Nobel laureate of India. Einstein argued that the truth or universe could be understood in its totality, if we have all the necessary information and mathematical capabilities. Tagore disagreed and argued that the universe we perceive is a truth relative to the nature and limits of our consciousness and intelligence. In Tagore's opinion, the limits of the human existential situation make the absolute reality *only partially accessible* to us. The truth we perceive will be just a *human truth* or human understanding and *not* the absolute reality. In the end, there was no convergence of views between these two great minds. However, Tagore seems to be right in the context of the ultimate reality that is unknowable, while Einstein was convinced of the absolute power of the human intelligence

(Ilya Prigogine and Isabelle Stengers, *Order out of Chaos: Man's New Dialogue with Nature* [Great Britain: Flamingo,1985], 293. Also, W. Heisenberg, *Physics and Beyond: Encounters and Conversations* [Harper Torchbooks], 51)

A cat is forbidden by the limits of its brain to understand Einstein's theory of relativity, even if it tries hard for its entire lifetime. Tagore seems to imply that human species (or any other life form) also suffers from some existential constraints. It is true even though it hurts human pride and chauvinism. The acute realization of such limits of the human thought and intelligence makes one feel a sort of *existential claustrophobia*. Some of our literary writers known for their philosophy of existentialism have betrayed such claustrophobia of the human predicament. Sometimes, one can't help wondering that our intellectual pride is nothing but a human vanity in the context of the universe as an *unknowable* entity.

To place in its proper context, intelligence is a very versatile and dynamic power that not only guarantees survival of life but also accelerates its progressive evolution. Yet beyond that, it seems to have no role in the larger scheme of the universe. The phenomenon of life having discerning properties of intelligence and feelings presents a stark contrast to the brute forces of the universe, which are intrinsically arbitrary, amoral, and neutral to intelligence. That is obvious in the universe, which is perpetually violent with black holes sucking up star systems and galaxies committing cannibalism by gobbling up other galaxies. It is infinitely merciful that such cataclysms occur in the immense vastness of space and in the timescales of millions of years in contrast to the extremely miniscule age of a few millennia of human civilizations on this tiny planet.

The functional utility of intelligence includes the acquisition and use of knowledge that is more efficacious for adaptation compared to the defense mechanisms of feelings, urges, and reflexes possessed by the living organisms. Yet we should not overlook the limits and negative consequences of knowledge. It is accumulative and has the inherent limits of *locality and relativity*. Against that perspective, Vedanta, the philosophic scripture of ancient India, counsels wise persons to transcend the urge to pursue knowledge beyond a point in order to liberate the mind from the stress and tension of mundane life. Vedanta means "end of knowledge" (*Veda* means "to know" and *anta* "an end"). Vedanta describes the pursuit of knowledge as a disease to be cured for experiencing oneness with the Ultimate Being manifested as the universe (Harald Fritzsch, *The Creation of Matter: The Universe from Beginning to End* [New York: Basic Books, Inc. 1984], 277-9).

Whether one is able to share the perspective of Vedanta or not, it seems certain that the pursuit of knowledge as an accumulative habit and psychological gratification is not much different from the greed and pursuit of incremental wealth. It does entail cost in terms of stress and frustration in life.

Let us put aside the discussion of that philosophical absolutism and focus on practical relevance for us. Such discussion is taken by people as a prescription for nihilism. Resorting to extreme skepticism or nihilism by rejecting everything as meaningless would indeed be an escapism and utter stupidity. For us, this is our precious world, our life, and all that we can claim to possess. We have to face happily and successfully our dimension of reality without being mired in the debate of virtual or absolute attributes.

The pertinent lesson for us from the discussion is to be humble and realize that our habitual belief in the absolute veracity of human perceptions and thoughts is presumptive. The existential bondage of subjectivity is a deeper constraint for us and to that extent we need extra caution to scrutinize our decisions and judgments that have critical impact on our life. The formidable forces of the universe and its immense time and space should make us feel the shame and pettiness of racial and ideological conflicts and violence on our tiny planet. We have to rediscover the virtues of empathy, love, and compassion for fellow beings as well as other life-forms. Though it is easier said than done, our endeavors in that direction will reduce stress, conflicts, and sorrow not only in our personal life but also in the lives of people around us.

SYMBIOSIS WITH EMOTIONS AND FEELINGS

It is essential to understand the interrelationship of thought, emotions, and feelings, which is quite intricate and mutually supportive. We have to go into this because understanding this interrelationship has practical implications for tackling emotional problems and stress. Being aware of the way these psychic forces operate gives us some command over them as well as an ability to diffuse their unyielding power.

There are at least four dimensions of this symbiotic relationship. The first is the constitutional connection. As we learned earlier, most of the memory images that flow in the body of a thought have emotive contents. For instance, the words representing images like *picnic, friend, father, wife, party,* and *accident* have contents that are more explicit emotively. On the other hand, the matter-of-fact words like *table, door, shoes,* and *road* may have less emotive contents, unless one has special emotional associations.

The second dimension of relationship is that thought acts as a vehicle to carry feelings and emotions and also as an instrument of their expression. Unlike the constitutional dimension that is rather implicit, this dimension is a matter of explicit experience in our daily life. Our feelings of anger, hurt, fear, wonder, and joy find expressions in our thoughts. As we know, the poets and literary writers give expressions to their feelings in more artistic and vivid thoughts. Thought, by means of language, is the most articulate form of communicating our feelings. We also do so through body language, gestures, and behavior, but thought again plays a very crucial role in shaping our actions and behavior.

The third dimension of relationship is the role of thought as a catalyst of feelings and emotions (see fig. 3.4). Normally, feelings and memory drive the activities of thought, as they are more powerful and intense elements of mind. Nonetheless, thought also becomes the instrument of generating and sustaining feelings and emotions. During a relaxed weekend, a sudden thought of going to the office the next day would unleash emotions and even anxieties of pending work and difficult interactions with some colleagues. More thoughts and memories accompanied with feelings will ensue, gaining a momentum of their own. On the other hand, in the midst of office work, a sudden thought of the approaching vacation will crowd the mind with pleasant feelings and daydreams about the exciting trip.

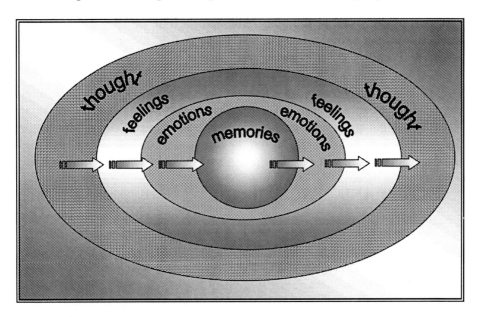

Figure 3.4. The two-way provocative actions of the mental processes. Memories provoke emotions, which result in feelings and finally thoughts. It can be also a reverse chain of action, wherein thought can lead to feelings, emotions and memories.

Let me clarify that, as discussed in the chapter on memory, the processes of thought, memory and feelings intertwine so closely that it becomes quite arduous to distinguish who triggered whom. These mental phenomena have mutually evocative as well as mutually reinforcing powers. These integrative processes are normally advantageous for survival, but also turn out to be quite exacerbating and painful factors in stress and anxieties. They act as mutual catalysts for one another, and the catalytic processes become more intense and rapid in stress and depression. Conversely, if the strength of one of them is dissipated, it would break their vicious cycle and bring a welcome relief.

The fourth dimension of relationship is the role of thought as an *errand boy* for feelings and emotions, which was discussed earlier.

THE ROLE OF THOUGHT IN STRESS

Since the role of thought in stress and emotional afflictions has been already mentioned in this chapter, a brief statement will suffice here. In our common experience, thought is one of the main culprits in the incidence of stress, anxiety, and depression. When one is caught up in the emotional turmoil of anger, agony, hurt or fear, the *winds* of thoughts blow fiercely. The negative memories and emotions continue to breed thoughts relentlessly and the thoughts, in turn, further deepen and prolong the pain and agony.

The functional characteristics of thought and its activities as a carrier, catalyst, and errand boy of feelings were discussed earlier. That speaks volumes about the critical role played by thought in the incidence of stress, depression and anxieties. As this chapter deals with the nature of thought, the remedial suggestions on how to cope with stress and the negative aspects of thought are discussed in the latter part of this book.

A CULPRIT AND BENEFACTOR

The portrait of thought emerging in this chapter might look startlingly negative, but let us look at some of the virtues of thought. Despite its limits, we cannot overlook the enormous role it plays in our life. It has helped us immensely to survive successfully in our long evolutionary journey. The early and exponential growth of our thinking ability gave us an exceedingly vast edge over other species in the fierce battle for survival. The growth of human civilizations since the ancient days and the dazzling achievements of humanity in science and technology are primarily because of thought. It would be impossible to sustain our daily life without the activity of thought, and we will definitely continue to depend on it for sustenance and advancement of our life in the foreseeable future.

All the same, it would be a partial truth if one ignores the other consequences of thought that mankind has suffered over millennia and will perhaps continue to do so, i.e., the wars, violence, exploitation, and miseries. Societies continue to be divided, at times, brutally in the name of race, color, religion and nationalism. The horrendous atrocities of the Nazis, Pol Pot, and other cruel autocratic regimes were the extreme manifestations of the dark side of the nature of thought. It is a very distressing fact that since the dawn of history, no other creature but man has been the most gruesome and violent to man. Human beings enjoy the dubious distinction of being the biggest predator on this planet causing devastating environmental problems with their unbridled commercialism and consumerism.

The positive and negative consequences of thought prove that thought is a double-edged instrument like a surgeon's knife, which can be used for bestowing life or snatching it away. However, it might be argued that the direct connection of thought with the positive and negative consequences mentioned earlier is sweeping and not well-founded. The wars and violence ensue from a set of complex reasons including man's greed and aggressiveness, while the progress of human civilization accrues from man's aspirations and desire for advancement. That is no doubt true, but as we discussed earlier, thought is the action-brigade of desires, aspirations, aggressiveness and greed of man. It is the thought that finally plans, executes and achieves the results, good or bad.

A legitimate question would also arise that if thought is merely a vehicle of intelligence and feelings propelled by memory, how can we hold it responsible for either conflicts and violence or all our great achievements? Here one has to bear in mind that, despite being a vehicle, thought would not exist in the absence of intelligence, feelings, and information stored in the memory. Thought is a systemic entity that comes into being due to its different constituent parts. It is akin to the car as a systemic entity that is nothing but the totality of its parts such as wheels, engine, fuel and body.

One cannot deny the fact that intelligence, emotions, feelings, and memories are the causative factors behind our actions and behavior. They are the masters and string pullers behind the scene, but the errand boy gets caught in the act by an onlooker. Among the hidden actors, emotions and feelings happen to play a more powerful role. Hence, the next chapter is devoted to that subject.

CHAPTER 4

EMOTIONS AND FEELINGS

Poetry may make us from time to time a little more aware of the deeper, unnamed feelings which form the substratum of our being, to which we rarely penetrate; for our lives are mostly a constant evasion of ourselves.
—T. S. Eliot

Emotions and feelings play a predominant and decisive role in our day-to-day life. At home in dealing with relatives, our behavior is imbued with feelings and emotions either in mild or intense forms. When, after a long time, you meet your affectionate mother or loving spouse, the tender emotions of love and joy overwhelm you. On returning home after a long business trip, when your sweet toddler manages to run up to the doorstep shouting, "Mummy, Mummy," the surge of intense emotion of motherly love engulfs your entire being.

On the other hand, the daily life in the family also presents situations that overpower us with anger or irritations. In the office or social gatherings, we remain well guarded against betraying emotions, even in provocative situations though we experience a variety of them ranging from joy and happiness to nervousness, irritation, and anger.

Experiencing emotions is just the beginning of the drama of life. The more crucial stage that follows is the unfolding of feelings in the form of our actions and decisions. Our thoughts and actions are governed and shaped by the impulses of emotions. Even when we perceive ourselves as thinking or acting coolly, emotions are quietly operating in the background as mood or disposition of the moment. Though we may not notice or recognize it, their ubiquitous and hidden presence is undeniably there.

We are all familiar with the obstinate nature of emotions. They are indeed very difficult customers to be handled. Many complications and troubles in life ensue from the unyielding and arbitrary forces of emotions. The problems of stress and depression are rooted in the inexorable nature of emotions. One feels helpless and spellbound against the force of emotions. For instance, when one is angry, it is difficult to act wisely. Similar behavioral lapses occur in the fits of other emotions.

No wonder, we tend to be wary of feelings and relegate them to a lower position in comparison to reason. That is, however, a flawed idea. It has been now well established that the role of feelings and emotions is much more crucial than we normally realize. In neurological research, it is discovered that our reasoning ability gets seriously eroded when the areas of brain responsible for feelings and emotions are damaged (Antonio Damasio, *The Feeling of What Happens: Body and Emotion in the Making of Consciousness* [New York: Harcourt, INC. 1999], 41-42).

Our reasoning ability is not only rooted in feelings and emotions but also governed by them. It is beyond doubt that they are the primary psychic forces, which govern the biomechanics of life in order to ensure its survival and well-being. Given their enormous significance in shaping and commanding the mental processes of thinking, reasoning, and memory as well as our behavior, it is essential to understand the nature and operation of emotions and feelings.

DISTINCTION BETWEEN EMOTION AND FEELING

It is necessary to clarify the words *feeling and emotion* to avoid a communication gap. As lay persons, often we tend to make no distinction in them. We use them interchangeably, which is evident in the linguistic usages like *feeling of anger* or *emotion of anger* and *feeling of* love or *emotion of love*.

Nonetheless, these terms are used for expressing different nuances. Emotion is considered a *more intense form* of experience than feeling. Emotions reveal themselves in a visible body language, while feelings, being less volatile, are accompanied with faint or no bodily manifestations. When the emotion of anger or fear ensues, our heart starts racing fast, breathing becomes shorter, skin begins to sweat, muscles become tense, and the body experiences emotional tremors. The brain dispatches fast electro-chemical messages, and the biochemical profile of the body undergoes changes to meet the emotional challenge.

Emotions seem to place the mind and body in an accelerated motion and that is why perhaps the word *emotion* originated from the Latin word *emovere*: *e* added with *movere*, which signifies motion. The great neurologist Dr. A. Damasio, however, makes specific distinctions between feeling and emotion in his brilliant book *The Feeling of What Happens: Body and Emotion in the Making of Consciousness*. In his opinion, emotions are a complicated collection of chemical and neural responses, forming a pattern, which involve both body and mind. Emotions are automated reactions that take place as bioregulatory devices to assist maintenance of life. They play out themselves in the theatre of the body and hence are visible to others in terms of distinct body language and behavioral reactions.

Dr. Damasio propounds that emotions occur first as unconscious and involuntary reactions of mind and body that subsequently get recognized and experienced by the conscious mind as feelings (see fig.4.1). That means one needs a conscious mind in order to feel emotion as a specific and explicit feeling. The ability to feel or own feeling as an organism's private experience resulted from the growth of consciousness that occurred later in the evolution. He believes that the biomechanism of emotions was evolved first in the course of evolution of life in terms of defensive mechanism of body.

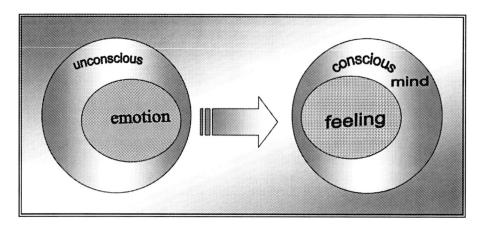

Figure 4.1. Emotion arises as an unconscious reaction of mind. When it reaches the conscious mind, it is recognized and experienced as a feeling.

The opinion of Dr. A. Damasio seems to be quite revealing. Yet it is also a fact that multiple sequences of emotions and feelings occur from moment to moment in swift cycles, which are perceived as overlapping and parallel. These cyclic processes make it difficult for a layman to recognize the fine distinction. Moreover, Dr. Damasio also adds that emotion and feeling are a *functional continuum*: an unconscious emotive response becoming a conscious experience of feeling after some microseconds. These factors account for why we are unable to distinguish between emotion and feeling except in terms of the degree of their intensity and impact.

For our practical purpose, I have used the word *emotion* in this book both as a separate process that is involuntary and as an interchangeable term with feeling. Let me also clarify that the qualifications of intensity and volatility mentioned earlier are applicable to both emotions and feelings and cannot be taken as the distinguishing characteristics.

BIOLOGICAL AND PSYCHOLOGICAL DESIRES

It is useful to understand the distinction of desire and urge vis-à-vis feeling and emotion. The words *desire, urge,* and *wish* are used often as synonyms, though they have their specific nuances. In general sense, these words stand for a state of mind and body in need of something at the physical or psychological level. For instance, when the stomach is empty causing a drop of sugar level in the blood, that information is signaled through the nervous system to the brain resulting in the desire for food. The brain generates the feeling of appetite which activates an organism to look for food.

It appears that a desire or urge in the form of a biological state of demand causes the brain to generate feelings that command the organism to action to fulfill the desire or urge. Desire or urge can generate multiple emotions, feelings and thoughts as instruments that lead to executive action or behavior.

The desires for food, sex, thirst, and sleep represent biological states of demand; but there are also the psychological states of demand like the desire to be a great writer, politician, business tycoon, or to own a more luxurious car. Such desires are generated because of psychological reasons that are connected with the social, cultural or individual factors. Unlike the biological ones, these desires are more complex, requiring a prolonged time-frame for fulfillment and account for most of our complications in life. Conversely, the lack of their fulfillment does not immediately and drastically upset the chemistry of body and harm it, but it results in long-term psychological afflictions like stress and depression. These afflictions affect the bioequilibrium of body and brain with grave consequences.

The other notable trait of the psychological desire is that it is incremental in its nature and often seems to be insatiable and breeding continuously. Its defining quality is *more and more*. For instance, if one succeeds in getting a bigger car, the next step is to hanker for more cars and models that are more prestigious. If you manage to become a millionaire, the desire to become a multimillionaire or billionaire is not far behind. The same applies to the desires for fame and power.

It is not a religious belief, but an actual experience of every one of us that satisfying a desire, particularly the psychological ones, is an endless task. This was aptly summed up in an analogy by Vivekananda, one of the great philosophers in India. He compared the fate of a man with that of a horse pulling cart on the road. Ultimately, both die in the harness—the horse on the road and the man on the path of seeking fulfillment of endless desires. This is the reason why practically all religions exhort people to curb desires.

Such characterization should not mislead us to think that desires are bad and one should strive to be free from them. The biological desires and urges cannot be eliminated except by gravely harming body and mind. These cannot be curbed also by any means, including religious beliefs, without causing psychic disorders. Conversely, an excessive gratification of biological urges is equally detrimental and indicates an obsessive disorder of mind. To be fair, most of the religions exhort against excessive gratifications. As against the biological urges, the psychological demands can be curbed or even eliminated through understanding or suppression.

The suppression and escapism routes are harmful as they lead to neurotic problems. But factual analysis and understanding of psychological desires would help avoid many complications. One has to be objective and intellectually alert to ensure that one is not suppressing such desires. One has to guard against the possibilities of self-deception because the human mind is very clever in cheating itself without realizing the harmful consequences of such action.

CONFLICT BETWEEN EMOTION AND THOUGHT

Let us look into some practical issues. We sometimes take a vow to rein in negative emotions and feelings, but get exasperated at our failure to do so. All of us experience the pain of our rational decisions being frustrated by the inner forces of emotions. We are at a loss to understand why our determination to act more rationally is thwarted. It is quite imperative to find out the causes behind this and remedies that are based on understanding and not on beliefs contrived to escape the facts of life.

What seems clear is that the decisions to rein in negative emotions are the *actions of our thought*. But thought seems to operate at a different level than that of feelings and emotions. Neurologists tell us that our thoughts, emotions, and feelings are generated by different regions of our brain. Is this the reason why thought cannot exercise a firm control over feelings and emotions? Although all regions of our brain are interconnected and act in unison, their influencing power upon each other is quite limited. Thought can diffuse the feeling that is very mild, but it is helpless before strong emotions. Rather, emotions and feelings overpower and command thought, as discussed in the previous chapter.

This suggests the need for a *direct action* in the regions of the brain responsible for emotions and feelings in order to influence them more effectively. Such an action has to be qualitatively different from suppression and self-hypnotism through autosuggestions and beliefs—religious or otherwise. Autosuggestions and beliefs provide transient results, since they are externally imposed actions. The initial euphoria wears off soon and one finds oneself back to square one. Such methods are basically unnatural and lead to mental distortions. Even, the drills of positive thinking are hardly different from autosuggestions and self-hypnotism.

EVOLUTIONARY SCHISM

The search for a direct action would require deeper understanding of the functional nature of feelings, emotions and their links with consciousness. Since this issue was highlighted briefly in the first chapter, we should go into more details to find out possible clues in the evolution of human brain. After *The Origin of Species* by Charles Darwin, it was well established that our body and brain have evolved by incremental improvements to adapt to environment. It means all parts of the brain were evolved not simultaneously, but gradually in response to the challenges of survival and changing circumstances.

In his brilliant book *The Dragons of Eden: Speculations on the Evolution of Human Intelligence*, the great scientist and astronomer Carl Sagan has captivatingly narrated the story of the evolution of human brain from the primordial time, when life was born first as a self-duplicating cell. Soon these cells called *replicators* began to multiply and started competing among themselves for the limited resources available in their ecosystem. That was the beginning of the endless battle of competition for survival—the mother of all battles that set off the unique course of evolution on this planet. Humans are the inheritors of that primeval legacy of competition in its all complexities.

Carl Sagan depicts a very fascinating, rather a disorienting picture of the modern human brain as the product of cumulative life processes of more than two billion years. Our brain still contains in itself the dispositional tendencies and vestiges of its long evolutionary history, particularly from the time of reptilian to mammalian eras. Since the different regions of our brain evolved to meet particular adaptive demands at various stages of evolution, they sometimes betray conflicting tendencies despite their symbiotic relationship. The human brain is thus not a monolithic and homogeneous structure, but a divided house with its discrete parts asserting themselves at times like sub-regional tribal lords. This is one of the factors why our behavioral patterns are often self-contradictory and inconsistent.

Neuroscientists categorize the anatomical structure of brain in three broad regions: the reptilian complex, the limbic system and the neocortex (Carl Sagan, *The Dragons of Eden: Speculations on the Evolution of Human Intelligence* [Ballantine Books], 59). The reptilian complex is the oldest region of our brain and hence, the remnant of the primeval time when life had proliferated in the form of reptiles in the initial stage of evolution. The ferocious reptiles of countless varieties ruled the earth for millions of years during that era. Some smart ones among them found it advantageous to grow limbs that can enable them to wage the war of survival more successfully. That necessitated development of *the limbic system* of brain marking the transition from reptiles to mammals. Later these new species developed the region of the brain called *neocortex* on the periphery of limbic system. Millions of years later, modern man emerged with the highly developed neocortex that is responsible for our abilities of thinking, reasoning, language and an enlarged memory.

The limbic system represents an enlarged growth around the reptilian complex and similarly the neocortex an enlarged growth upon the limbic system (see fig. 1.1, chapter 1). The neocortex is the largest section of the human brain representing about 80 percent of its mass. The ancient parts are at the lower base forming the inner core of the brain. It is necessary to stress the point made by Sagan that the reptilian complex and the limbic section of our brain are now not functioning exactly the same way they did millions of years ago, otherwise we would be behaving like dinosaurs and wild cats (Carl Sagan, *The Dragons of Eden*, 80, 199). Fortunately, it is so because at each stage of evolution, the physiology of the older regions underwent changes. The new regions also began to exert some assimilative influence and control on the old ones. The neocortex, by virtue of being the largest area, has a more predominant role in our life and behavior.

Unfortunately, the primitive parts of the brain have not totally lost all their intrinsic tendencies. For instance, as pointed out by Sagan, the reptilian complex is significantly responsible for our aggressive, ritualistic and hierarchical tendencies. He believes that these tendencies characterize a great deal of our bureaucratic and political behavior. The limbic system is largely responsible for the emotions of fear, love, attachment and kinship. The parts of the brain called pituitary gland, hippocampus, amygdala, hypothalamus and thalamus are integral to the limbic system (see fig. 4.2).

Amygdala is known to be the seat of fear and frenzied behavior. Dr Antonio Damasio has described the case of a young woman whose both amygdale were damaged in an illness. Consequently, she betrayed no emotion of fear at all (*The Feeling of What Happens*, 62). Animals like cats and monkeys were petrified in the state of fear when their amygdala was stimulated with an electric pulse.

Mammals and birds devote longer time caring for their young than reptiles and therefore the qualities of altruistic behavior and love are believed to originate from our limbic system. It is the mammalian legacy that humans have inherited. The neocortex endowed us with the abilities that distinguish us as human beings, such as complex reasoning, anticipation of future, prolific memory, abstract thinking, and language. Unfortunately, the price we paid for the very useful ability of anticipation is worry and anxiety.

It is pertinent to note that the divisive characterization of brain on functional assumptions in terms of reptilian complex, limbic system, and neocortex is an oversimplification due to the following reasons: Firstly, there are no absolute and clear-cut divisions in the functions of various regions of the brain. Neuroscientists have observed a great deal of overlapping and duplication of tasks among these regions. For instance, memory functions are distributed in the neocortex as well as the hippocampus of the limbic system. Feelings of empathy, wonder, compassion, pride and guilt are located in the neocortex, while fear is in amygdala of the limbic section.

Secondly, as discussed in the previous chapters, the mental phenomena of thought, emotions, feelings and memory operate in an integral manner, besides acting as evocative factors for one another. Thirdly, there are still puzzles and intriguing areas of ignorance concerning multiple functions of several parts of the brain. This is so, notwithstanding the commendable achievements of neuroscientists in unraveling the secrets of brain.

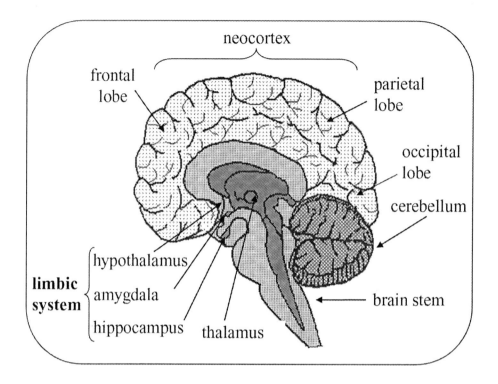

Figure 4.2. Different parts of the brain

THE CREATIVE FORCE BEHIND RELATIONSHIPS

Why did life in its evolution acquire this dynamic but volatile mechanism of emotions and feelings at all? Life perhaps would have been quite simple and serene without all the melodrama and mortifications that are the products of these psychic forces. It is a matter of utmost interest to find out why the phenomenon of life needed this mechanism. That will help us to understand the complexity of the nature and operational modalities of emotions and feelings. The awareness of their functional secrets would provide a balanced perspective to deal with these elemental forces on which life hinges so critically.

The drama of life, *full of sound and fury* with its turbulent history, owes its existence to the inexorable forces of emotions. It was under the spell of emotions and feelings of anger, fear, hurt, greed, pleasure, or pride that empires were built or destroyed and wars were waged with either the primitive weapons of stones and bones by our primate forefathers or with nuclear bombs by the modern man.

People have sacrificed their lives and everything in love for fellow human beings, tribe, nation, or ideologies. Feelings and emotions were behind our noblest and selfless actions and thoughts. Perhaps life would be a dull and worthless drudgery without the bliss of joy, pleasure, fun, and myriad entertainments that are made possible only because of our emotive abilities. Conversely, they have been also the perennial source of violence, societal divisions, and psychological conflicts.

The most valuable and indispensable part of our life is interpersonal relationship that is driven and nurtured by our emotional bonds. In fact, our cultural interdependence and the emergence of human societies as such would have not been possible without the cementing glue of feelings. Human societies began to emerge initially as primitive hordes and later as tribal groups. But the family system originated earlier as an immensely significant step forward in evolution. The cohesive forces behind this were again emotions and feelings.

Though some reptiles had developed the traces of family bonds, the mammals that emerged later began to devote a longer time of their lives in caring for their young. The mechanism of emotion acquired greater varieties and subtleties in mammals that, in turn, took forward the institution of family and enhanced the chances of survival of their young ones. The stronger emotional bonds among primates and particularly the human beings with their young, old, and companions have enormously enriched the family institution with unique cultural and moral values.

Directly or indirectly, the feeling of fear appears to have played the most crucial role in governing the course of evolution of life. It is indeed a primordial feeling with a distinctive place in the repertoire of feelings and emotions. Our instinct or passion for knowledge seems to have originated at the altars of fear. The fear of violent injury and death goaded our primate ancestors to be constantly on guard against any predators lurking in the bushes nearby. The fear of death, starvation as well as the wild and unpredictable forces of nature spurred them day and night to gain knowledge of the elements of nature, the predators and prey, the foraging and hunting grounds.

The primordial fear taught the advanced species that sustenance of life and its welfare were predicated on *knowing* things. Knowledge enhanced vastly the prospects of their self-protection and progress. They learnt the first lesson of the dictum—that knowledge is power as well as the panacea for all problems in life. No wonder that mankind is now at the threshold of knowledge society with astounding growth of information technology.

EVOLUTIONARY TOOLS FOR PRESERVING LIFE

It is obvious that sustenance and well-being of life would not have been possible without the vital forces of emotions and feelings. They are the dynamic instruments that set in motion the biochemical processes to ensure the integrity of life. Let us take the instance of fear that grips us when we come across a poisonous snake while walking in the woods. The fear seizes us instantly; our breathing becomes faster and heartbeat accelerates to pump more blood to the body for extra energy needed to jump off or run away. Our muscles become tense in readiness for action. These bodily changes are geared to protect life from fatal dangers. It is evident that emotions of fear, anger, and aggressiveness were evolved as defense mechanisms.

During the occurrence of emotion and feeling, both body and brain act in perfect unison as one with constant feedback of information. Emotions of fear, guilt, mental hurt, sorrow and joy are manifested through body language. On the other hand, emotions also work quietly without bodily manifestations when occupied with the ceaseless task of maintaining the biochemical balance of the body. Imbalance in any part of the body is sensed as a feeling of being unwell, tired, or something unusual. Such indications of the bodily state would not be possible in the absence of emotive sensors. When your finger is hurt with a kitchen knife, the feeling of pain leaves a lasting memory to remind you not to mishandle a knife in the future. It plays a role in guaranteeing our protection in the future.

Earlier, a reference was made to Dr. Antonio Damasio's view that feeling is recognition and owning up of emotion as one's private experience by the conscious mind. This entailed several advantages. The organism that is able to experience feeling would have the capability to understand the feelings of others. That will enable the organism to anticipate and manipulate feelings of others to its own advantage. For instance, the feelings of fear, sorrow and pain are used by autocrats to control people. Expressions of ferocity and aggressiveness are used by animals to create the feelings of fear and insecurity in others. Similarly, feelings of joy and happiness are induced in others as a reward or for gaining something. Good intentions are also conveyed by showing positive feelings.

Not only human beings but other animals also manipulate feelings of others to achieve their goals. When your pet dog wants to have something to eat, it comes wagging its tail. It caresses its body on your leg and licks your hands. It is trying to create a pleasant feeling in you so that in return you offer some food. Animals exhibit feelings *purposefully* through postures and body language to convey signals to others. Many animals like cats, dogs, and monkeys show teeth aggressively to convey a message that they would bite with their big sharp teeth. They do this to create fear when they feel threatened or when they wish to threaten other animals.

Human beings have acquired much more sophisticated and complex ways to convey emotive signals and create desired feelings in others to achieve their aims. For instance, evolutionists believe that the threatening action of showing teeth by animals has been modified by humans into a clever gesture of smile. A human being shows teeth with smile to convey the subtle message to other person that "I have the teeth that can hurt you, but I would not do so because I like you." On the other hand, we clench teeth in anger to convey anger or aggressive feelings like the other animals do.

It is perhaps logical to assume that many forms of life, which do not have enlarged consciousness, would possess only the defense mechanism of emotions but lack a conscious experience of feeling or a subjective awareness of the state of emotion. That raises a question: if these forms of life could carry on with their survival for millions of years without the capacity to feel the feelings consciously, why did the advanced species like human beings acquire the mechanism of *my feeling*. Why did we acquire the capacity to know feelings? Why did the *Eve of life* eat the forbidden fruit of knowledge, which resulted in her banishment to the tumultuous realm of sorrows and joys?

Fortunately, the life force acts with its innate intelligence and not under the sway of temptation like the mythological Eve. However, in doing so, what were the advantages for our species except to enjoy the feelings of happiness, but at the same time pay the price of suffering a myriad of sorrows?

The advantages of the biomechanism of feelings are the same as those of having the enlarged consciousness: our ability to understand the sufferings or happiness of others from our own experience. The qualities of empathy, compassion, altruism, pity, and sacrifice for others arise out of our ability to experience feelings not only in ourselves but in others as well.

The most crucial advantage that accrued to the life forms was the ability of anticipating sorrows and joys that might occur in future. This led them to act in advance, unlike the other species that have emotions only in response to immediate provocations and act on the spur of the moment. The ability of feeling accrued many benefits of not only improving the chances of survival but also building our civilizations. Human passion for knowledge was behind the immense progress in science and technology.

This leads us to the question of relationship between feeling and consciousness. Though it will be explored in details in the next chapter on consciousness, a brief mention would not be out of place here. Our feelings and emotions are *closest constitutionally* to consciousness in terms of their absorptive quality, impulsive force, and global reach that encompasses the entire brain and body. This can be grasped clearly in comparison to thought that has weaker power and diffused impulse. One can easily bring thought to a stop or change it at will, which is not possible in the case of emotions and feelings. They have a much stronger grip on our mind and body.

This closer relationship of consciousness with feelings and emotions might offer us some clues to tackle them more effectively through power of consciousness.

INTELLIGENCE AND EMOTIONS.

The question of relationship between intelligence and emotion has been an age-old controversy. The common belief is that emotions and feelings are antithetic to intelligence. Emotions are perfunctorily treated as irrational, blind and impulsive. Such notions are prevalent largely due to the fact that the ability of intelligent actions gets eroded when emotions and strong feelings seize the mind. Emotions and feelings are often looked down upon as human frailties and infirmities. In contrast, intelligence is considered calm, cool and superior.

Some recent research has proved that these are flawed notions. The antithetical division of intelligence vis-à-vis emotions and feelings is presumptive and baseless. According to neurological studies, intelligence is a perceptive power that is quite integral to emotions and feelings and not an independent mental faculty. In fact, intelligence gets gravely undermined when certain parts of the brain responsible for emotive occurrence are damaged in illness or accident.

In this regard, the renowned neuroscientist Dr. Antonio Damasio and his colleagues have made very revealing discoveries in their research work. They have gleaned direct evidences from clinical cases to prove that the patients, whose emotive parts of the brain were damaged, had lost the ability to make certain intelligent decisions. They failed to foresee intelligently the long-term impact of their actions concerning their job, personal relationship, or future. Consequently, they lost their jobs repeatedly and could not hold on to steady relationships. They, however, performed efficiently their skills in technical areas, accountancy, and language. The conclusion reached by Damasio was that the emotive areas of the brain play an essential role in the functioning of our intelligence, which enables us to make wise decisions involving future and social relationship.

Concerning the relation between intelligence and emotions, there is another view prevailing among some psychologists. Daniel Golemen, in his well-known book *Emotional Intelligence*, has put forward a concept of emotional intelligence (EQ). In his opinion, it is a distinct category of intelligence embodied in emotions and therefore different and superior to the intelligence operating in the form of thought like IQ. He defines IQ as inherently limited to mathematical and linguistic skills, while EQ as a wider and instantaneous reach to grasp complex issues like human relationship. It enables one to empathize and act more wisely in social relations; and persons having EQ are far more successful in life.

His definition of EQ matches with the intuitive perception that operates instantly without having to go through the circuitous route of thinking. It is evident in our experience that innate intelligence functions routinely in the slow process of thought but occasionally in the intuitive mode of instant perception or insight.

Carl Sagan points out that the right hemisphere of the brain functions in an intuitive or instant mode of pattern recognition. In contrast, the left hemisphere operates in a slow, analytic mode. The right hemisphere processes information instantly by simultaneously accessing several inputs, while the left hemisphere does it in a linear mode by accessing varied inputs sequentially (*The Dragons of Eden*, 177).

The discovery by Damasio confirms in a way, if not totally, what Golemen has propounded in his book. But does it mean that our emotions of fear, anger, love, sorrow, pleasures and joy are inherently imbued with the type of intelligence mentioned by Damasio or with EQ propounded by Golemen? As we know, these emotions operate as a response to an immediate situation and hence their role in intuitively safeguarding our future with intelligent decisions seems difficult to establish conclusively. Such emotions in daily life do not often turn out to be rational or intelligent acts and we repent for our emotional outbursts and for not having acted more wisely. These emotions frequently end up in complicating life and causing the problems of stress and depression. Certain fears like that of boss, some people or situations and the emotions of anger and aggressiveness cause troubles in life. In this context, the expression "emotional intelligence." would sound a contradiction in terms.

Notwithstanding their negative and unintelligent aspects, emotions as a bio-defense mechanism do have inherent rational qualities. But here again, their rationality operates in the immediate or short-term context and does not encompass an intuitive foresight and perceptual wisdom of EQ. In sum, our emotions betray some irrational and arbitrary qualities as well as the short-term intelligence as a defense mechanism; but not the intelligence that foresees long-term consequences.

However, this would contradict what the two distinguished experts have stated about the connection between intelligence and emotions. Let me attempt to clarify the over-lap in understanding the intuitive intelligence or EQ vis-à-vis the symbiosis of intelligence with emotions. Firstly, in all fairness, Damasio does not say that the specific emotions of fear, sorrow and anger embody intelligence as their defining quality. Instead, he concludes that damage to the regions of the brain responsible for emotions causes impairment of a specific variety of intelligence. For this, he has cited a clinical case of the patient who had lost the ability to experience fear. As a result, she was unable to foresee negative possibilities in striking a relationship with an acquaintance and strangers who were untrustworthy. She was incapable of precautionary behavior that ensues from the feeling of intuitive fear (Antonio Damasio, *The Feeling of What Happens: Body and Emotion in the Making of Consciousness*, 62).

Further, on the basis of clinical evidences, Damasio feels that emotions and core (nonverbal) consciousness appear to share the same neural infrastructure. Many experts believe that intelligence is an intrinsic quality of inner consciousness. Logically, therefore, damage to the neural ensemble responsible for emotions would result in erosion of intelligence or core consciousness. This would apply in the case of every human being without exception.

On the other hand, Golemen does not propound that EQ arises inherently from the repertoire of emotions. If it were so, everybody having emotions would possess EQ, which is not the case. That is why he says that only those people having EQ are likely to be more successful in life. Perhaps, the qualification *emotional* in EQ is a cause for confusion. EQ is, no doubt, a distinct quality of intelligence, but what presumably led Golemen to use that nomenclature was the fact that emotional intelligence operates in the same impulsive and instantaneous manner as emotions do.

The clinical evidences of Damasio imply that everybody has the intuitive intelligence which foresees the problems likely to happen in future, but it is undermined following damage to the emotive regions of the brain. That would differ from the concept of EQ of Golemen who implies that only some persons are endowed with EQ. This difference can be reconciled by an assumption that, as it happens in the case of IQ, everybody has EQ, but in varying degrees. In other words, some may have a more developed EQ than others. Since people having lower IQ are commonly characterized as not smart or intelligent, those having lower EQ would be presumed to be lacking it altogether.

Be that as it may, the preceding discussion at least underlines the close symbiotic relation between emotions and intelligence. The popular notion that subordinates emotions and feelings to intelligence is misleading. This also bears out the fact that the intuitive variety of intelligence is similar to emotive occurrence that does not rely on the circuitous process of thoughts. Such intelligence and our repertoire of emotions also have a common source of origin.

The deeper connection between the intuitive intelligence and emotions suggests that an increased access to such intelligence endows the ability to tackle the excessive and inexorable aspects of emotions without undermining their noble and defense qualities. This raises two questions. How can one have an enhanced access to such intelligence? How can an enhanced access enable one to tackle emotions without suppression or psychological coercion? These are very crucial questions for the practical purpose of dealing with stress and anxieties. We will address them in the latter part of this book.

ROLE IN STRESS AND DEPRESSION

What are the ingredients of stress, and anxiety? It is obvious that emotions and feelings are the raw materials, which make up these afflictions. Memory and thoughts continue to fuel and stoke them up. Let us examine stress which is primarily based on fear linked to an individual or situation. For example, one is afraid of a boss in office, which might be due to a fear of his short temper or losing job. The memory of bad experiences in past and the tendency of anticipating such possibilities feed the emotion of fear. This gives rise to a vicious cycle of stressful thoughts and anxiety. A sense of insecurity is primarily made up of fear involving uncertainties in life. Fear is accompanied with the feelings of sadness and pain.

A stressful state of mind may lead to either frustration followed by self-pity or aggressiveness and anger. Some people tend to respond with self-pity that may result in tears and weeping. Such actions are intended to earn sympathy and support; but a failure to elicit that response might lead to more sorrow, depression, or anger.

Some experts advise that one can be free from negative feelings merely by venting them. In their opinion, one should box a bed pillow repeatedly for venting anger or cry to dissipate grief. This does not sound to be wise advice because it does not tackle the underlying causes and would not bring a durable solution. For instance, an attempt to express anger does not give you relief; rather it would further stoke that feeling. Given the fact that emotive acts leave behind strong imprints in memory, any repetition and prolongation of emotions and feelings would leave deeper marks and lead to a behavioral pattern. You might end up forming a habit of doing so and exacerbate emotional problems. The right course of action is to try and understand why we behave the way we do.

Let us understand how different mental phenomena mutually support and intensify each other in stress (see fig. 4.3). When a stressful state of mind persists, the initial emotion of fear evokes emotions of sorrow, self-pity, frustration, aggressiveness and anger. Our common experience tells that compared to thoughts, emotions leave behind deeper marks in memory. The repetition of emotive occurrences, which is a usual pattern in stress, accentuates the impact on the mind and deepens the memories. In stress, the repetitive cycles of emotions, memory and thoughts come into play. They feed on each other and gain more strength.

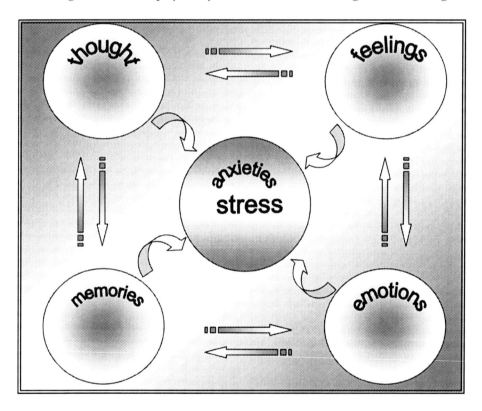

Figure 4.3. Anatomy of stress: Negative emotions, feelings, memories, and thoughts act as ingredients of stress and anxieties. They also act as provocative factors for each other. The straight arrows in the graphic indicate the mutual evocation of the mental processes.

In fact, thought and memory are held captive by emotions. Stressful emotions actually seize the mind and drain off its energy. When such stress persists for a long time, depression occurs as a continuing phenomenon. The stronghold of emotions in depression neutralizes and cripples the ability of rational thinking.

Neurologists tell us that emotions and feelings temporarily skew up the neural circuits of the brain and that is the reason why clear and rational thinking becomes quite difficult in strong emotions.

Given the fact that emotions are the prime mover and commanding force in stress and depression, any rational decision of thought to overcome strong emotions does not make much impact. The clue to resolving such mental impasse lies in tackling emotions directly as they are not amenable to any action of thought. An attempt to loosen the hold of the emotive affliction with counter emotions, like sorrow with joy, does not bring a lasting solution. A clever juggling with emotions and counter emotions, including the religious ones, is nothing but escapism. In such cases, the emotional problem lies hidden, continues to vitiate the peace of mind covertly, and distorts our behavior. That is why the drills of positive thinking do not make any lasting impact and the initial enthusiasm and hope wear off sooner than expected.

In an attempt to get rid of emotional problems, people sometimes embrace religious or mystical beliefs. Unfortunately, such attempts are nothing but a respectable psychological cover-up. This should not be misconstrued as condemnation of religious beliefs. The ritualistic adoption of ideologies and beliefs, however cogent and sublime, cannot bring about a transformation of mind and freedom from psychic problems. Only a sincere exploration with an open mind, which leads to direct understanding, can bring a lasting peace and unfetter the energy of mind.

There is a possibility of seeking freedom from anxieties and stress by more access to the power of consciousness. Such a possibility is based on the fact that our nonverbal consciousness shares the same neural infrastructure being used by emotions. More access to inner consciousness results in an amazing benefit of dissipating the rigid grip of emotions. This will be discussed in the latter part of the book.

BACKGROUND EMOTIONS AND FEELINGS

All of us are quite familiar with the manifestations of emotions and feelings in tumultuous and placid forms. They are experienced explicitly in the realm of conscious mind; but if we look within us with deep awareness without the interference of thought, we would discover a vague background of feelings. That is a subterranean layer of feelings at the periphery of conscious mind and beyond that lies the unconscious mind. Even though they operate in the twilight zone between the conscious and unconscious mind, they make their impact felt at the conscious level and thus manipulate our behavior.

Normally, we tend not to notice or recognize our background feelings and emotions as such, but we do it differently by calling them moods. When I say I am not in a good mood, I refer to the background feeling of sorrow or unhappiness over something which I may or may not be aware of. Similarly, the day before my long-awaited vacation begins or when something good happens to me, a steady layer of background feelings of joy pervades my mind. That means I am in a good mood, ready to help and cooperate.

The diverse moods we experience can be divided in three categories: positive, negative, and neutral. The cheerful, happy, enthusiastic, energetic, and friendly moods are positive while the negative category includes angry, irritated, bitter, sulky, sad, and melancholic moods. The neutral variety includes serene, peaceful, and tranquil moods, which indicate mental equilibrium and the absence of strong feelings.

We are under the influence of one mood or another all the time. In fact, if you are deeply watchful, you will realize that our consciousnesses is normally not in its virgin purity because thoughts, emotions and feelings of one kind or the other prevail in it almost ceaselessly. Thoughts are clearly recognizable, but that is not the case with emotions and feelings, particularly those which are mild, vague and intertwined with thoughts. Emotions and feelings can pervade our mind in three ways, namely, volatile, placid and vague. The vague feelings fall into the category of background feelings.

In sum, consciousness remains turbulent or noisy practically all the time with the activities of thoughts, feelings and memories.

Let me add that this book later deals with how to reclaim the sublime purity of consciousness without intrusion of thought and feelings. Such a technique is outlined not as a pursuit of some romantic ideal or mystical fascination, but as a practical and rational way to eliminate stress. It also helps in diffusing the background emotions and feelings.

There are several factors that shape our moods. Normally, the experiences and events in the immediate past stretching back to a few days make up our moods. Memory and thoughts also change and manipulate our moods. Furthermore, the physiological state of our body has a significant effect on our moods or background feelings. If the body is tired, unwell or suffering from some problem, it results in the lack of a good mood. One gets easily irritated or upset. It means the biochemical state of the body has to be stable to feel good and energetic.

Experts tell us that our brain ceaselessly monitors the physiological state of body through the nervous system. The maintenance of a balanced chemical profile of the body is accomplished through physiological reactions, which are largely automated. Though such monitoring and housekeeping tasks are performed involuntarily at the unconscious level, they also affect our moods. This proves that a healthy body helps us by generating positive moods.

When one has taken an antibiotic or potent medicine, one is likely to get easily irritated. The reason is that the drug acts as an external interference to the physiological processes of the body. Therapeutic drugs affect the chemical profile of the body and brain in a complex manner and can make one oversensitive. In sum, there are innumerable stimuli, both internal and external to body, which act as contributory factors for background emotions or moods.

We should not succumb to pessimism with the notion that our moods are shaped by biological and genetic factors beyond our conscious control and hence nothing can be done. These factors really account for a very small share in making our moods. In contrast, our thoughts, memories, habits, aspirations, prejudices, and psychological desires are the predominant factors. Our attitudes and mental conditionings, which are our own makings to a large extent, play a significant role in the induction of feelings and moods. This suggests that much scope and hope do exist for action on our part to shape our moods and destiny.

In conclusion, it should be borne in mind that background feelings and emotions, though less perceptible, play a very crucial role in shaping our behavior and in contributing to our success and failure in life. These innocuous looking background feelings operate like a gentle breeze, but can gather momentum to turn into an emotive whirlwind. Despite their apparent vagueness, the background feelings do exert cumulatively a greater impact on our life than we normally realize. Our interactions at home, in the workplace and in social life are largely the products of our moods that affect our relationship. It is not an exaggeration to state that our individual future is built on the 'bricks" of moods in a gradual and cumulative fashion.

ANXIETIES AND WORRIES

The terms *anxiety* and *worry* are commonly used to convey the sense of being in a state of mental disquiet and tension arising from uncertainty of the future and fear of possible mishap or failure. These words are used for conveying different nuances. The word *worry* is used to convey a milder state of anxiety. For instance, one worries about fulfilling one's responsibilities while taking up a new job. A student has anxiety about failing in the examination. Anxiety is marked by persistent worries and represents an acute state of mental unease. On the other hand, stress is understood as an acute state of mind beset with frequent worries and anxieties, while depression is a pathological case of excessive and prolonged stress.

Even though, there might be different views on the meanings among experts and lay persons, the terms: *worry* and *anxiety* are often used interchangeably. But for our practical purpose, it is not essential to debate their precise meanings. Rather, the point to be noted is the common factor of fear that underlies these mental phenomena. Fear, even in its mild form, is accompanied by sorrow, gloominess, and a sense of insecurity.

We have to recognize the significant fact that negative emotions form the ingredients of anxieties and worries, which betray an imbalance in the biochemical state of the body. Further, the persistence of the cycles of negative emotions and feelings continue to compound the imbalance. Consequently, the biomechanism of our body and brain is put under stress to function at an accelerated pace like a car running at the highest gear. That multiplies the possibilities of extra wear and tear. It explains the modern scourge of increased prevalence of old diseases like tuberculosis, diabetes, asthma and new ones like heart attack, high blood pressures and cancer

The phenomena of anxiety and worry also affect the efficiency and energy levels of the brain. They rob the brain of its natural spontaneity, equilibrium and cheerfulness. Such mental disturbances, which are so routine and frequent in our lives, do have cumulative costs in terms of negative impact on our health and quality of life. One wonders whether ignoring them as natural and unavoidable is wise. Of course, certain worries and anxieties might be inevitable or difficult to be avoided, given the uncertain world we live in.

Yet it is also an irrefutable fact that most of our anxieties and worries owe their existence to our attitudes, habits and morbid tendencies of seeking power and pleasures and not to the genetic or hereditary prewiring of our brain. It is irrational to carry on life complacently in the belief that our daily habits of anxieties and worries are natural and nothing can be done.

There is a vast scope for achieving freedom from the perpetual bondage of anxieties and worries and for making our life more cheerful and energetic. This is not a religious or spiritual belief, nor is it a dream. It is a goal of immense practical value that is achievable, provided one is determined to outgrow fossilized attitudes and ideas.

There are, of course, no easy shortcuts for such transformation. However, as indicated before, one has to be on guard against the common pitfalls of suppression and escapism through beliefs and ritualism. Unfortunately, our mind is cunning and adept at such psychological deceptions without realizing the detrimental consequences for itself.

BACKGROUND ANXIETIES AND WORRIES

Not only are anxieties and worries the ingredients of stress and depression but also a persistent nuisance in our daily lives. Though these are experienced normally at the conscious level, they also occur in vague forms. Hence, one is not able to experience them vividly and identify their causes. These are called background anxieties and worries which arise from hidden memories and psychological insecurity about future events.

Many people experience background anxieties on waking up in the morning. Some carry on and experience them frequently in the course of the day. These anxieties also spill over into sleep and dreams. One can sometimes link them up causally with past or future events. In fact, background anxieties operate as a habit or autonomic behavior in most human beings. This can be partly traced to the anticipatory tendency that is prewired in the brain to prepare an organism for uncertainties and exigencies of life.

Background worries are also vestiges of evolutionary conditioning of mind. Our forager/hunter ancestors had to face constant dangers from predators and the ubiquitous reptiles. Such fear and anxieties were perpetually on their minds either in conscious or implicit forms. Consequently, these were prewired in our brains as defense behavior in the evolutionary process.

If you consciously develop the sensitivity to observe your inner self, you will be able to feel background worries, particularly when you wake up in the morning. They have to be distinguished from the explicit worries of the day, which you can easily identify; for instance the worries concerning pending work, an important meeting or likely tussle with a colleague. Background worries are quite vague and foggy and can be recognized only with a deliberate effort. Yet their impact on the conscious mind and our behavior is decisive. They overshadow our conduct and distort our actions.

Even though the foggy feelings of worries are manifestations of our anticipatory behavior, we also discover in hind sight during the day that these feelings were not actually warranted in many instances. Background worries often represent the tendency of our brain for reflex and habitual behavior that is not necessarily rational. Notwithstanding the usefulness of the anticipatory behavior, such worries do have a cost in terms of stress. Why should we not aim to outgrow this evolutionary junk and face our future prudently in the daylight of the conscious mind? Instead of being driven by the dark forces of background worries, we must change and rely on the volitional and discretionary power of intelligence.

Though that is easier said than done, it is not a futile vision, for at least two reasons. First, the immutable rationale of evolution demands to shed off the past junk and adapt to new and better ways. Since the strength of background worries is much weaker, it is easier to outgrow them. Second, most of these worries are habitual behavior arising from subjective factors as well as cultural and social conditionings. In fact, it is possible to live life practically without these worries.

SHAPING HUMAN DESTINY

For our practical purpose, what do we conclude from the evolutionary legacy? The first point is the unfortunate fact that our brain is an admixture of different parts that have evolved in response to the adaptational needs at different stages of our evolution. Despite several symbiotic linkages among them, these parts have limited control over one another.

A more fundamental question arises relating to genetic determinism from the evolutionary history of the brain. If the discrete regions of the brain are bound by their inherent tendencies, how can we change them? Many people, therefore, tend to believe in fatalism; and practically all religious ideologies reinforce such beliefs, citing an argument of divine determinism. The arguments of fatalism and genetic determinism in absolute terms are myopic.

Of course, one cannot deny the fact of genetic heredity consisting of latent potentials that might manifest or remain dormant depending on the external environment and actions of the organism itself. Given their prodigious intelligence and enlarged consciousness, human beings are endowed with a greater willpower and foresight to shape their behavior and destiny by overcoming certain genetic influences. In fact, in our daily life, we frequently defy our genetic tendencies. The adoption of family planning represents a defiance of genetic urge and so do many of our social and moral values.

The assumptions that emotional afflictions, anxieties and worries are natural and immutable betray a mental block. In upholding the arguments of a prefixed destiny and genetic determinism, we miss the governing principle of evolution that is gradual and incremental improvement. Life, the unique creation in the universe, works on this crucial principle that was invented not by chance or divine determinism, but through the hard logic of survival.

Intelligence, the highest virtue of life, knows that adaptation is the panacea for all problems. It means developing new abilities and behavior that can enable us to surmount the vagaries of nature. Once you live by a belief in predeterminism, you are negating the fundamental principle of life and its evolutionary growth. Fatalism is a futile escapism and a debilitating ailment that corrodes the dynamism of human mind.

Humanity, I think, is capable of shaping its destiny by determining the pace and direction of its evolution. In fact, the question here is not just of capability, but the inevitability faced by humanity to do so in order not to hit the dead end of its evolution. The complacency in the immortality of our species and faith in our technological power are fundamentally flawed.

We, as an advanced species, can ensure our long-term proliferation and progress through an enlightened approach to take our destiny in our hands; instead of reacting to circumstances and forces that are created by Nature or ourselves while drifting along. Cut-throat competition, rampant commercialism and unbridled consumerism with their devastating impact on environment are some of the brute forces created by us. We need to evolve a wiser and more foresighted approach for the sake of our future generations.

Something believed to be natural does not necessarily mean that it is unchangeable. Even the patterns of mental phenomena like thought, emotions, feelings, worries and anxieties are amenable to long-term changes for the better without resorting to suppression. The firing patterns of neurons that constitute these mental processes are intrinsically dispositions not drastically different in biomechanism from our common habits. They can be influenced with persistent and penetrative use of the power of consciousness—the overriding creative force.

The invention of consciousness was actually a quantum jump in the progression of evolution ushering in unprecedented potentials. It offered a unique freedom of action to break out of the shackles of genetic rigidities and chart out our destiny in the midst of this seemingly indifferent universe. *Natural* is a relative term in time and space. Millions of species that got bogged down in their biological shortcomings were fossilized in time and became extinct.

Our evolutionary journey till the *underdeveloped consciousness* of mammalian era was, as if, through a dark tunnel; but the acquisition of an enlarged consciousness was like arriving in the sunshine of an open landscape with vast freedom and new opportunities. It constituted a new paradigm of our future evolution with new potentials not to be lost in the lure of gratifications of consumerism and commercialism. This leads us to the issue of consciousness in the next chapter.

Chapter 5

Consciousness

Our normal waking consciousness, rational consciousness as we call it, is but one special type of consciousness, whilst all about it, parted from it by the filmiest of screens, there lie potential forms of consciousness entirely different.

—William James

The journey into our inner world in the previous chapters led us to the subterranean world of memory, thought, emotions, and feelings. We also touched upon the symbiotic relation of intelligence with these mental phenomena. It was intended to be a preparatory phase before embarking on the more crucial task of finding some practical ways to address the problems of stress and depression. However, our inner journey is not yet complete.

The next pertinent and fundamental question arises—whether the psychic forces of memory, thought, emotions, and feelings have a common ground from where they emerge? Is there a common foundation from where they derive their operative strength? If we find out the deeper source of their energy and understand its functional modality, it would perhaps be easier to tackle their negative and painful manifestations that forebode many of our troubles in life.

I suspect the answer to this lies with the elusive entity we refer to as consciousness. The question of consciousness, therefore, has to be explored. Let me clarify that this issue is discussed here not from any academic perspective or for intellectual gratification, but in the context of the practical purpose of the book to tackle the problem of stress.

THE QUESTION OF CONSCIOUSNESS

What is consciousness? This question has bothered humanity for centuries. Even in modern times, despite the spectacular achievements in science and technology, the answer to that has remained elusive and vague, and might continue to be so in the foreseeable future. One of the hurdles, being faced by scientists and experts, is the fact that they cannot place the phenomenon of consciousness under their microscopes for scientific scrutiny.

Nonetheless, many scientists and philosophers have expounded conceptual ideas on the nature of consciousness; and entering into that debate would be like daring to enter a wild forest fraught with dangers. This debate is characterized by a broad divide with many finer shades on both sides. One group of experts believes that consciousness, though enormously complex, is computational and can be explained like any other phenomenon. They have offered different perspectives of consciousness as a cognitive phenomenon or perceptive phenomenon. Many of them follow a step-by-step approach or what is termed in science as a reductionist method.

The more well-known expert among them is Dr. Francis Crick, the Noble laureate who unravelled the secrets of DNA. In his book *The Astonishing Hypothesis: The Scientific Search for the Soul*, he has put forward the view that our sense of self, our joys, sorrows, memories, ambitions and free will are nothing but the behavior of vast ensembles of nerve cells. We, as a psychic entity including our consciousness, are just a bundle of neurons. Personally I see much truth in what he has stated. It is time to demystify and bring down from the high pedestal mind and consciousness that are commonly believed to be nonmaterial mysteries.

Dr. Crick feels that if we can adequately understand all integrated processes of how one sub-faculty of the brain functions, such as vision, that would make it easy to move ahead and unravel the secrets of the entire brain and consciousness. With the help of research, he has proceeded to explain the complex task of vision and how its multiple aspects are processed and synchronised by different regions of the brain, which finally enables us to experience images in their complexities of color, size, motion as well as cognitive and emotive contents. He has focussed upon the thalamus and other contiguous parts of the brain stem that are believed to play a crucial role in the making of consciousness. However, he admits some real problems being faced in grasping *the holistic dynamics* of not only the more complex issue of consciousness, but even the sectoral functions like vision, smell and other perceptual processes.

There are several other experts who feel that consciousness can be understood by explaining how cognitive and behavioral functions are performed by our brain. But, they have not made spectacular headway in resolving the issue. They encounter mysteries of *the integrative globality* of consciousness as well as the properties of *awareness* and *understanding*.

In contrast, the experts on the other side of the divide hold the view that consciousness is noncomputational and any physical account of mental processes, sectoral or otherwise, cannot explain the mysteries of consciousness. In support of their view, they cite several problems that have eluded explanations, such as the questions of *understanding, awareness*, and *subjectivity*. No satisfactory answers are available as to how these phenomena, which are the intrinsic properties of consciousness, occur in the brain in the first place. The cognitive theory merely accounts for how cognitive processes take place, but falls short of explaining the unique property of *understanding* and *generic intelligence*.

The issues of subjectivity and ownership—*my* feeling, *my* thought, and *I*—have remained as baffling as ever. *I am I*, and *you are you*, but why can't *I* be *you* or vice versa? How does the exclusive owner of thoughts, feelings, and experience—the sense of self as such—come into being? The explanation of self as a collective embodiment of autobiographical memories and future intentions merely relates to the consequential properties that build up at the subsequent stages and keep varying with the age. But how the construction of the primordial sense of self or the subjective owner takes place from moment to moment still defies explanation.

Neuroscience has made spectacular progress in unravelling the secrets of how various regions of the brain function and their symbiotic relations. The latest computer technology and brain-scanning devices have made it possible to observe the ceaseless activities of neurons as well as the electrochemical processes behind the phenomena of memory, emotions, feelings, and thinking. The secrets of how the brain transmits messages within itself and to other organs of the body have been revealed. A great deal of fruitful research has been done in unravelling the cerebral processes behind vision, auditory, olfactory and motor functions.

Notwithstanding all these successes, the mysteries of how the physical processes and neural patterns turn into the subjective experiences of self, color, shape, smell and sound still remain unresolved. How do the electrochemical processes produce the sentient properties of intelligence, awareness, and understanding? The knowledge gap is yet to be bridged on how the material processes give rise to nonmaterial phenomena of subjective experiences.

Given such blind issues, Colin McGinn, a philosopher at Rutgers University, made the following arguments in his book, *The Problems of Consciousness*. Consciousness is an essentially subjective feature of the world and cannot be grasped by the current science that explains things from an objective, nonpersonal angle. He goes on to say that explanation of consciousness is "cognitively closed" for creatures like us. When it comes to consciousness, we are at the evolutionary stage like that of the cats and squirrels trying to comprehend quantum mechanics!

There is one more aspect of this problem. Since understanding is an intrinsic property of consciousness, our attempt to understand it would mean consciousness is trying to understand its own self, and consequently, we confront the problem of what is called *irreducible subjectivity*. This is referred to as the enigma of *observer* and *the observed* merging into one process. In quantum physics, such a mental impasse occurs wherein the observer (mind) affects the state of the observed (subatom) and as a result one is denied the complete understanding of the quantum event.

In fact, some scientists believe that consciousness is brought about through the quantum mechanism within the micro structure of neurons. One more argument is advanced on the strength of an intriguing aspect of quantum reality called *nonlocality*. When the state of one subatom at the quantum level is changed, it affects the state of its counterpart irrespective of any distance between them. It appears as if these subatoms are aware of each other. This has led some scientists to propound that ultimately the universe is *self-aware* (*The Self-aware Universe*, by Dr. Amit Goswami, a professor of physics at the Institute of Theoretical Sciences at the University of Oregon). It is argued that since awareness is a property of consciousness, the later can be explained in terms of a quantum phenomenon.

Many scientists believe that the quantum argument is a leap of faith and cannot explain consciousness. The nonlocality cannot be assumed to be awareness; it might be a connectivity of some unknown force or energy in the universe like gravity or magnetism but more pervasive and powerful. Besides, quantum events are observed at the temperature closer to absolute zero (-273.15 Celsius) and the brain does not function at that level. Nonetheless, the well-known scientist Roger Penrose has made very comprehensive arguments in favour of the possibility of consciousness arising from the quantum dynamics in the microtubules of the brain cells (Roger Penrose, *Shadows of the Mind* [London: Vintage, 1995], 369-76).

Be that as it may, the universe is obviously something immensely vast and distant beyond our individual reach. But in contrast, our consciousness is within our bodily courtyard. We wrestle with it day and night, and hence, we need to make sense of it, at least, in some practical terms. Let us put aside the complex issues involving the metaphysical pessimism of philosophers and *cognitive myopia* imposed by our evolutionary limits.

The latter part of this book deals with practical methods of reducing stress, which are based on the use of awareness as the core of consciousness. Therefore, it would be useful to have some pragmatic perspective of the power of consciousness and how it is related to emotions, feelings, thought and memory, which play crucial role in anxieties and stress.

AN ENTITY WITHOUT THOUGHT AND MEMORY

Before we attempt to form an idea of consciousness, let us begin with the examination of our experience of *being conscious*. It represents a state of mind that is capable of interacting or responding to objects in the external world on its own or otherwise. It means one is awake and not asleep or unconscious as in a coma. In deep sleep our conscious mind does not function, but when we are dreaming, a different state of consciousness operates. In dreams, we think, feel, and speak, though often these actions have a bizarre nature because the flow of our consciousness is weak and unable to impose a more logical order.

Normally, we are conscious or aware of one thing or another from the vast array of objects in the external world or biological phenomena in our mind and body, such as our thoughts, feelings, memory, and experiences. Being conscious of something means establishing a mental contact or relationship with it. Obviously, that is not the totality of consciousness as such, but it is an act of consciousness in the sense that without consciousness the action of being conscious of something is not possible.

When we focus our conscious mind purposefully on something external or internal, it is called *attention*. In other words, attention is a focussed application of consciousness. A more intensified attention constitutes *mental concentration*. There is one more dimension of consciousness, namely, *awareness*, which has a central place in the theme of this book as an instrument of tackling anxieties and stress. This is the crucial connection why this abstruse subject of consciousness is raised in this chapter.

Let me clarify the meaning attached to the word *awareness* in this book. It is *a neutral flow* of consciousness devoid of any activities of thought and memory. Such pure awareness is referred in this book as *nonverbal* consciousness. We are aware of the environment and political developments around us. This type of awareness signifies merely possession of information or knowledge, and not the awareness that is the core and defining quality of consciousness. The difference between attention and awareness is not very wide. Attention is an intensified effort directed purposefully to an object, while awareness signifies a steady flow of consciousness with or without purpose.

For instance, one is aware of a colleague sitting on the next chair. One can be simply aware of the colleague's presence without any specific thoughts, which is possible for a few moments but soon our mind is invaded by thought and memory. One begins to think about past experiences and images concerning the colleague. It is our common experience that our thoughts and memories are ceaselessly active in our mind and it is nearly impossible to stop them beyond a few moments. Both of them also act as catalysts for each other.

However, if you make an effort to suspend your thought activity for some seconds, you would notice that your memory has also stopped operating. In life, we have many experiences, though very brief, when the interference of thought and memory ceases and we get immersed totally in a nonverbal pure experience of sensations or feelings. In fact, all our memorable moments of pleasures, particularly ecstasies are such pure feelings. Instances of such deep pleasures include sexual joy, eating delicious food after a day of fast, or meeting a beloved friend after a long time.

Music has universal and overwhelming appeal for all human beings because it instantly knocks off thought and memory and transports you to the realm of pure feelings, though unfortunately for a short while. Soon thought and memory invade the pure sensations. No wonder everyone says that music touches the core of our heart—consciousness, which is not a poetic but a factual statement. Our consciousness is the fountain-head of undiluted sensations. The scenic beauty of a snow-clad mountain, the starry vastness of the night sky, the grandeur of the ocean in the morning glory of the sun—all these bring the spell of pure joy and awe without the pollution of thought and memory.

Unfortunately, thought is an agent of adulteration of our pure and deep feelings. The mind habitually hankers for prolonging the process of pure joy, which is made possible with the help of thought and memory. But that is a stale recreation, an act of reliving the past moments of joy. In order to gloat over a joy of past, memory and thought labour hard and evoke each other. For this, we use our imagination which is nothing but a joint venture of memory and thought to revive feelings.

Consciousness is in essence the primordial feeling or sentient impulse of *virgin awareness* that is devoid of thought, memory and any specific feeling or emotion such as joy, sorrow, anger, love, or sympathy. Such pure consciousness or awareness is nonverbal.

Many scientists and psychologists associate short-term memory with consciousness. They believe that short-term memory is essential for sustaining consciousness. That is not quite accurate. Pure consciousness is an independent and foundational impulse emanating from moment to moment. What the short-term memory does is to carry forward the impression of previous moment. It is the nature of memory to link up images and sensations moment by moment to provide integrity and continuity to our experience. That is how memory creates our sense of a stream of consciousness and self. It would be wrong to say that memory creates consciousness. It merely creates *an impression* of a flow of consciousness.

THE CONSCIOUS AND UNCONSCIOUS MIND

Consciousness in its entirety has two broad divisions, namely, the conscious window and unconscious window. The conscious window stands for the conscious mind that generates and sustains the activities of thought, explicit memories, language, and specific feelings of joy, sorrow, anger, and sympathy (see fig. 5.3). The unconscious window includes memories, emotions, dispositions, and reflex actions, which are implicit and not accessible to the conscious mind (see fig. 5.1). The roots of our anxieties, worries, stress, and emotions are in the subterranean world of the unconscious. For the limited and practical purpose of this book, I have made no distinction between the unconscious and the subconscious.

Earlier in this chapter, I indicated a third division of consciousness referred as *nonverbal consciousness*. It is an interim state between the conscious and unconscious mind. I have maintained the conceptual distinction in the following manner. Thoughts, explicit memories, and reason operate in the conscious mind and represent the verbal state of mind. On the other hand, the nonverbal consciousness is pure awareness devoid of thoughts and explicit memories. It also includes a pure feeling or sensation that is unadulterated by thought (see fig. 5.2)

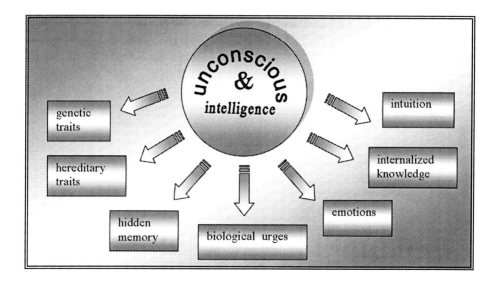

Figure 5.1. The mental phenomena arising from the unconscious, which is imbued with innate intelligence.

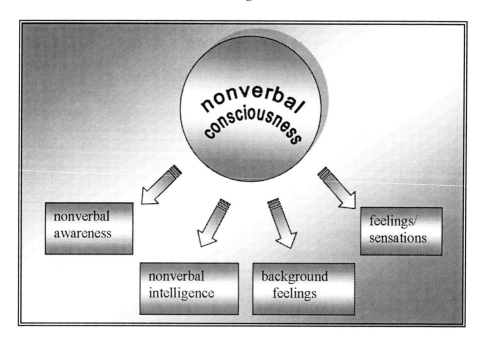

Figure 5.2. The mental processes arising from the nonverbal consciousness that is an interim state between the conscious and the unconscious mind. Feelings/sensations are in the nonverbal state namely, without thought.

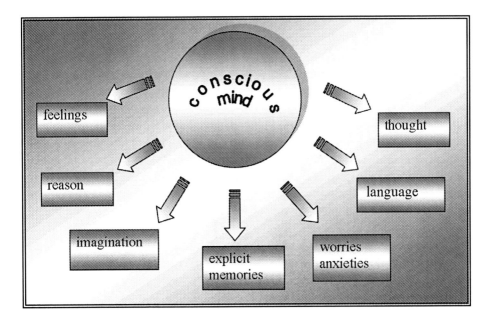

Figure 5.3. The mental processes arising from the conscious mind.

In the nineteenth century Sigmund Freud and Carl Jung put forward specific concepts of the unconscious and subconscious mind. They wrote extensively on the powerful influence of the unconscious on behaviour. Their focus was directed mainly toward therapeutic significance of the unconscious for behavioral and emotional problems. In comparison, the approach of neuroscientists and other experts in modern times has been much more comprehensive. They have brought about more scientific understanding of emotions and their linkage with intelligence and the role of the unconscious in sustaining the vast array of activities of the conscious mind.

The nonvoluntary activities of the brain to maintain and monitor the entire biomechanism of body, including vital organs, are in the realm of the unconscious window. The conscious mind emanates from the unconscious and hence the former depends for its existence on the latter. The unconscious exists in the absence of the conscious mind as it happens in coma, vegetative state, or under anaesthesia.

Of course, neuroscientists and experts provide clarity and subtle distinctions, but it is a self-evident experience that consciousness operates at both the conscious and unconscious levels. The repetitive actions at the conscious level are internalized and stored in the unconscious. That is how we acquire a vast array of reflexes and skills like car driving, and learning a language. Our habits, inhibitions, and defense reflexes in the face of danger are an internalised repertoire of the unconscious mind.

The human mind is bound by innumerable conditionings and a range of internalized behavior that can be divided in two broad categories. First is the acquired category of mental conditionings shaped through circumstances, social influences and individual actions. The second category includes our genetic prewiring through evolutionary grind and the hereditary traits. One can make distinctions and describe all these as different phenomena in terms of genetic programming of the brain. However, the prime mover and the main actor of the drama of life is consciousness. Thus in its fullness, consciousness can be equated with the life force that encompasses every cell of the living organism.

These points would enable us to perceive the intricate forces that govern not only our external behavior and actions, but also the mental processes of thought, memory, emotions, and feelings. Our anxieties, worries and stress are products of their interplay.

COGNITION AND CONSCIOUSNESS

One has to recognize the fact that the act of being conscious or aware is different from the act of cognition. The process of cognition consists of different stages involving several regions of the brain. Consciousness, on the other hand, is a wave like impulse occurring from moment to moment.

The process of cognition involves first establishing a contact with an object in terms of physically seeing it, say a bird. It means *being aware*, which is an act of consciousness. The optical image of the object is flashed in the brain, which is processed and verified by memory in the light of innumerable images of past experiences concerning other birds. Intelligence joins the process to identify the image in the context of earlier knowledge with the help of thought and memory. At the end of this process, one recognizes the bird. It is thus clear that cognition is a mental process of recognizing an object or event and gaining knowledge.

It is an interesting question whether the cognitive process can take place in the absence of consciousness. I think it is not possible because, firstly, the process cannot be sustained without being aware or conscious of the object, which is an act of consciousness. The process of cognition can happen by establishing an ongoing contact with an object. But a sole act of contact in terms of seeing would only bring in the material image of the bird as the mechanism of camera does. That is not sufficient.

The physical image on the eye lens and its transmission by the optical nerves to the brain are simple material phenomena. These are clearly distinct from the representational image that is experienced as part of consciousness with the integral elements of emotions and feelings. The cognition process is not possible without transformation of the material image into an experiential correlate permeated with consciousness. In other words, the image has to be encompassed in awareness and become an indistinguishable part of consciousness.

We have to distinguish knowledge from consciousness. In the earlier instance, we noted that at the end of the cognition process what accrues is knowledge, which is consigned to memory and becomes the reservoir of knowledge for future use. Though knowledge is an end product of cognition, it is not limited to that alone. We accumulate knowledge through press media, books, interacting with others, and during our daily activities. Of course, during the process of gaining knowledge, we use our judgement to evaluate the information by using our reasoning power and cognitive ability; but often we also act on faith and belief in the authority of others.

The action of being aware of something per se is not knowledge, but its combination with memory becomes knowledge. At the same time, it is also a fact that conscious act leaves behind an imprint in memory that can serve as knowledge.

In sum, consciousness is not a consequence of cognition, but cognition is the consequence of consciousness.

THE MOTHER OF ALL FEELINGS

The nonverbal sensation of subjectivity can be described as *pure* consciousness because that is how we experience it by extricating it from the entanglement of memory, thought, and the specific, transient feelings such as joy, sadness, and fear. Yet emotions and feelings seem to have relatively much more closeness with consciousness in their intrinsic nature and mode of operation. It is not far from truth to say that consciousness is a *foundational feeling* that operates continuously and has no specific or volatile contents as is the case with the transient feelings, such as sorrow and joy.

Our transient feelings have, at a time, only one constituent element like joy, sorrow, fear, or anger. The transition from one feeling to another is often very quick giving us the impression of multiple emotive contents. Our short-term memory creates such a flawed perception. In contrast, thought and memory have more than one ingredient. Thought is a combined product of memory, intelligence, emotions, and feelings, while memory contains feelings, ideas, and information in the form of images. This would suggest that thought and memory are twice removed from consciousness compared to feelings, which have constitutionally only one shade of difference with consciousness.

Feelings and emotions are also transient and erratic occurrences, which need internal or external stimulus. That contrasts with consciousness, which operates from moment to moment and requires no stimulus. Consciousness, in its wider entity of having both the conscious and unconscious windows, operates as long as an organism is alive. This substantiates the view that consciousness is not far removed from life force; rather both are one and the same.

Earlier it was mentioned that at a time feeling has only one specific ingredient of joy, sorrow, or anger. Let us go a bit further and inquire whether a feeling can exist without its specific content. What happens when one eliminates the content of a feeling, namely, joy or sorrow? Obviously the joy or sorrow will vanish. Thus feelings cannot exist without their specific contents. But when specific feelings and thoughts do not operate, we do not become unconscious. We experience a nonspecific and inclusive feeling or sensation of *being*. This primordial feeling without any contents of thought, memory, and specificity of joy, sorrow, or anger is the pure and nonverbal consciousness. The deeper experience of consciousness suggests that it is a *raw feeling of existential subjectivity*. In sum, consciousness is the mother of all feelings.

THE GLOBAL QUALITY OF CONSCIOUSNESS

If you observe very carefully, you will find that the nonverbal consciousness underlies and encompasses all mental activities. Since the impulse of nonverbal consciousness pervades the entire brain, it is called a *global* quality of consciousness. In its absence, the activities of thought, memory, reasoning, and feelings cannot be sustained. The implicit and hidden operations of emotions, feelings, and memories will also cease when the unconscious segment of consciousness is non-functional.

The global underpinning role of consciousness is evident in other ways. The mental processes like emotions, feelings, thought, and memory are intrinsically imbued in the primordial feeling of consciousness. On careful observation, you will find that when you experience the feeling of joy, sorrow, or anger, your consciousness submerges and becomes one with that specific feeling. At the time of anger, *you are anger*—one entity and not two, namely *you* and *anger*. Only a moment later, you recall that you were angry, which is an act of memory only.

The same is true in the case of other mental activities of thought and memory. It appears as if pure consciousness assumes the specific and transient forms of feelings, thought, or memory.

In other words, the stream of pure consciousness that is an *all-inclusive, nonspecific subjectivity* becomes an exclusive entity having specific and turbulent contents such as joy, sorrow, thought, or memories. The pure or nonverbal consciousness can be metaphorically compared with the placid and calm water underneath the surface of an ocean, while the myriad feelings and emotions of fear, anger, sadness, or pleasure are alike the waves and turbulence on the surface of the ocean. The operations of thought and memory also represent turbulence in the ocean of primordial consciousness. Basically it is the same water assuming different forms with varying patterns and degrees of force. The fits of overwhelming emotions like anger and fear are the high waves of the ocean of consciousness in a stormy weather. Let me clarify that this description is not just poetic.

The foregoing explanation underlines the point that is crucial in the theme of this book: consciousness is an *overarching force* or *prime mover* of all other mental activities. Hence an increased access to it will empower us to deal more effectively with anxieties, stress, and depression.

The global trait of consciousness might be challenged on the grounds of an anatomical argument in the following way: Firstly, certain parts of the brain stem, the evolutionarily ancient region of the brain, are believed to be responsible for creating consciousness because when they are damaged, a person becomes unconscious. That would be cited as the local characteristic. Secondly, mental activities like thinking, feelings, emotions, and memory are handled by disparate regions of the brain. Hence, it can be argued that these processes stand on their own. Thirdly, it is a matter of our daily experience that when one activity, like thought or emotion, is operating, it eclipses operation of other mental phenomena including the nonverbal consciousness.

Notwithstanding these points, the primary fact remains that all the mental activities would not be sustained, even exist, without consciousness in its wider form having both the conscious and unconscious windows. Secondly, the global role of consciousness operates irrespective of the fact that only a certain region of the brain is the causative factor of conscious window. Thirdly, the evolutionarily modern regions in the neocortex are an extension of the nonverbal consciousness. Further, the neurologists tell us that all our conscious activities, even those originating in the neocortex, are not possible when certain areas of the brain stem are damaged. That indicates the global underpinning role of consciousness, despite its localized origin in certain anatomical sites. This wider reach of consciousness is also the matter of our daily experience.

MEMORY AND CONSCIOUSNESS

In order to use the power of consciousness for eliminating stress and depression, it is quite crucial to bear in mind the distinction between consciousness and memory. As mentioned before, many neurologists and psychologists believe that short-term memory is essential for consciousness. That is not a complete truth. Consciousness, the primordial impulse, is the foundation of all mental processes including memory in all its varieties. It is the prime mover of all mental activities, whether voluntary or nonvoluntary. Memory has no role in the creation of consciousness that is an independent entity in itself. We can, in fact, experience the pure consciousness in the form of inner, nonverbal awareness devoid of memory, thought, and emotions.

When the experts say that short-term memory is essential, they indicate its role in sustaining the continuity of the sense of consciousness. The wavelike pulse of consciousness emanates from moment to moment, but the short-term memory carries forward in time the image of the experience of each moment. It is the short-term memory that creates this experiential link.

The role of memory is significant in terms of the continuity of our experience of anything including the sentient pulse of consciousness in its verbal or nonverbal forms. Further, memory is the binding glue of all our experiences and our processes of reasoning and language. It binds together the constituent parts of a single thought as well as the flow and the accumulative perspective of several thoughts, which endows us with the analytic skill.

Much more significant is the cementing role of memory in the construct of our sense of self. All of our experiences and self-images beginning from our early phase of life till our ripe old age are strung together by memory to build the edifice of our autobiographical self. The architecture of our autobiographical self will fall apart in the absence of memory. We would be utterly disoriented and lose our individual identity as it happens in the case of persons suffering from wide-ranging memory loss or the last stage of Alzheimer's disease.

The close connection of consciousness with memory would logically mean that the actual size of memory would have a significant bearing on the operative aspects of consciousness. Does it mean that more developed memory might suggest more access to consciousness? Though this is a debatable point, a couple of points can be clarified easily. Memory as the reservoir of information and knowledge is very crucial for the operation of consciousness as an instrument of intelligence or understanding. The more information, the better the understanding of a given situation. It is evident that when memory is impaired, intelligence, which is the intrinsic property of consciousness, also gets crippled.

Further, the perceptive horizon or reach of consciousness increases with a larger memory. That is evident when we compare human beings with other animals. All forms of life have wide variations in their memory power, and that has direct linkage with their abilities to act intelligently and anticipate future. Perhaps, it would not be human arrogance to assume that the lower forms of life, which are endowed with much less memory, operate at a narrow span of the conscious mind in contrast to human species, which has prodigious memory.

THE QUESTION OF SELF AND CONSCIOUSNESS

Earlier we discussed that very substantial loss of memory would cause disorientation and disintegration of our sense of self. This leads us to the important issue of self, which is intrinsically connected with consciousness. The question of self has remained an intriguing issue and, in fact, a mysterious experience. In simple terms, our sense of self divides into two segments: the biological self and the psychological self. Our physical body—which includes brain, biological urges, desires, and reflexes—makes up our biological self. We have images of what we are physically—tall, short, handsome, fair, or dark.

The biological self is a simpler affair when compared to the psychological self, which is enormously complex. The concept of psychological self includes our autobiographical memories, prejudices, aspirations, dreams, and multiple images of what we think we are—a great writer, a powerful politician, an eminent intellectual, or a spiritual personality. On the other hand, we have negative images of self, which include our perceptions of our deficiencies and failures. Unfortunately, life is not a simple affair in black-and-white. Therefore, we suffer from a combination of negative and positive images of self at one time or the other. We have both the happy and nagging aspects of our psychological self.

The preceding elucidation is nothing but a description of self, but that does not resolve the question of how the behavioral patterns of neurons in the brain give rise in the first place to the *subjective owner* of all the experiences, memories, aspirations, failures, and successes. How does the mysterious self that perpetually goes through the myriad experiences of sorrows and joys, pain and pleasures, elation and depression come into being? The subjectivity of "I" or the ownership as "myself" is the most baffling thing. It is the primeval force—*the big bang* on earth—that has unfolded the unique drama of life full of sound and fury. The foundational feeling of "I," devoid of personal name and autobiographical memories, presents the biggest bafflement or qualia.

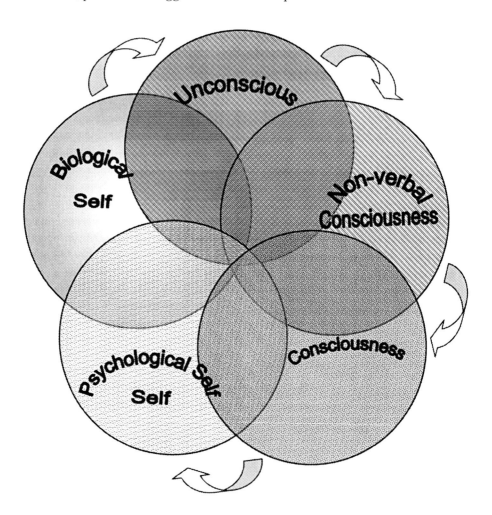

Figure 5.4. The architecture of self.

Neuroscientists and philosophers use the term *qualia* for certain subjective experiences that are irreducible and inexplicable. For instance, consider the *redness* of a red object or the *sweetness* of a sweet thing. Of course, we understand these qualities relatively by making comparison between red and green or sweet and bitter, but we cannot say for sure what is essentially green or bitter. Those are the irreducible properties described as qualia. For me, nonverbal "I-ness" has remained the most puzzling enigma.

Some philosophers and religious persons go to the extent of propounding that *self* is nonexistent, an illusion. Buddhism describes self as an illusion. It says, when you hold a firebrand in hand and wave it speedily in a circular fashion, an illusion of a fiery circle is created. Similarly, an illusion of self is created with the ceaseless movements (activities) of mental processes of thoughts, emotions, and memories.

Hinduism preaches a goal of transcending the sense of self as a means of uniting with the Ultimate Being (Para-Brahman) and also as a *nirvana* (freedom) from all problems of mundane life. Hinduism has a branch of philosophy called *maya* (a Sanskrit word) that is more than 2,500 years old. It considers the external world and self as *maya*, which means something that exists and does not exist at the same time. It is like when you witness a magician's trick of cutting a woman in two pieces, you see it as a reality, yet it is not an actuality. *Maya* is a reality virtual to a particular dimension of existence. It is a virtual and not actual reality. The world is thus an illusion, a vast collection of images, which changes depending on the perceptive power of biological senses or viewing devices. Incidentally, this reminds of Albert Einstein's quote: "Reality is merely an illusion, albeit a very persistent one."

Modern science might not totally reject the philosophical perspective of *maya*. The contradictory puzzle of *maya*—the state of existing and not existing simultaneously—is not without a parallel in the modern physics. It is similar to a quantum cat paradox contrived by the great scientist Schrödinger. In the quantum physics, the electron is neither a wave nor a particle until a measurement is made on it. Similarly, in Schrödinger's box contraption, the cat can exist in two quantum mechanical states—dead and alive. The cat is both dead and alive at the same time, until an observer opens the lid of the box to gaze at it. An act of observation makes the electron or the cat adopt one of the two states. It is an enigma of the quantum reality, which still puzzles scientists.

Whatever the truth, *self is* our daily and perennial experience that is tangible beyond any doubt. We wrestle with it every day, every moment of our life. The biological self with its shape and defined boundary is the physical reality beyond any question. It is the anchor and central reference point of all our experiences, thought, feelings, and actions. It is the owner of our joys and sorrows, our pain and pleasures. We cannot disown it or wish it away, even when we feel like doing that.

Let us get back to the issue of connection between self and consciousness. Self is the consequence or product of consciousness. It is the consciousness that causes and holds all the mental processes, including its *central reference point*, the sense of self. Our sense of self is deep rooted. It is verbal as well as nonverbal, conscious or implicit. In other words, it is entrenched in both the conscious and unconscious segments of consciousness. Even in the state of coma when our explicit sense of self is absent, the nonverbal and subconscious impulse of self as a sentient entity remains functional, along with its body of hidden memories, reflexes, and mental conditionings.

THE BINDING PROBLEM

The conscious experience per se of anything by a living organism is, in fact, an amazingly complex phenomenon. We are so used to this ubiquitous phenomenon in the humdrum of daily life that we do not realize its mysteries. Unfortunately, it is a habit of mind to turn everything experienced easily and frequently into a trite and mundane reality. We lose the sense of wonder and beauty when we are exposed frequently to unique objects. That is why many mysteries of life that unfold every moment around us go unnoticed by our minds. No wonder that we are bored so easily and pervasively in our life, and keep foraging perpetually for excitement and gratifications. The unbridled consumerism comes to our rescue and keeps feeding our pastimes.

Let us examine the issue of conscious experience and its complexities. Our act of seeing a tree on a landscape seems to be a simple experience, but in reality it is not so. It is rather a highly complex phenomenon that comes into being by binding together many diverse elements of sensory perceptions. The image of a tree in our mind actually consists of many features, like its size, location in a particular background, colors, and the smell of its leaves, flowers, or fruits. The image also includes feelings of beauty, wonder, or pleasure that are evoked by the sight of the tree. These numerous sensory perceptions are made possible through electrochemical activities of several regions of the brain with the external support of various sense organs of the body.

In fact, the brain works on the principle of division of labour. It is like the Barbie doll factory where many workers divide their skills and make different parts like hands, legs, head, eyes, hair, and clothes, while somebody else puts all the parts together to create the doll. In regard to the image of the tree, a logical question would arise: how do the disparate sensory perceptions that are processed by several parts of the brain bind together to create a complex and holistic experience of the tree? This important issue was raised first as a *binding problem* by Francis Crick when he turned his attention to understanding the phenomenon of consciousness.

The act of seeing a tree is not just a flat two-dimensional experience like seeing a photograph generated by computer or camera. It is a multidimensional and superbly integrated experience of emotions, feelings, smell, sound, motion, and colors. But why does the experience not remain broken down in the brain as disparate elements of sensations, which are generated in variations of time and space? Though these variations are of very miniscule degrees, they are quite significant nonetheless.

The binding problem has intrigued many scientists who are still looking for an explanation. William James argued that consciousness proceeds in a *flowing, ever-shifting manner* and the objects of conscious experience possess a "fringe" that blends them into each other. It seems that he was aware of the binding problem in some sense and offered a possible explanation. The idea of fringe is, however, not verifiable and does not provide a convincing answer for scientific scrutiny.

It appears that the problem of binding perhaps owes its existence to the reductionist methodology of science, which requires breaking down of a complex phenomenon into smaller parts and scrutinising them in a step by step approach. In the physical sciences, it has worked quite well, but in the case of consciousness, it is yet to prove its success. Quite remarkable research has been carried out on sectoral issues, for instance, on the subject of vision by Francis Crick himself. Such research has advanced understanding of the enormously complex processes concerning the actions of vision and olfaction that otherwise look so simple. It has, however, not met with full success in unravelling the secrets of consciousness and the question of binding.

In my view, it is not unreasonable to assume that the global property of consciousness is responsible for binding various sensory phenomena in the brain. The nonverbal consciousness *holds in itself* all mental processes like memory, thought, feelings, and emotions. Crucially, more important than that is the fact that consciousness is solely responsible for the mysterious phenomenon called *experience*—a sentient act. The electrochemical processes construct the myriad images of vision, olfaction, and other sensory facets, but it is the consciousness that lends the property of experience—a subjective feeling—to the images. The foundational property of *subjective experience* that underlies all those material processes of brain is the binding canvas.

I have earlier stated that the nonverbal consciousness can be experienced as a wavelike impulse from moment to moment. In fact, it flows continuously without the help of memory. However, we find it quite difficult to feel this nonverbal consciousness for more than a few moments, because memory keeps flickering to recall an experience. The act of memory to take a print or image is spontaneous and simultaneous with the occurrence of an experience, but that is basically a nonverbal and nonintrusive act. What is intrusive is the second aspect of memory, namely, the act of recalling, particularly in the instance of short-term or working memory.

The purpose of this explanation is to suggest that the *continuous flow* of the impulse of nonverbal consciousness underlies all brain processes and acts as a binding or continuity factor. Further, it seems each and every neuron holds, as its primary property, the potential of an impulse that is part of the flow of consciousness.

The binding problem also exists at another level in the makeup and play of feelings, emotions, memory, and thought. All our thoughts are embedded with some emotions and feelings either in an active or implicit manner. Feelings are often embedded so mildly in thoughts that we hardly recognize them. The binding phenomenon occurs in multiple ways in the following instances. Thought is constituted by the blending of nonverbal memory images, verbal correlates, and intelligence. The images of memory include blending of multiple sensory elements, feelings, and emotions. Our linguistic ability is made possible through blending of nonverbal images, verbal correlates as well as intelligence, emotions, and feelings.

All these disparate sets of sensory processes occur in different regions of the brain but they bind together in unique ways to create astonishing products of combinations and complexities, such as thought, language, and memory images. Mental stress, depression, anxieties, and worries are also astounding combinations of different psychic entities. We are so used to these miraculous facts that we hardly marvel at them. However, the epicentre of all these miracles is consciousness, which is the magical fountainhead of life.

One cannot totally rule out a contradictory view that the binding phenomenon is nonexistent and merely a perceptive illusion as it happens in the motion film mechanism. A series of still pictures on the reel of a motion film are projected in such a rapid manner that our mind is not able to process and recognize them as separate pictures. On account of the micro time gaps, these still pictures overlap and merge together in the ongoing visual processes of mind, and that creates the binding impressions resulting in the experience of lifelike dynamic scenes.

Neuroscientists tell us that our abilities of recognizing and experiencing at the conscious level is extremely sluggish in comparison to the high speed of external stimuli, sensory phenomena, and the electrochemical processes that take place within our brain and body. These experts have observed that neurons get activated and fire in just a few milliseconds to create sensory images, but in contrast the delivery of the experience of the images at the conscious level takes a few hundred to thousands of milliseconds.

The sluggishness of the conscious mind might account for blurring out of the micro time gaps between actual occurrence of sensory image and its recognition at the conscious level. Similarly, the time variations in processing of different sensory aspects of color, smell, size and motor action as well as in their deliveries will be blurred out and overlap at the conscious level to create the binding impression. Does it imply that the binding issue is a mere rapid juxtaposition of different sensory perceptions like the rapid screening of serial pictures in a motion film?

Can one stretch these arguments to speculate that consciousness or its global property is an illusion like the binding impressions due to the sluggishness of our experiencing ability at the conscious level? This might come closer to the Buddhist line of thought that self is an illusion like the ring of fire produced by the fast circular motion of a burning stick. The metaphor of the burning stick can be arguably applied to consciousness and the binding problem by stating that these are also illusions created by the ceaseless mental activities with micro time gaps. But what is the truth? According to neurologists, since consciousness has an actual seat in the brain stem, one cannot call it an illusion. Also, consciousness is the self-evident hard fact of our daily experience.

If the mechanical argument of motion film is applied to the inner functioning of the brain, it would mean that our thoughts, memory, linguistic ability, and multidimensional experiences are mere rapid juxtapositions of disparate sensory perceptions. For instance, the makeup of thought would be juxtapositions of feelings, nonverbal images and verbal correlates. Our experiences would be juxtapositions of images with visual, audio, olfactory, emotive contents. However, any mechanical process with its inbuilt arbitrariness and rigidities will result in random juxtapositions or binding. The element of randomness would jeopardise the high degree of intelligent symmetry and integrity that otherwise exist in the makeup of mental processes of thought, memory and language. Our coherent experiences having multiple, harmonious features would not be possible under such a mechanical principle.

In contrast to such a chaotic scenario, the human brain is extraordinarily efficient in generating amazingly complex but coherent products of thought, memory, feelings, and emotions. Hence, logically it necessitates the existence of an entity which ensures appropriate juxtapositions and binding of the innumerable sensory features caused by random stimuli. This entity is no other than consciousness. But how does it do that? Intelligence, which is the integral property of consciousness, performs the task of harmonious juxtaposition or binding of the sensory perceptions.

Can human beings, in the light of the principle of juxtaposition, produce a machine that is similar to human brain? Some progress has been made by experts in producing mechanical sensors of smell and touch. As in motion film, one can possibly use the method of rapid juxtapositions of material sensors to mimic a coherent experience of human brain. Even if one achieves an immensely complex task of rapid and coherent juxtapositions in a machine, it will lack *the sentience* of feeling or subjective experience, which is actual, and not virtual or mechanically contrived. The insurmountable gap of knowledge faced by experts is how to create in machines *subjective feeling* and the property of *understanding* that is dynamic and nonlinear. Moreover, since the instrumentalities of feeling and understanding are not possible without consciousness, we are back to the point of full circle.

ENHANCED ACCESS TO CONSCIOUSNESS

We began this chapter with the hope that exploring the question of consciousness might offer us some clues to tackle the problems of stress, depression, and the inexorable force of negative feelings. There is no doubt that consciousness is the common ground from where our thoughts, emotions, feelings, and memory emerge. It would stand to logic to say that more access to and dependence on the power of consciousness would make it easier to address emotional problems.

The question that arises next is whether it is possible to enhance our access to consciousness. Though some experts might doubt it, it is possible in the light of the following. Firstly, William James, whose insights and seminal writings in the nineteenth century remain unsurpassed even now, mentioned that spiritual persons have "more access" to their consciousness. Even by overlooking the issue of spirituality that experts might question, the possibility of human beings acquiring more access to the power of consciousness cannot be dismissed. Let me clarify that the term *access to consciousness* stands for "application of the power of consciousness."

Secondly, don't we access our consciousness in some measure in our daily life? When you become conscious of your anger, its force is dissipated. When you become aware of your mistake, you try to correct it. The more one is conscious of the fullness of a given situation, the more one is likely to succeed in tackling it.

When you focus your awareness on the strategy of your rival, you understand and cope with it better. Whenever we try to resolve any difficult problem or issue, we intensely focus our power of consciousness. This reminds us of the point made earlier that attention is a mode of consciousness.

In all these instances, we are actually accessing our power of consciousness in varying degrees and denying reflexive or impulsive actions. It might be argued that in these instances, we are accessing our innate intelligence, but as discussed earlier, intelligence and awareness are inherent and inseparable properties of consciousness.

Let us look at this from a slightly different perspective. The mental processes of thought, memory, feelings, and emotions are *specific and transient manifestations* of pure consciousness. Those are the operational modes of nonverbal consciousness. However, when more intelligence is imbued in these mental processes, their operational qualities are of a higher order, which would mean an increased application of the power of consciousness.

All of us have developed different levels of abilities to apply the power of consciousness. As we know, very significant differences exist in our individual abilities of memory, analytic thinking, feelings, and empathy. Even brothers and sisters have often notably wide differences in their abilities. The levels of such abilities and sensibilities differ substantially between literate and illiterate persons, criminals and honest social workers, or poets and stock brokers. The reasons for this are connected with the circumstance of life—the cultural and social environment. Much more important than these external factors is the way we individually react and shape our personality as well as our destiny.

The different points made in the foregoing paragraphs substantiate the issue that is central to this chapter, namely, access to consciousness is not a belief or mystical point. It is what everyone does in the daily life, though in different degrees. These points amplify and support the actual possibility of more access to consciousness implied by William James.

Though all of us have the natural scope to enhance our access to the power of consciousness, the unfortunate fact remains that we tend to forego such a possibility and confine ourselves to a narrow periphery of our consciousness. Practically all our problems at both the individual and collective levels germinate from our habitual confinement in *narrow bands of consciousness*. The instances of such problems are psychological conflicts and emotional afflictions at the individual level, while terrorism, violence, and societal conflicts at the global level.

The confinement in a narrow periphery of consciousness results from our tendency to live by switching over to automation of habit and reflex action. This tendency extends beyond the routine and repetitive actions that are necessary to get on with our daily life. It encompasses the way we think and react with emotions and feelings. The bulk of our thoughts and emotional reactions occurring in such autonomic mode are much larger than we ever realize. That is in addition to the reflex behavior that results from our cultural and social conditionings of mind.

The more obvious and gross examples of habitual thoughts include our rigid beliefs, superstitions, and social prejudices. People are ready to sacrifice their own lives or take lives of others when possessed by deep-rooted reflex thoughts and beliefs. Innumerable evils of our present day like terrorism and social fragmentation arise from that.

It is a sort of habitual inertia of mind to slip into automation that we were used to during our long evolutionary past as lower forms of life. The evolutionary course of life has been from the autonomic behavior that was prewired in the unconscious, to the innovative and more intelligent actions arising from the enhanced consciousness. Our evolutionary journey, since the origin of life as a self-duplicating cell till the mammalian era, had been as if through a dark tunnel of unconscious automation. With the accrual of expanded consciousness at the human stage, life seems to have arrived in an open landscape of sunshine and opportunities of conscious choice.

This would imply that we should make conscious and enlightened choices concerning our future as a species rather than allowing the blind forces of evolution to grind slowly and determine our destiny. The problems of environment, global warming and terrorism arising from unbridled commercialism and consumerism suggest that the human race is drifting along with short-sightedness, unmindful of its long-term future.

Expansion of consciousness or more access to consciousness means freedom from the blind forces of nature that control us from within. These evolutionarily older tendencies of reflex and autonomic actions continue to assert themselves in our thoughts and emotions more frequently and surreptitiously than we actually realise.

Let me add a clarification on my depiction of reflex actions as blind and negative factors. It should not be misconstrued that all reflex actions of our brain per se are negative and restrictive, because many of them are crucially important for sustaining and protecting life, such as fear of fire, height, or snakes. Our biological drives that are essential for life also generate reflex and prewired patterns of behavior. Many of our instinctual expressions of emotions and feelings are meant for protection and advancement of life.

A step ahead are the reflex actions that we consciously master for convenience and advancement of life. These are actions internalized by mind through repetition such as our professional skills. Such internalized and automated actions are meant to ensure better efficiency and save time in the exigencies that might threaten life.

Our journey in order to familiarize ourselves with the inner world of thought, memory, emotions, feelings, and consciousness has ended here. We would explore practical methods of tackling stress and anxiety from the next chapter onwards. These methods are based on accessing and using the power of awareness, the defining quality of consciousness. I should, however, caution the readers that these methods have to be tried with actual practice and personal experience to judge their effectiveness. A mere theoretical or intellectual scrutiny will not convince the reader. Of course, comprehensive evidences from research by various scientists and medical institutes have been cited in the latter chapters, which, I hope, will convince a skeptic.

Chapter 6

Expansion of Inner Awareness

*Or the waterfall, or music heard so deeply
That it is not heard at all, but you are the music
While the music lasts.*

—T. S. Eliot, *Four Quartets*

The majestic beauty of great mountains has the awesome power to immobilize our mind by knocking off the swarms of thoughts and anxieties, which ceaselessly haunt us. During my stay of a few years in Geneva and Vienna, I often drove around the enchanting mountains and lakes. It was an escape that I passionately looked forward to, from the verbose but non-communicative world of diplomacy. The scenic beauty of the Alps is captivating from a vantage point in the city of Montreux overlooking Lake Geneva. A drive farther south in the mountains is simply unforgettable. Also in Austria, the Alps and the serene lakes particularly in the southwest of Salzburg are gorgeous and a treasure of cherishable memories.

It was, however, my encounter with the Himalayas in Nepal that left me speechless. I drove from Kathmandu on the road winding up the hills to reach a lonely teahouse ahead of Nagarkot, a small village. It is the closest point about fifty kilometers from Kathmandu for watching the sunset in the Himalayas. It was my first trip to the place, though I did visit it several times later during my three-year stay in Nepal. When I reached the place, the sun was about to go down, and the sky was absolutely clear without a speck of cloud. The top of the hill I stood upon was overlooking a misty valley that spread across the cascading foothills. Above the deep, misty valleys rose the mighty Himalayas in a panoramic magnificence of innumerable snowy peaks. Beyond the foot hills, the long chain of mountain peaks filled the entire horizon in a semicircular expanse. The peaks pierced the deep sky with their astounding heights. Some of the snow-clad peaks had started to glisten in orange and light pink with the caressing touch of the soft sun.

Though this description is gleaned from the memory, my actual encounter was a unique experience. My mind was totally submerged, and it became one with the immensity of the awesome beauty unfolding beyond the stretch of the misty valleys and the cascading chains of foothills. Soon with the approaching twilight, the dark blue sky, the majestic mountains, the valleys, and I appeared to melt into an infinite oneness. The utter silence of the place immobilized my mind, wiping out even the noise of thought. I could feel the sound of the footsteps of time in the midst of the immense space, which engulfed the identity of everything around.

One time or the other, most of us have encountered such overwhelming awareness that wipes out our thoughts and memories for some moments. In the fullness of its primordial sentience, our consciousness immerses in the splendour and charm of the scenic beauty silencing the mind totally. Of course, such blissful experience does not last for more than a few seconds, but there can be exceptional cases like that of the great poet William Wordsworth, who could retain such extraordinary state of mind for a longer time. Also, some monks and Yogis practicing meditation have the capacity to allow the pristine pulse of consciousness to prevail by disengaging their minds from the transient processes of thought, memories and emotions. However, that, I believe, can be possible for several minutes only at a stretch. The great Indian philosopher J. Krishnamurti claimed to have an ability to remain "without any movement of thought" for even a couple of hours!

The narration of my encounter with the Himalayas highlights the phenomenon of total awareness and its silencing power over other mental activities. It knocks off thought, memories, and the ordinary feelings. The only mental process prevailing at the time is the primeval feeling of pure consciousness or being. Though silenced at the initial stage of experience, thought and memories invade the mind after some moments and we start making exclamations to articulate our experience or comparing with similar experiences in past. We even continue to derive joy and gratification by gloating over the memories of the experience, which is nothing but a replay of the memories to prolong the pleasure.

In fact, thoughts and memories are the spoilers of pure sensations and feelings. All our engrossing experiences of joy, wonder, or sorrow are marked with the absence of thought and memory. Even when you listen to the music that deeply touches your heart, there is no encroachment of thought and memory. In *Four Quartets*, T. S. Eliot says, "You are the music while the music lasts." When we start judging and evaluating the quality of music, it means both thought and memory have taken over the place of pure awareness of music. The deep joy of music and the fulfillments of our acute biological urges represent the undiluted sensations and feelings that universally hold inexorable appeal. The point to be noted is that inner awareness represents pure sensation, which is the foundation of all mental processes.

WIDENING THE HORIZON OF AWARENESS

The possibility of increased access to consciousness has been discussed in the earlier chapter. Now, let us explore some practical ways of doing it. Since consciousness manifests itself in the form of awareness, an increased access to consciousness would mean expansion or deepening of awareness. This, in other words, means using the power of inner (nonverbal) awareness, which is the intrinsic property of consciousness. It may be noted that such awareness is the main instrument of the practical method that is outlined in this chapter.

Of course we do use the power of consciousness or awareness in our daily life. Unfortunately, we do it only occasionally. When we feel deep pity for a beggar, or we are moved by the tears of someone whose child has died, our inner awareness expands and reaches beyond our narrow self. The same thing happens when you appreciate the reasons why your colleague has become upset and angry with you. Compassion for others is a resultant quality of expanded consciousness, and so is empathy. The expansion of inner awareness means widening the horizon of understanding—the central quality of our consciousness. It means detachment from the narrow self-centred individuality.

An endeavor to expand inner awareness would entail the following actions:

- ➢ Develop a habit to focus inner awareness on all activities of daily life.
- ➢ Avoid impulsive judgments and actions.
- ➢ The proverbial advice "Think before you act" is good, but go one step ahead to pause, and focus your power of pure awareness before you crank up your machinery of thought.

- Identify and put the brakes on the habitual and reflex thoughts and judgments, which occur more frequently than we realize. Note that inner awareness is an antidote to habitual thoughts and reflex feelings.
- Identify and be aware of the prejudices and past conditionings of mind involving individuals, places, or activities. The act of awareness loosens the hold of the rigid patterns of reactions.
- Do not rule out the probability of valid reasons for someone's actions that were found to be irksome or painful.
- Practice empathizing with others.
- Be compassionate, as it not only opens the door for better understanding but also brings joy, harmony, and peace in you and others.
- Avoid routinely identifying yourself with your thoughts, feelings, emotions, and beliefs. Learn to question them and practice a judicious detachment.
- Intuitive judgments and actions are useful but do not place blind faith in them.
- Living intelligently means increasing reliance on inner awareness of our actions and mental activities.

The series of actions outlined above represent expansion of inner awareness, but readers would react in dismay that such wise prescriptions are meaningless because they do not work in the real life. The stubborn question of how to do all that remains unanswered.

THE LIMITS OF POSITIVE THINKING

Admittedly, such advice is not different from the drills of positive thinking and spiritual guidance in countless books. The lucid exhortations in such books give the readers an initial thrill of having found panacea for all problems in life, but that belief fades away sooner than expected as one realizes that things are not as easy as made out. Unfortunately, the patterns of our thoughts, worries, and anxieties are too stubborn and unyielding.

These mental phenomena often have an autonomic force that is far greater than our willpower and determination. The play of memory is equally intrusive and obstinate. We desperately wish to forget our mental hurts, failures and mortifications. We wish to get rid of the haunting worries and anxieties, but unfortunately we find ourselves helpless. Why are we condemned to such an autocratic and oppressive regime of our psychic world? Why are our desires and efforts to live in the bliss and joy of spontaneous life thwarted?

The reasons are not far to seek. Our decisions are mere products of our thoughts at the conscious level, which is just the tip of the iceberg. Our thoughts play out their drama and incessant cacophony in the spotlight of conscious mind, while our emotions, feelings, memories act as the prompters and string pullers in the darkness behind the stage. Our thoughts act on the surface and do not have any sway over the subterranean operators.

Our decisions and rational thoughts constitute mere tinkering from the edge of consciousness and therefore, they fail to disentangle the hard-wirings of the brain at the deeper levels. Of course, we can repeat our suggestive thoughts over and over again for months and years as a drill of positive thinking and perhaps succeed in refashioning our habits and tendencies. However, that is external imposition of discipline and not a transformation brought about by understanding of the workings of our psychological self at the deeper levels.

The serious shortcoming one can find in the counseling of positive thinking is that it seeks to address mainly the symptoms such as negative patterns of thoughts and feelings but fails to make a person face and deal with the causes behind the symptoms. Such counseling normally includes suggestions like be confident and believe in yourself; look at the positive aspects of life and your personality; remember your successes; do not allow your failures to overshadow your actions; adopt optimistic attitude; do not allow the negative emotions of anger, sorrow, and frustration to distort your perceptions and actions; avoid prejudices and hasty judgments; be objective in your judgments; think before you act, etc.

Others offer spiritual planks like "You are the sacred soul that is metaphysical and transcends the frailties of mundane life! You are the part and parcel of the omnipresent God and hence, above all sins and infirmities of life." Some other offer recipes in a scientific garb like "You are a quantum self distinct from the thoughts, feelings, and worries."

All these are clever and seemingly intelligent attempts to escape the hard fact of actual self. Unfortunately, no amount of gloss can hide the harsh reality of self. The naked truth is that we are indivisible and not different from our thoughts, emotions, feelings, and memories. It is not possible at all to run away from them with the help of ideologies and beliefs couched in spiritual or scientific jargon. There is no way but to face our self and the facts of life, however ugly they might be. The only path available to us is to try and understand them, even though that is an enormously daunting task.

In retrospect, one might retort that the serial actions to expand consciousness, mentioned earlier, are not different from the drill of positive thinking. I cannot but fully agree with that remark. Yes, such advice and sermons have an insignificant impact on our habit of getting stressed and swept away by the force of negative emotions. So let us look for a long-lasting and effective means of dealings with these problems.

AWARENESS MEDITATION

All of us struggle in our lives to outgrow the predicament of haunting worries, anxieties, and stress, which strongly defy common sense and intelligence. Our mortification in life extends beyond that to include dispositional tendencies of impulsive actions, succumbing to self-pity or anger where cool reaction would have been a right course of action. Our mental hurts were often uncalled for in the hindsight of rational judgment, but we invite them impulsively. It is an intriguing puzzle that we are often the ones, rather than others, who inflict the severest agonies on our own selves.

I have also struggled a lot in my life and went begging for answers from books on psychology, philosophy, and positive thinking. These books seem to provide promises of solutions and solace but in actual terms, leave us where we were. In the course of such endeavour, one loads oneself with a great deal of knowledge and information to dish out and impress others. Unfortunately, knowledge has little impact on our mental conditionings and proclivities. People know that smoking cigarettes can lead to cancer and other ailments or that the propensity for getting easily stressed can cause health problems. Yet that knowledge does not free them from such habits and tendencies.

In my search, I have found the power of inner awareness as an amazing tool to tackle stress and anxiety in a lasting manner without having to resort to any psychological escape or self-hypnotism. The method that is effective for expanding our inner awareness or enhancing access to our consciousness is what I call awareness meditation, which is linked to the ancient tradition of meditation in India. I came across the knowledge of meditation in 1963 when I happened to read the lectures on Raja Yoga by Vivekananda, the great Indian monk and philosopher. Since then I have practiced meditation. The other great Indian philosopher and thinker who impressed me profoundly was J. Krishnamurti, though he vehemently denounced the traditional practices of meditation.

There have been many methods and varieties of meditation since the ancient days and hardly anyone can now claim much originality in evolving a new variant of meditation. I have struggled to understand the nature of our mental phenomena and resorted to meditation as an exceptional tool to do so. In the process, I have evolved a modified variant of meditation that I call awareness meditation. My amateur interest in astronomy, evolution of life, and neurology led me to look at meditation in a spirit of scientific research. Such an approach made me question the concepts and practices associated with different traditions of meditation. Some of the traditional varieties are based on compulsive mental concentration, while others involve repetitive drills of reciting sacred words. I have attempted later to outline their positive and negative aspects.

Let me clarify that I do not claim much originality in my concept of awareness meditation. My contribution lies perhaps in the new scientific approach and synthesis of the old and new in the light of substantial research done by neurologists and other scientists. I have tried to describe not only the method of this meditation but elucidated the mental processes during the meditation. I have attempted to explain how it brings about a slow and silent transformation of mind that enables one to live life more intelligently, with remarkable reduction of anxieties and stress.

Let me add a few words for skeptics. It surprised me to learn through print media like *Time* magazine and *Washington Post* that nearly 15 million people practice meditation in the USA alone, including many well-known personalities. This popularity is largely owing to the extensive research carried out by many scientists and medical institutes around the globe confirming enormous health benefits of meditation. I have endeavoured to analyze and explain how the psychology of meditation works and how it is linked to the miracles that the entity of consciousness works in our daily life to make us what we actually are. Let me urge the skeptics and rationalists to look at this issue with an open mind and a spirit of inquiry.

DIFFUSION OF INTELLIGENCE

Before I take up the question of awareness meditation, let me touch upon the incidence of "fragmentation of attention or diffusion of intelligence" that is so common in the way our mind operates. It is relevant to know for two reasons. First, it is an aberration from the application of inner awareness, which siphons off a good deal of our mental energy. Second, holistic attention without encroachment of parallel mental processes is very crucial in tackling stress, anxieties and depression. One needs highly focused attention and concentration of mental energy to perceive with requisite clarity the activities of mind that are so elusive and subjective.

Let us observe the quality of our attention in the instance when we are engaged in a serious talk with other persons. The quality of our listening is often deficient and marked with divided attention owing to simultaneous interference from thought, emotions, and play of memories. While listening, the parallel process of these mental activities goes on in order to judge and look for counter arguments against the speaker. At times, we feel impatient to respond in anticipation before even the speaker finishes what he or she has to say. The machinery of our mind keeps clattering in an effort to detect or imagine the motives and strategy of the speaker. Memory keeps feeding and affecting the process of listening with prejudgments and biases. Emotions of annoyance, sympathy, or boredom intrude upon the process of communication between the listener and the speaker.

Of course, it would be unwise to rule out these parallel processes as unwanted intrusions, because we need them to anticipate and judge and thus arrive at some understanding of what is spoken to us. Therefore, what is being questioned here is not the general requirement of these mental processes, but their parallel timing, overlap, and consequent distortions brought about in the quality of our perceptions and mutual communication.

Such parallel streams of mental activities evidently show how attention or operation of our intelligence gets divided and undermined resulting in fragmentation of our energy. Wouldn't it be more efficient to operate without allowing such dissipation of mental energy? Wouldn't that improve our mutual communication and make the world more harmonious with better understanding of each other? It is unfortunate that we are normally so preoccupied with ourselves that we hardly have the time and desire to listen to others in the fullest sense of the term.

The next question that arises is whether we can really listen and communicate without such fragmentation of attention and diffusion of intelligence. Of course, we are not strangers to the holistic attention or total awareness that we apply in the moments of crisis, emergency or deep pleasures. Also, occasionally when we have intense concentration of mind, it is marked with that quality of attention. I have no hesitation in saying that it is quite possible to listen with total attention as a norm. Fragmented attention is rather a matter of habit and reflex action that one can change with determination and effort, though that is easier said than done. However, it becomes much easy with the help of awareness meditation. I would even add that, after long experience of awareness meditation, holistic attention becomes the way your mind normally functions and prevents dissipation of its energy.

THE TRADITIONS OF YOGA—BENEFITS AND PITFALLS

The art of meditation as the most important element of Yoga was evolved around three thousand years ago during the Vedic period in ancient India by religious persons and ascetics called Yogis (practitioners of Yoga). The word *Yoga* signifies *union*, which is expected to take place with Para-Brahman, the Supreme Being. The word *Yoga* is normally associated in the minds of people with certain exercises and body-postures to improve health by enhancing the circulation of blood and vitality in all parts of body. But in fact, Yoga has several branches of disciplines and ideologies such as Jnana Yoga, the Yoga of spiritual knowledge; Raja Yoga, the Yoga of meditation; Bhakti Yoga, the Yoga of devotion and love; Kundalini Yoga, the discipline of activating certain nerve centers in the body to attain spiritual liberation; Karma Yoga, the ideology of liberation through enlightened actions;

and lastly the Hatha Yoga, the discipline of body postures and exercises, which is commonly known all over the world (see fig. 6.1). There is also a branch of Yoga called Tantric Yoga, which has lapsed into occultism and obscure rituals.

In ancient times, the underlying essence of all Yoga traditions was to discipline and prepare the body and mind for attaining spiritual enlightenment to unite with the Supreme Being. One would realize from the various prefixes of the word *Yoga* that those branches were in fact different paths leading to that singular goal. Each discipline has its own philosophy and practices, which must be understood and followed, in my opinion, with an open mind and intellectual scrutiny. One should be extra careful to avoid ritualism and a doctrinaire approach.

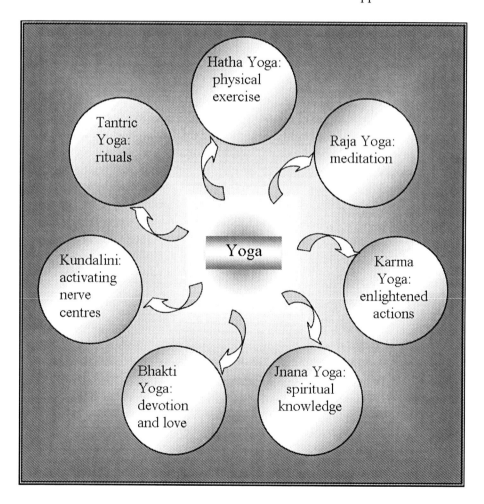

Figure 6.1. Various disciplines of Yoga.

The ideologies and practices in these Yoga branches have their own limitations as well as some exaggeration of benefits to attract followers. The truth and validity of the philosophies and rituals of some Yoga disciplines, particularly Tantric Yoga and Kundalini Yoga, are not yet established scientifically. Mere fascination and craving for mystical solutions and spiritual ideologies to compensate one's inadequacies can be detrimental physically and psychologically.

There are countless books on Yoga available everywhere around the globe in practically all languages. Unfortunately, teaching of Yoga has nowadays become a very profitable profession, given the predominance of commercial interests on the part of many writers and teachers. Therefore, one has to be discreet in identifying a teacher who has genuine interest and long years of Yoga experience combined with an open mind. Let me add a word of caution that one must avoid blind faith in the name of Yoga and adopt a scientific approach. One should not be taken in by clever teachers who smuggle in scientific vocabulary to merely impress and attract followers.

Let me also point out some pitfalls that one should avoid while choosing Yoga teachers or practising it independently.

The importance of unflinching faith in the guru (teacher) was quite exaggerated in the ancient Yoga traditions and spiritual ideologies in India for both the right and wrong reasons. The right reasons were related to the fact that various Yoga branches are specialized disciplines and practising them without the help of a well-experienced teacher might result in some harm to body and mind. For instance, the Yoga of body postures, if performed hastily or wrongly, can result in stretching a muscle and there have been incidents of hurting the backbone or neck. The postures called *sirshasan* (headstand) and *sarvangasan* (shoulder stand) are no doubt quite beneficial; but according to a medical research, if performed longer than forty seconds, these postures can harm the blood capillaries in the brain and cause headache. Such postures are risky, and the possibility of hurting some parts of the body is strong in the absence of proper knowledge and guidance of a teacher.

Some persons initially use the guidance and training of a teacher for a few months and then carry on the practice of Yoga on their own with the help of books or videocassettes. Such practitioners should bear in mind the following: One should be careful and take precaution not to be overenthusiastic, hasty, and abrupt in performing Yoga postures. One should acquire some basic knowledge of the physiology of the body and how one can avoid harm to muscles, limbs, or nerves. Yoga is meant to circulate blood and nutrients slowly to each and every part of the body, including the brain and thus enhance vitality and strength. It is not meant for weight reduction or bodybuilding.

In order to ensure benefits and avoid mishaps, the Yoga postures have to be programmed wisely in correct order and duration based on the knowledge of human physiology and structure. The postures need to be planned in such an order as to give exercise to different parts of the body through gradual and sequential turns, and to avoid repetitive patterns, which might be harmful. The bending and twisting of limbs and backbone should be gradual, slow and alternate in different directions to avoid overstretching. It is imperative to provide a few moments of relief and relaxation to the used muscles by a pause or a variant posture. Sudden force and vigorous jerks can be quite harmful in Yoga postures. In other field of exercises, it is believed that there is no gain without pain, but in Yoga pain is pain and no gain.

Nonetheless, it is proven beyond doubt that Yoga postures are very balanced sets of exercise with many benefits that accrue after regular practice of some months. The health problems of backbone, spine, knees, headache, joint pains, and arthritis can be avoided even in old age by regular Yoga exercises. It slows down the aging process. Young people can increase their vitality and retain their youth for more years through Yoga.

Let me mention the wrong motives for exaggerating importance of the tradition of a guru. Unflinching devotion to guru is overemphasized by some teachers to safeguard their self-interests through monopoly and subservience of their disciples. The instances of exploitation of disciples by unscrupulous teachers are not rare. The traditions of secrecy and blind faith in a guru have caused significant damage in terms of discouraging research, innovation and spread of Yoga knowledge. It has also abetted the obscure elements of occultism and mysticism to creep in and exploit people.

One must have a questioning mind and should not be deceived by tall claims of supernatural powers of Yoga like walking on water, reading thoughts, foretelling future or clairvoyance. Many persons are lured into Yoga and meditation with the claims of supernatural powers, which are nothing but delusions and tricks. Also, the promises of attaining union with the Supreme Being and liberation from the limitations of the mundane world are questionable and mere make-believe.

Similarly, the claims of Yoga powers to heal all types of diseases should be taken with a pinch of salt. It would be utterly unwise to shun modern medical treatment for serious illnesses and instead depend solely on Yoga's *miraculous* powers.

Of course this should not be misconstrued as a denial of many health and mental benefits of Yoga, which are truly remarkable. Fortunately, with the spread of knowledge of Yoga around the globe in the last few decades, extensive scientific research has been carried out confirming profound benefits of Yoga on mind and body, particularly in reducing stress and depression. People suffering from hypertension, heart ailments, and psychological problems have found notable relief by practicing certain types of Yoga, particularly meditation. No wonder popularity of Yoga has spread not only to schools and colleges but even to some large commercial firms that provide Yoga and meditation facilities to their employees.

PRECAUTIONS IN MEDITATION

Let me warn against the dangers of wrong meditation too, which could be even worse than the physical Yoga. The meditation that prescribes certain drills of mental concentration on an image of a god or a spiritual master and fixing one's gaze for a long time on a candle or small spot, can cause stress on optical nerves or the brain leading to headaches. Many techniques of meditation focus on coercive concentration and training of the mind with the aim to control thought and other mental processes like desires, emotions, and biological urges. Such practices are definitely harmful. The human mind is very dynamic and buzzing constantly with activities and any attempt to discipline it by prolonged repetitive drills like reciting sacred words is akin to locking up an energetic and playful child in a room.

Such arduous practices are essentially repressive and can make the mind dull, creating an illusion of peace for some time. They cannot bring about a healthy transformation that can enhance the flow of natural energy and spontaneity of mind and body. Any discipline to suppress biological urges and mental processes is not only futile, but can also lead to psychic maladies. Our biological urges, emotions, and thoughts are the integral biomechanics for protection and sustenance of life. They cannot be suppressed for a long time by any coercive discipline and willpower without causing abnormalities. However, what one should avoid through understanding and wisdom is obsessive gratification of biological urges and desires.

It should be noted that the awareness meditation described in this chapter is not a suppressive practice, nor does it involve the action of selective will power to negate and suppress thought, feelings, or desires. Rather, it requires one to face oneself honestly and intelligently.

This would raise some pertinent questions: What is a right meditation? What are its main elements? This would entail an endless debate in view of the following reasons. Meditation abounds in diverse personal perceptions and experiences that defy objective characterization, and thus, it becomes a fertile ground for divergent claims. The multiplicity of Yoga and meditation traditions further complicates the task. Besides, there has been a large proliferation of experts and teachers in the field who seek to have their own brand names and protected clientele. Mystification and occultism have also been the tricks of the trade.

In the backdrop of these compounding factors, I have endeavoured to elucidate awareness meditation in the following parts of this chapter with as much clarity and objectivity as possible. I am not sure that will make satisfactory answers to those questions. However, the honest advice one can offer is to rely on one's own critical judgment and open mind in the pursuit of meditation. Additionally, I have gleaned the following suggestions and precautions from our preceding discussions, which will help the readers in their search for a right kind of meditation:

- First, question yourself honestly, why do you wish to pursue meditation?
- Meditation should be pursued with the aim to live life more intelligently without stress and anxieties.
- Meditation is meant to help you see the facts of life and complexities of your self as such and not escape them. It should not be used as self-hypnosis, which is nothing but self-deception.
- Meditation aimed at suppression of thought, feelings, desires, or biological urges would lead to psychological disorders.
- Do not suspend your critical judgment and spirit of inquiry.
- Your mind will perceive as real what you believe in and meditate upon.
- Beliefs camouflage facts of life and are pitfalls on the path of true meditation.
- Beliefs are often psychological escapes from the realities of life or contrivances to lure followers.
- The repetitive drills of reciting words and practices aimed to negate and suppress thoughts, feelings, and memories can make the mind dull and languid, giving an illusion of inner peace.
- Fixing gaze for a long duration on a candle or small spot may cause harmful stress on optical nerves and the brain.
- Mental concentration for a long time on an image, a word, the centre of forehead may stiffen and stress nerves and cause headaches.
- A wise and experienced teacher is essential in both physical and mental Yoga.
- Do not be guided by absolute faith and total obedience to gurus, who are ultimately human beings with their own limits and shortcomings.
- Pursuit of meditation for seeking domination over others is delusive.
- The claims of attaining supernatural powers through Yoga are false and deceptive.

THE JOURNEY WITHIN

Swami Vivekananda, a great monk and philosopher of India, who had the truly modern mind, described meditation as a *journey within* for inner quest. In his opinion, the Western man looked around and marvelled at the secrets of the physical world, which motivated him to undertake his journey outward for exploring the world of physical objects. The superb achievements of the modern age in science and technology are the results of that outward journey of the curious human mind.

On the other hand, the Eastern man thought to himself, *The physical objects like the rivers, the mountains, the sky and stars are far away from me. I have layers and layers upon me, namely the biological body, thoughts, desires, feelings, and emotions that daily toss me around from one extreme to the other. What are these mighty forces governing me?* He, therefore, undertook his journey within in search of himself. That brought about a great variety of religious and philosophical thoughts marked with profound insights and intellectual depth. The ancient scriptures like Upanishads and Vedanta of Hinduism as well as the Buddhist holy books are some of the superb examples of such inner exploration. Meditation as one of the disciplines of Yoga was a product of this inward journey.

The quest of man to discover himself still goes on. The inner journey is evident in the abundant research that is being carried out to make sense of consciousness and how the brain functions. The outward journey aims to discover our place in the vast mysterious universe. One aspect of that journey is the search for other planetary systems, stars, and galaxies, and to unravel the enigma of how the universe originated in the first place. Pursuits of science and technology are other horizons to look for answers to our earnest age-old questions.

In the midst of this, we have hurdles and challenges on our path, such as the problems of environment and the gradual destruction of the planetary ecosystem, which threaten the very existence of life on earth. On the other hand, the problems of stress, anxieties, and depression have become universal and acute. They are the biggest killers in modern times.

THE TECHNIQUES OF AWARENESS MEDITATION

Let us now focus on the techniques of awareness meditation as a means of tackling stress and other emotional afflictions. The elements and guidelines narrated here are based on my experience of several years. As stated earlier, awareness meditation includes some elements from the traditional practices of meditation and I do not claim full originality. However, the techniques and guidelines given here are evolved after careful exploration and scrutiny and would accrue benefits that are tangible and long lasting. A spirit of inquiry and a critical mind are quite essential in pursuing this meditation. The practitioners should bear in mind that this is their own journey on the path of meditation to discover the world of their inner self. They should avoid blind faith in the knowledge borrowed from others, including this author.

The persons suffering from respiratory diseases, slipped disc, and cardiovascular or similar illnesses must consult their family doctors before attempting Yoga exercises or meditation. Meditation practice narrated here is not meant to replace medical or psychiatric treatment needed by someone.

A healthy body is an important requirement for starting meditation practice. The body and mind are closely linked; rather, they are inseparable parts of one system. If the body is ill or suffering from pain, it is hard for the mind to function in an efficient manner. Meditation demands alertness and application of mental energy, which is possible at the optimum if one is healthy and happy. Maintenance of good health requires a well-regulated life with physical exercise, and intake of nutritious food. It is advisable to avoid alcoholic drinks and smoking because of their harmful effects on body and mind.

I have enumerated first the physical aspects like body posture and health guidelines before discussing the mental techniques of awareness meditation.

PHYSICAL ASPECTS

Different sitting postures are recommended in the ancient tradition of meditation. Figures 6. 2-4 give an idea of such postures. However, there is no rigid rule. One can choose any sitting posture; but the important point is to keep the head, neck, and backbone in one line without any curve. This facilitates easy breathing and a smooth flow of blood to the brain and enhances its energy level. The second point is that one should feel comfortable and relaxed in whatever posture that is chosen. One should not force or overstretch legs or any part of the body to suit a posture. In the beginning, many persons will find it difficult to remain in a steady posture; but with the practice of a few days, one will feel comfortable.

One common posture (fig. 6.2) is called *sukhasan* (a Sanskrit word), an easy cross-legged posture. The second posture (fig. 6.3) is *vajrasan*, which can be done by kneeling down and sitting on the heels with erect backbone and neck. The third posture (fig. 6.4) is *padmasan* or a lotus posture, which is uncomfortable and difficult. I would not recommend it unless you are already adept at it. You may choose any sitting posture that is easier and can make some adjustments to feel comfortable. However, do follow the points made in the preceding paragraph.

Figure 6.2. Cross-legged posture (sukhasan).   **Figure 6.3.** Steady posture (vajrasan)

Figure 6.4. Lotus posture (padmasan)

The physical aspects of meditation are enumerated below:

- Choose a stable and safe platform that is hard or soft to suit your convenience. A chair might become risky if one dozes off.
- The place of meditation should be quiet and without any disturbance.
- The body should be alert, steady, and comfortable.
- Body and mind should be fresh and energetic.
- Usually, morning is chosen for meditation when mind and body are full of energy. This does not rule out other times in the day if one is inclined.
- The stomach should be light; therefore, meditate before a meal or a couple of hours after a meal.
- Coffee or strong tea goads your mind artificially into alertness, and one should avoid it before meditation. Instead, a small helping of fresh juice or fruits would be good a few minutes before meditation.
- Get adequate sleep of about seven hours a day with a regular routine.
- Avoid smoking and alcohol that harm both body and mind.
- One might feel drowsy and not focused while meditating immediately after hard exercise or when the body is tired and weak.
- A healthy body is necessary for meditation. It is advisable to have regular physical exercise and moderate food habits, meeting the nutritional needs of body.
- Try to avoid watching highly violent and thriller films that overexcite and disturb mind with negative emotions like fear and sorrow.

The next step after sitting down in a good posture for meditation is a breathing exercise called *pranayama*, which is not compulsory but is recommended because of the following reasons. If you observe carefully, you will realize that thought and emotions have strong connections with breathing. Breathing becomes short and fast during intense emotions and stress. It slows down when the mind is attentive and calm. That is why people are advised to breathe slowly and deeply when they are emotional, angry, or nervous. Slow and deep breathing supplies more oxygen in the blood to meet the requirement of the accelerated biomechanics of the body. At the same time, it also stabilizes heart rate and the hyperactivities of the body.

Experts tell us that we are habituated to a shallow and easy breathing and consequently use only 20 percent of the lung capacity. In a research, it was discovered that people living in the mountains have deep breathing habits with higher intake of oxygen and consequently, they have remarkably less incidence of heart stroke and other cardiovascular problems.

The ancient Yogis were aware of this linkage, and therefore, they devised pranayama to regulate and deepen the breathing. This exercise has not only a very soothing and serene impact on mind, but accrues impressive health benefits. Deeper and more regulated breathing accelerates blood purification by increasing the supply of oxygen and makes the lungs stronger. Pranayama exercise is aimed to stabilize mental processes and improve physical health as well.

There are several types of pranayama exercises described in the ancient literature. Some of them would be strenuous and tiresome particularly for old or weak persons and hence, should be avoided. Persons suffering from respiratory or other illnesses should consult their family doctors before attempting pranayama.

Pranayama for about ten minutes is quite beneficial in preparing the mind for meditation. The capacity for attention and inner awareness is enhanced with a steady, deep and slow-paced breathing. It may be noted that the underlying essence of all diverse breathing exercises of Yoga is only one, namely, to increase the depth and length of inhalation and exhalation by reducing their frequency and stabilize the breathing at a slower and deeper pace. A common and easy variety of pranayama is narrated below. It has four consecutive phases without any break:

- The first phase, after sitting down in an erect posture with a totally relaxed body and mind, start inhaling the air through both the nostrils in a slow and steady pace. Avoid filling up your lungs quickly; rather you should take as much time as possible to fill your lungs in a steady manner to their maximum capacity. This phase should last from three to fifteen seconds depending on your capacity and comfort. At the initial stage, you will be able to manage shorter inhaling durations but over time, with regular practice, your capacity will increase. The crucial rule to be borne in mind is that you should never strain your body and mind beyond your comfort limits.
- The second phase, try to withhold and retain the intake of air in your lungs as long as possible; the duration could be two to ten seconds depending on your comfort level.
- The third phase, exhale the air in a slow and steady pace with as much duration as you can manage comfortably. The duration could be from three to fifteen seconds.
- The fourth phase, after complete exhalation, keep the lungs empty by withholding the inhalation process for some time, say two to ten seconds without subjecting yourself to any discomfort.

The actions in the second and fourth phase can be performed by either keeping both the nostrils open or closed with the fingers of one hand.

There is another easier variation of this exercise. Instead of keeping open or closed both the nostrils as stated above, one can use only one nostril alternately for inhalation and exhalation in the first and third phase by closing the second nostril with fingers of one hand. In the first phase, you have to inhale through one (right) nostril while closing the other one with a finger. Second phase, close both the nostrils by pressing fingers for retaining the air intake. Third phase, exhale the air by opening only the left nostril. Forth phase, close both the nostrils to keep the lungs empty by preventing inhalation for a few seconds. The second cycle will start with inhalation through the left nostril and repeat the process alternately and sequentially. The durations of inhalation, retention of air in the lungs, exhalation and empty lungs should be uniform to the extent possible.

These four phases have to be repeated without break for ten to fifteen times or a bit more, depending on your inclination. It is advisable to start at the minimum with gradual increase without unduly straining oneself. One can have two or more such breathing sessions a day, but at least once a day prior to meditation session is advisable. You would soon realize that the breathing exercise makes you feel light, alert, and inclined for meditation. Over a period of time, it also enhances your capacity of focused attention or inner awareness.

These days, there are many experts on pranayama in India, but one name that comes to my mind is Swami Ramdev, who is an honest and selfless monk with a great deal of expertise. He is known to have cured even very serious illnesses with his techniques. He has established a large research facility on Yoga and pranayama in the town of Haridwar in North India. His experiments with pranayama are remarkable and worth looking at with an open mind. His weekly teaching sessions are hugely popular all over India.

THE MENTAL PROCESS

Now after having completed the breathing exercise, pranayama, we may begin the actual meditation aimed at gradually expanding the ability for inner awareness. Following are the guidelines for the mental process of meditation:

- ➢ Close your eyes after choosing your posture and performing pranayama.
- ➢ Mind and body should be steady, calm, and restful.

- Try to be aware of your breathing and heartbeats and then the whole body as one unit.
- Allow the mind and body to relax and calm down further.
- Awareness meditation is an effort at total relaxation of mind and body to such an extent that even the machinery of mind, namely thoughts, memory, and emotions also slows down gradually to enhance peace of mind.
- Allow your inner awareness to unfold and spread in its all-inclusiveness. It means you would switch over to the neutral mode of observation. In that, you do not make any choice in favour or against any thought, feeling, or memory. In other words, you are in the choiceless awareness.
- The overall single governing force in your mind is inner awareness or nonverbal consciousness, which is the vital essence of your self, undiluted by memories, thought or specific emotions and feelings.
- Do not try to control your mind against or in favour of anything.
- Give up all efforts at directing or manipulating your mind. Be effortless in the full sense of the term.
- Do not attempt concentration, which is a resistive action to prevent other mental processes and may make the nerves tense and rigid.
- If any thought, worries, anxieties, or feelings creep in mind, let them float on their own. Do not attempt to control them, nor should you participate in them.
- Do not make any choice among them, as it would mean participation.
- Do not make any judgment of good or bad, right or wrong, as that would mean an act of thought and memory.
- You are a choiceless or detached observer.
- You are a spectator, not an actor nor a director, in the theatre of mind.
- Never repress the painful or unpleasant thoughts and memory.
- Do not pursue pleasant thoughts and memories.
- Do not get frustrated with the rush of thoughts, memories, and feelings; just relax.

THE HYPERACTIVE BRAIN

Let me hasten to add that I would not slur over and ignore the enormity of the task described above. The billions of neurons in our brain ceaselessly churn out thoughts, memories and feelings. Neurologists have very aptly compared the neurons with noisy brokers in a hectic stock market. The Yoga scriptures have compared the human mind, which keeps shifting almost incessantly from one process to the other, with a wild monkey jumping from one branch of the tree to the other. It is always on the roller coaster of thoughts, memories, and feelings. The task of being a neutral observer is an antithesis of such an operative frenzy. The endeavour of our willpower to allow inner awareness to prevail becomes a lonely voice in this wilderness.

However, let me caution that one should not be dejected by the hordes of thoughts and memories that stampede the mind during the initial phase of meditation. The experience during the initial few weeks would be tough and, at times, frustrating. At first, our body finds it hard to sit down in an erect and fixed posture because we are used to easy postures curving our back. Our body resists the immobilization of the fixed posture. It rebels in the form of sensations of itching and twitching of skin, urging the body to fidget and resume normal movements. Such bodily protestations would divert the mind and dissuade it from meditation. Do not worry; such bodily tantrums will slowly subside and disappear after a week or so.

During the initial period, another war is being waged on the frontier of mind. When we try to allow inner awareness to prevail, the army of thoughts, memories, feelings, and desires invades our mind. Our mental hurts, joys, and myriad experiences come alive, and before we realize, our mind is already drifting in the stream of thoughts and memories. One finds it almost impossible for the choiceless observer to exist and operate even for a fraction of second. Even if you succeed in unburdening the observer (inner awareness) of thought, memory, and feelings, its existence is still very transient and flippant.

The torrential flow of thoughts and memories sweeps off the observer in its strong currents. The emotional and stressful events of past may take hold of the mind. It might become a painful and tormenting journey in dark memory lanes. On the other hand, the observer might vanish in the memories of a picturesque and eerie caravan of happy events. It gets hijacked by the memories of past pleasures or imagination of gratifications yet to be fulfilled. All this melodrama would make one feel utterly hopeless and frustrated. My advice is that this is a common experience of all of us, but do carry on with regular meditation for some days or a few weeks and you will be amply rewarded.

The reasons for the incessant activities of human brain are not far to seek. Our brain is an exceptionally sensitive organ that operates constantly in response to inexhaustible stimulations from objects and events of the external world as well as our internal urges, desires and memories. Also, the biological state of the body, that keeps varying, and our hidden emotions and feelings stimulate ceaseless activities of mind. Further, as discussed in chapter 4, our thoughts, memories, and feelings are not only intertwined inextricably, but act as mutual catalysts to reinforce and multiply each other. That complicates the operation of the neutral observer.

Unfortunately, we are the victims of the technological age of supersonic jets, entertainments, omnipresence of commercial advertisements, and the frantic pace of life, which makes our mind hyperactive. Before the arrival of mobile phones, when one stepped out of the house for activities like walking down to the place of work, enjoying a picnic or a walk in the nearby garden, one was left alone in peace. But now we are robbed of that privacy of a few moments for ourselves. The number of external objects that keep constantly bombarding our mind with sensory stimulations has proliferated immensely. The cutthroat competition, mental tension, and pressures of life drive the machinery of thoughts, memories and emotions into a frenzy of high-gear activities.

However, it would not be wise to live with stress and drift along with the notion that these are realities of life that cannot be altered. Our state of anxieties and worries should not be taken as existential predicament that is immutable. If you subscribe to the ideology of determinism and accept this as your fate, you are denouncing the central principle of evolution, namely, constant adaptation and improvement to ensure survival and enrichment of life. Stress and depression in the modern age are the silent killers that are more sneaky and dangerous than the wild predators encountered by our primitive ancestors. We have to tackle these psychic aberrations and overcome this daunting challenge of our time.

PRACTICAL GUIDELINES

Despite all the difficulties, including boredom and disinclination, in the initial phase of meditation, you will do well not to lose heart and take it as your discomfiture. Also, avoid agonizing over it and repressing the flow of memories. Face them with the strength of your awareness or inner intelligence. In fact, after the steady practice of a few weeks, your body would slowly discover the irresistible joy of a serene and soothing effect of meditation on its biochemistry and the mind begins to look forward to it every day. Let us see how the tide begins to turn and what benefits, though slowly, you will begin to reap.

Some practical advice would be useful on how to carry forward the practice of meditation. At the initial stage, your session should last about ten minutes once or twice a day. It is alright if you feel like continuing a few minutes longer, but without feeling any stress on your nerves. It is imperative to be regular so that your body and mind start getting tuned to meditation. If you have to miss it for a day or two due to some reasons, that does not matter.

After four to six weeks, you can increase the session to fifteen minutes but only if you can do so without taxing your mind and if you really feel inclined to do so. It should be borne in mind that if you get a headache or stressed after the session, it means you are forcing your mind and resorting to the resistive action of concentration. Any such coercive practice should be strictly avoided. The fundamental principle is that your mind should remain completely relaxed during the entire session and feel deep peace and happiness after the meditation.

When you find that your neutral observer does not come about or gets swept off in the intrusive flow of thoughts, memories, or feelings, do not worry. Let these mental processes play out in full. However, when you get even a momentary reprieve, you should remind yourself that you are only the spectator of the drama on the stage of consciousness. When you are a spectator, you are in the state of inner awareness, which is your anchor. A time will come after long practice, when you will remain anchored in the awareness, even in the midst of the high waves of thought, memories, or feelings.

After the practice of a few months, you will notice that the incidence of thought, memories, and feelings has started getting reduced and their obstinacy weakened. The ground on which you are standing, namely, inner awareness seems to become a bit firmer, though still slippery and transient. You are no longer like a straw in the winds. The clouds of memory, thought, and emotions begin to get thinner and scatter away, giving way to the sunshine of the choiceless observer to flicker. A new strength of detachment and perceptions of the workings of our psychic self slowly emerges. The background worries and anxieties, which are hidden, will dissipate and even vanish, bestowing upon the bliss of inner peace that you had never experienced before.

The door will begin to open into a new vista of life filled with a sense of liberation and spontaneity unfettered by the usual anxieties and psychological fears. In your workplace and daily life, you will feel more focused, energetic, and decisive. The intrusive thoughts and emotions will cease to invade your mind, enabling your innate intelligence to operate.

The horizon of your inner awareness that earlier remained fully engulfed and absorbed in "me," the narrow self, will expand to empathize with others and appreciate their views and feelings. You will not rush impulsively to defend your actions, but weigh them with detachment and the strength of your inner awareness. Of course, the old tendencies and habits will creep in occasionally, but there is no denial of the amazing changes in your behavior. The unique thing you will notice is that you have ceased to inflict psychological torments and restrictions on yourselves. All this will evidently accrue profound benefits of health and harmony in life.

After a year or so, one can increase the duration of meditation session to half an hour or even more subject to the precautions advised earlier. By this time, if you are proceeding correctly, meditation becomes a matter of real joy. Every day, the mind and body look forward to it earnestly. Also, within five to ten minutes after starting meditation, your mind will enter in a relaxed "twilight state," which we experience just before falling asleep. This state is marked with increased theta brain waves. It is followed by a state similar to non-REM (absence of rapid eye movement) sleep, which is dreamless and deeply relaxing. This state is achieved by Yogis within just ten to fifteen minutes in meditation. Normal human beings usually achieve such a deeply restful state of mind only after two hours of sleep in the early phase of night. Hence, after meditation, the Yogi gets the same level of deep relaxation, which normal persons get after deep sleep of a few hours. In the state of meditation, the Yogi does not fall asleep but remains anchored in deep awareness.

Let me clarify that the correlation between the duration of one session and how long one has been practicing meditation is approximate and not precise like a rule. For instance, one year of meditation experience does not necessarily mean the daily session has to be for half an hour or more. It may vary with each individual depending on the way he meditates, his age, health, regularity and life style. So increasing or decreasing the duration of a session will depend on one's own sound judgment, bearing in mind the safeguards mentioned in this chapter.

SOME SAFEGUARDS

Given their seriousness, let me reiterate these safeguards that must be adhered to very carefully:

- ➢ If you are suffering from any illness, consult your doctor before embarking on meditation practice.
- ➢ Your mind should remain totally relaxed during the entire session.
- ➢ If you feel uncomfortable, tense, or disinclined, stop the session without any regret, and wait for the next day when you are fresh and ready.
- ➢ If you feel a headache, unfocused, or do not get the benefits, such as deep peace and relaxation, after regular meditation of about four to six

weeks, it indicates that you are not able to meditate correctly, and you must discontinue or reassess your method of meditating.
- If you are getting more emotional or unhappy during or after meditation, it may mean that you are not observing with detachment your feelings, mental hurts, and sorrows and are instead pursuing them with active involvement.
- The continued preponderance of thoughts, memories, feelings, and emotions may mean that you are not anchored at all in dispassionate awareness. If not very serious, it can be overlooked in the initial period of a few weeks. However, it should soon begin to diminish day by day, ushering in happiness and inner peace, which last for several hours, if not the entire day. In fact if you do meditation correctly, such emotional preponderance will not be there at all even in your early phase.
- Do not get frustrated with the obstinacy of thoughts, feelings and memories because frustration itself is the creation of thought and expectations.
- The strong and persistent desire to achieve quick progress might sometime work as a hindrance to meditation. You should adopt a patient and investigative approach.
- Meditation does not bestow supernatural or mystical powers. Such claims are nothing but deceptions, and such expectations are self-delusions.
- There is nothing mysterious about some persons seeing unusual lights, colors, images, or similar experiences while meditating. These are transient dreamlike phenomena caused either by beliefs and cravings for supernatural or by activation and tickling of optical nerves and hidden memories.
- Beliefs and strong desires work as autosuggestions and self-hypnosis to make you see what you strongly wish, but that has no realistic value at all. Avoid being sidetracked by this.
- If you feel drowsy or fall asleep while meditating, do not mind; it is normal particularly in the initial period of some months.
- Meditation is not the type of emotional purgation or catharsis that is achieved by seeking to relive painful feelings or by gloating over past or future pleasures. Conversely, such attempts can reinforce memories and strengthen the painful feelings or cravings.

Some clarification on the question of sleep is necessary. It is not a worrisome matter if one feels drowsy or falls asleep while meditating. In fact, it is called Yoga-nindra (*nindra* means sleep). It can happen on account of reasons like inadequate sleep and tiredness. In some scientific studies, sleep of seven hours a day was found to be ideal and quite beneficial to health. In contrast, a routine with one or two hours more or less sleep had negative effects. Sleep deficiency is a widely prevalent problem of modern times, because of our hectic pace of life and plethora of entertainment avenues. Not only during the initial phase, but any time one can get into Yoga-nindra. The habit of regular sleep and "early to bed and early to rise" is very helpful for meditation.

Another cause for Yoga-nindra is the lack of necessary mental energy during the early phase of meditation. The brain is not used to exerting the extra energy required for meditation or for trying to remain in inner awareness. This may cause fatigue to the brain resulting in drowsiness or sleep. The brain, however, acquires necessary strength and energy after the meditation practice of a few weeks and then the incidence of Yoga-nindra would not happen. There is no mystery here; the brain gains the necessary strength in the same way as any part of the body does through an exercise. Such extra energy and strength of brain will remarkably enhance your capacity for mental work in the office. You will not require frequent cups of coffee or tea during the workday to spur your brain into alertness. The incidence of yawning and mental fatigue will become a thing of past.

There is another but a better variety of Yoga-nindra, which is somewhat similar to the twilight period of a few minutes preceding the actual sleep. A notable difference, however, exists between such Yoga-nindra and the ordinary twilight sleep. The role of reasoning power and logical thinking is considerably weakened or wiped out in the ordinary twilight sleep and consequently nonverbal images and blurred thoughts seem to float in the mind like straws in the wind. Also, the ability of conscious recognition of verbal and nonverbal images is suspended.

In contrast, this Yoga-nindra has some distinct features. The eerie floating of verbal and nonverbal images is practically nonexistent or negligible in Yoga-nindra. The Yogi in Yoga-nindra remains anchored in inner awareness, and therefore, the images in his mind are largely nonverbal and stringed with some logic. Also, in deeper meditation, there are no images at all; nonverbal awareness prevails.

Let me clarify that being anchored in inner awareness is not necessarily uniform and uninterrupted. There is often a brief loss of awareness, which actually means moments of total rest akin to sleep and hence it bears the name Yoga-nindra. The inner awareness, however, keeps reestablishing itself in a recurrent fashion even after being interrupted momentarily. These issues will be easier to grasp for an experienced meditator.

In conclusion, we have dwelt upon several aspects of awareness meditation as a specific method of expanding the reach and horizon of inner awareness. In other words, we looked into the practical ways of gaining more access to our consciousness and using its properties of intelligence and understanding to tackle stress, anxiety, and depression. The focus of this chapter, however, was limited to the physical and mental aspects of the meditation. In the next chapter we would look into the benefits as well as the scientific aspects of how it works and makes its benign impact on one's personality without having to resort to escapism or suppression.

Chapter 7

Benefits of Awareness Meditation

*Our knowledge is a torch of smoky pine
That lights the pathway but one step ahead
Across a void of mystery and dread.*
—George Santayana

Traditional meditation has now wider acceptance among the public including many well-known politicians, actors and intellectuals around the globe; but still some western experts view it with suspicion or dismiss it downright as nonscientific stuff. Many term it as obscure and mystical ritual that is being practiced by gullible people and preached by vested interests for exploitation. Some scientists even summarily denounce it as Oriental nonsense!

In this chapter, I present the findings of several research studies on meditation. Several neuroscientists, psychologists, and medical institutes carried out these studies independently. Most of these experts were taken by surprise to discover a wide range of benefits that related to not only stress and depression but also to cardiovascular diseases, the aging process and disorders affecting memory, attention, and sleep. Even more striking was the evidence that meditation bolsters the immune system. This explains why meditation has curative effects on many illnesses.

Logically, the antistress benefits are the most critical in view of the fact that persistent anxieties, stress, and depression are the causative factors of several serious illnesses. There is no doubt that these afflictions have wide-ranging negative effects on health and our immune system. The inevitable question arises: how does meditation lead to antistress benefits? Some experts might suggest that it must be a sort of faith healing, but that is not the case at all.

The answer is linked to the way meditation slows down and streamlines the activities of certain regions of the brain that become hyperactive to create stress and depression. It also rewires the brain in the long run to bring about a functional equilibrium in the cerebral regions, which are responsible for persistent anxieties and stress. Neuroscientists with the help of the latest brain-scanning devices have observed the benign workings of meditation minutely.

Therefore, this chapter is devoted to the workings of meditation and how such wide-ranging benefits accrue. I have tried to provide extensive details of the scientific studies. In the latter part, I have explained how awareness meditation is a more effective and intelligent method compared to the traditional practices that are quite prevalent now. Some methods of how to effect emotional cleansing and live life more intelligently are elucidated as well. I have no doubt that anyone practising regular meditation with an open mind would be able to experience such benefits directly. I hope that this will provide enough food for thought to the skeptics who tend to dismiss meditation as an obscure practice.

AN INSTRUMENT OF INNER INQUIRY

Let me begin with a background of how meditation originated in several religious sects around the world and evolved independently as a comprehensive system in ancient India.

Humanity has been struggling since the dawn of history with the fundamental questions of its place in this vast and mysterious universe as well as the powerful forces that govern the inner and external world. The basic human urge to investigate and seek answers to these existential questions has been behind the origin of meditation as an instrument of inquiry in ancient times. Of course, religious and philosophical thoughts also led to a pursuit of meditation.

Meditation as an effective method of contemplation arose independently in different societies around the world; but Hinduism deserves credit for evolving it into an elaborate system with unique traditions. The Christian monks known as the Desert Fathers, the Jewish tradition of Cabalism, the Muslim Sufis, and many religious sects across the world used meditation for spiritual pursuits. The Buddhist scriptures since sixth century BC prescribed meditation for monks to understand the nature of self. In fact, Buddha is believed to have achieved enlightenment while meditating under a banyan tree. During the same era, Jainism in India also attached similar significance to meditation. This must have happened because of not only the influence of Hinduism, but also the fact that Buddhism and Jainism were originally the offshoots of Hinduism and then developed as independent religious ideologies.

It is obvious that meditation as a practice arose out of a normal trait of human behavior, namely, contemplation. In the daily life, all of us resort to a kind of meditation when we focus attention to tackle a given situation that is complex. Scientists and experts actually use it more often in a nonsystemic form when they struggle with the problems that elude easy answers.

Meditation was developed as an elaborate system of contemplation in ancient India. The central spirit of various traditions of meditation continues to be inner inquiry and the overriding aim was to ensure mental equilibrium and robust mind. The wider acceptance of meditation in many countries since the dawn of human history to the present day testifies the validity of the point that meditation is a sane and healthy practice. The occult and mystical practices that later crept into it have created negative perceptions of meditation among the experts and scientists. Hence, it is imperative to differentiate the facts from fiction and place meditation on a sound footing with research and a scientific approach.

Fortunately, noteworthy progress has been made over the last few decades in terms of scientific research on the effects of meditation. The increasing popularity of Yoga all over the world has attracted the attention of many psychologists and neurologists, which led them to conduct research. The latest technological devices helped them to observe directly the electrochemical processes in the brain of meditating monks and other volunteers. This has provided reliable evidence on the positive effect of meditation.

The scientific evidence and direct experiences have led to a surge in the popularity of Yoga and meditation. It was earlier confined to India and some Eastern countries, but has now spread across the Western countries of Europe and America. According to media reports, around 15 million people in USA alone practice some form of meditation. Given the increasing conviction and demand, many hospitals, schools, colleges, social clubs, hotels, and government offices have started offering meditation facilities. Some business organizations found it quite effective for stress reduction. They noticed increased productivity and improved behavioral patterns among their employees. Many doctors now advise their patients to practice meditation to reduce anxieties and stress.

Let me clarify that the findings of scientific research are fully attributable to awareness meditation because it is essentially a variety of traditional meditation that has been refined to ensure long-lasting benefits and avoid dangers of practices, which encourage self-hypnotism and repression of desires, feelings, and thought. It does not include mentally coercive and rigid drills like repetitive recital of sacred words or fixing gaze on an image. Unlike other practices, the awareness meditation lays emphasis on detached observation as well as understanding of the mental processes and how the psychic self operates in daily life. It is more scientific and effective, but demands more intellectual alertness and efforts.

THE ANCIENT ORIGIN

The term *meditate*, signifying contemplation, is indicative of the genesis and underlying purpose of meditation. As indicated earlier, though it was prevalent as a practice in other religious sects around the world, meditation first evolved into an elaborate system of contemplation and inquiry in the ancient India. Around three thousand years ago, it was developed as one of the disciplines of Yoga. The Sanskrit word describing the process of meditation was *Dhyan*, which meant "deep attention or mental concentration." It was intended to be an instrument to help understand the self, purpose of life, and ultimately unite with the Supreme Being.

It is a remarkable fact that meditation evolved in ancient India as a way of life, particularly for pupils and older people to enhance their ability of attention and mental equilibrium. During ancient times in India, life was divided into four asrama, (the Sanskrit word for a phase or stage of life). The first phase of life from childhood until adulthood at the age of twenty-five years was called *brahmascharyasram*, meaning celibate life. It was meant for leading a celibate life in pursuit of education and knowledge. This period was supposed to be spent with the teacher, often away from the parents.

The second phase was *gruhasthasram*, when a person was expected to get married and raise one's own family. The age for this extended from twenty-five to fifty years, and one was expected to enjoy the pleasures of family life along with carrying out responsibilities toward the society. The third stage was *vanaprasthasram* from the age of fifty to seventy-five years, which was meant for being away from the family to acquire religious wisdom. The last phase after the age of seventy-five years was *sanyasthasram*, when one was required to renounce the mundane life and become a monk to spend time meditating on spiritual matters and to seek union with the Supreme Being.

These stages of life were recommended guidelines and not necessarily followed by everyone. Meditation was supposed to be a major part of daily routine in the third phase, and intensified in the last phase. It was also taught to the youngsters in the first stage of *brahmascharyasram* in order to help them sharpen their minds and increase their concentration on studies.

This system of life contributed to establishing meditation as an important discipline for mental and physical health. It also gave rise to proliferation of meditation practices that were quite easy but stereotyped to suit the common person, such as repetitive recital of sacred words and concentration on images of gods and goddesses. The Yogis (practitioners of Yoga), who devoted their life to philosophic contemplation, preferred more difficult forms of meditation involving intense concentration and hard mental discipline.

It would not be out of place to add a few words on Vedas and Upanishads, which helped establish the traditions of Yoga and meditation. These scriptures represent the most brilliant creative works of humanity in very ancient times. They were composed more than three thousand years ago in ancient India by meditating Yogis and philosophers. The Vedas and Upanishads contain amazing philosophical insights and explore the questions relating to the creation of the universe as well as time and space.

The word *Veda* in Sanskrit means "to know" and the Vedas literally means the book of inspired knowledge. The most outstanding scripture among them is Vedanta, which signifies "end of knowledge" (*Veda* means knowledge and *anta* means end). As indicated by its name, it explores the limits of human knowledge and thought in understanding the ultimate nature of the universe and consciousness. It emphasizes the need for transcending the blinkers of thought and knowledge to have insight into the mysteries of self and creation. Human thought and knowledge are defined as relative processes that construct a kind of virtual reality in the limited dimension of human existence, and not ultimate reality

In order to give a slight idea of the intellectual depth that pervades in the Vedas, let me quote one of the translated verses of *Rigveda*. An attempt is made in this stanza to grasp the essence of the Ultimate Being as the one and the only reality that prevailed before the universe was created with its properties of time and space. The reach of the contemplative vision that is evident in this verse is simply amazing, given the fact that it was composed in very ancient times, when the knowledge of solar system and universe was just primitive, to say the least.

> There existed no death, nor did immortality then;
> > There prevailed no glimpse of night, nor of day;
> That One breathed no external breath,
> > But his own nature;
> Other than Him, there existed no beyond.

THE BENEFITS OF MEDITATION

Having dwelt upon a historical background, let us now deal with some concrete issues that have practical value for tackling stress and depression. These relate to the various benefits that accrue from meditation in the short and long term.

First, I will enumerate the benefits and then dwell upon research work and how meditation actually affects the working of our brain.

- It reduces or eliminates stress and brings inner peace.
- Over time, it frees one from the habit and reflex behavior of getting stressed.
- One experiences freshness and inner joy throughout the day.
- One feels focused and one's ability of attention increases considerably.
- The energy that was being siphoned off in anxieties and worries is restored and available to the mind.
- One experiences an enhanced flow of mental and physical energy for practically the whole day and the common fatigue disappears.
- It confers a high level of health of both body and mind.
- The aging process of body and mind slows down.
- It brings about a remarkable emotional cleansing—catharsis.
- Endows a power of detachment that results in a better understanding of one's thoughts, feelings, and behavior.
- One learns to act more intelligently and objectively instead of being bogged down in subjective feelings and thoughts.
- The background worries and psychological fears, which are hidden, diminish considerably in the long term.
- The tendency of mind to get easily irritated or hurt vanishes or diminishes quite significantly.

- The "me" that is often aggressive, vulnerable, and constantly struggling to defend itself sheds its psychological baggage and subjective submergence.
- It enhances the capacity to empathize with others, resulting in better interpersonal relationship and reduction of mental conflicts.

It may be noted that the benefits mentioned here are definite possibilities that can be realized, if one meditates regularly and correctly. Some of these benefits like feeling more focused, calm, and deeply relaxed can be realized within two or three weeks. In the initial phase, such a mental state lasts only a few hours after meditation, and the old habit of reacting stressfully comes back in the latter part of the day. However, the duration of inner peace increases as one continues the practice for months. After a few years of regular meditation, a meditator retains effortlessly such mental equilibrium throughout out the day.

The other benefits involving behavioral changes, like freedom from background worries and the habit of getting hurt or angry accrue after a long period and not in the initial phase. Those are deeper mental conditionings, which require rewiring of the neural activities of brain and hence a longer time to dissipate. Of course, there are always situations in life that are provocative and challenging enough to exasperate even an experienced Yogi and might cause pain and sorrow, but such reactions are remarkably reduced in frequency and intensity. In addition, one's emotive resilience expands significantly, and one is able to switch over faster to a steady and normal mode of behavior.

However, it should be borne in mind that the span of realizing all these benefits is correlated with one's mental profile, determination, intellectual alertness, and the way one meditates. The kind of circumstances one is placed in and one's quality of life can have an impact on the durability of meditation results. Highly challenging and stressful circumstances, such as the loss of a job, breakup of close relationship, and a hostile boss, are, no doubt, too strong factors to maintain one's mental equilibrium. In such a scenario, one should increase the duration and frequency of meditation in the course of the day, which will definitely give renewed strength to the mind to withstand the stress.

Most meditators will confirm that frequent and longer meditation during a crisis provides a good deal of mental detachment and resilience that enables one to cope with the stressful situation more effectively. It infuses hope and motivation to look for solutions, instead of being bogged down in pessimism. In a situation of deep sorrow and mental turmoil, emotions work like a vortex that slowly drags a person deeper into stress and depression. Persons, with such afflictions, find themselves helpless, and their ability to reason objectively is eroded.

According to studies, meditation diminishes or even blocks the uncontrolled flow of sensory inputs in the brain, which fuel negative emotions and stress. Further, the action of meditation amazingly restores our ability of objective reasoning, clears the emotional fog and helps oneself to pull out of the morass of sorrow and depression. One would wonder how meditation works such a miracle. The answer lies in the way meditation changes the electrochemical profile of the brain. We will later go into the details of how the functioning of various parts of the brain undergoes change in the meditative state.

STRESS AND VITAMIN DEFICIENCIES

A great deal of research is done on how stress slowly and silently does its diabolic work and seriously damages both body and mind. I was impressed in particular with the writings of the well-known nutritionist in the USA, Dr. Adelle Davis. She relied on a vast body of research across the globe and showed that stress caused vitamin deficiencies, and acute deficiencies are the primary causes for majority of our illnesses, such as heart diseases, diabetes, haemorrhoids, digestive disorders, paralysis, and vertigo. Of course, that does not rule out hereditary reasons and other causative factors. She observed that the body's requirement of vitamins and minerals increases manifold in order to cope with the heightened biochemical activities induced by excessive stress. Consequently, the body quickly exhausts the available stock, and the deficiencies that subsequently occur affect the health and functioning of various organs.

Davis has cited research experiments showing marked recovery by patients from several serious diseases after intake of enhanced doses of vitamins. For instance, high dozes of vitamin B6 cleared less acute haemorrhoids in a few weeks and even saved some acute cases from the requirement of surgery. A regular supplement of extra vitamin B complex prevented exacerbation of nonhereditary type diabetes. Many patients of vertigo found remarkable relief with regular intake of vitamins, particularly B complex.

In the early 1970s, Davis was the first who strongly advocated the use of folic acid, a part of vitamin B complex, for pregnant women. In her opinion, an acute deficiency of folic acid can be dangerous for a growing baby. It can cause underdevelopment of the embryo and the child might be born with defective organs like a hole in the heart, deafness, and even brain retardation. That was corroborated later by other experts. Consequently, only now some developed countries have made it obligatory for doctors to prescribe folic acid for pregnant mothers along with other nutrients.

Davis observed that supplements of potassium along with vitamins resulted in marked improvement in some cases of paralysis at an early stage. She did not rule out that some cases of cardiac arrest might actually be paralytic seizures due to acute deficiency of potassium. The animals that were fed only sweet and salty diet in experiments, developed acute deficiency of potassium and paralysis within three to four days. However, they recovered soon after generous supply of potassium.

For more details and accuracy, the interested readers are advised to refer to her books *Let's Eat Right to Keep Fit* or *Let's Get Well*. It should be also noted that there are many medical experts who are against the regular use of vitamin supplements and strongly disagree with the vitamin therapies advocated by Davis. Some other medical experts feel that she overstated the use of vitamins, but still there is considerable truth in what she has said.

Even though the medical experts are divided on the use of vitamin pills, at least two facts are well established in science. Firstly, persistent stress conditions accelerate our biochemical processes to the highest gear, which results in vitamin deficiencies. Secondly, such deficiencies are behind many of our ailments. In other words, stress is the mother of many diseases. In the face of these facts, we have two choices before us. First choice is to deal with the stress-related ailments by resorting to a drug treatment or vitamin supplements, which is a controversial issue in the opinion of some experts. Yet it would be reasonable to use vitamins for therapeutic purposes in exceptional circumstances under the guidance of a doctor.

However, given the perennial and universal affliction of stress in the modern age, it would be unwise to depend permanently on drug treatment or vitamins to avoid stress-related deficiencies. The golden rule is not to load our bio-system with external chemicals and vitamins, at least not on a regular or long-term basis. The second choice before us is much wiser and healthier, namely, to reduce or eliminate the stress itself—the primary cause of deficiencies and ailments. Meditation not only makes that possible but also bestows inner joy and happiness.

STRESS AND ACCELERATED AGING

Let me now provide some details of the research that has discovered substantial evidences to support the stress-reduction value of meditation. In

1967 Dr. Herbert Benson, a professor of medicine at Harvard Medical School, gathered thirty-six transcendental meditators in his lab to measure their heart rate and blood pressure. He found that during meditation, they consumed 17 percent less oxygen, lowered their heart rate by three beats a minute, and increased their theta brain waves that occur in the state of deep relaxation.

These results were corroborated by the American physiologist R. Keith Wallace—from the University of California, Los Angeles—who conducted a series of experiments in late 1960s on young meditators. He found evidence of significantly positive changes in heartbeat, breathing pattern and blood pressure. The state of relaxation experienced by the meditators was found to be more profound than deep sleep. Also, such a state of relaxation was achieved by them much more quickly—within ten to fifteen minutes after starting their meditation session—compared to a few hours of sleep we take to do so.

Emotional equilibrium and a life without stress will not only improve health but also minimize the wear and tear of the body. Hence, it is quite logical to assume that it will slow down the aging process of the body as well. In the late 1970s, Wallace focused his research on the impact of meditation on the aging process. He used the indicators of biological aging like blood pressure, vision, and hearing, which normally decline with age. He found that all these indicators improved significantly, arresting the aging process in those who had practiced meditation for a few years.

He also observed a notable difference between the biological age and chronological age of the long-term meditators. Dr. Wallace concluded that those who meditated regularly for less than five years had an average biological age five years younger than their chronological age. Those who had been doing it for more than five years had average biological age twelve years younger than their chronological age. Others have subsequently corroborated these amazing benefits.

In the USA, Dr. Jay Glaser and Dr. Deepak Chopra have gone even further in their research on meditation and its impact on the chemistry of aging. They worked together on the possible linkage of a steroid called DHEA (Dehydroepiandrosterone) with human aging. Dr. Chopra has made the following observations in his book, *Ageless Body, Timeless Mind*. DHEA is the only hormone that declines in a straight line with the age. Its level peaks during prime youth in the midtwenties and declines at an increasing rate after menopause. It falls off to a mere 5 percent of a person's maximum by the last years of life.

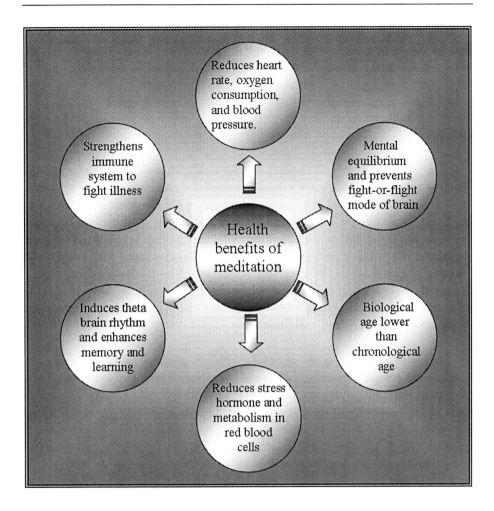

Figure 7.1. Health benefits of meditation found in research by medical institutes and independent scientists.

Another significant fact is that this hormone is a precursor of stress hormones such as adrenaline and cortisol, and hence when body produces these stress hormones, it has to use up some quantities of the reservoir of DHEA that nature has endowed us at the time of birth. Its depletion corresponds with the incidence of stress resulting in the biological aging, but not directly with the chronological aging. This leads to a logical conclusion that one can keep up one's DHEA levels by avoiding stress and thus slow down biological aging.

Dr. Glaser compared the DHEA levels of 328 meditators to those of 1,462 nonmeditators. In all the women's groups, the meditators had higher levels of

DHEA, and eight out of the eleven men's groups showed similar results. He found that the meditating men above the age of forty-five had 23 percent more DHEA, while the women 47 percent more. Dr. Glaser concluded that DHEA levels in meditators were equivalent to those of the people younger by five to ten years. These significant findings confirm the similar conclusions by Dr. Wallace.

IMPACT ON ILLNESSES

There have been several research studies on the impact of meditation on the immune system. Dr. Mehmet Oz, director of Columbia-Presbyterian's Heart Institute, established that meditation prevented the fight-or-flight behavior of our brain, in which the adrenal gland floods the body with the stress hormone called cortisol. Meditation also slows down the metabolism in red blood cells and suppresses the production of cytokines, the proteins associated with heightened immune response in the stressed-out persons such as students taking exams. Studies have shown that meditation reduces heart rates and cuts down hardening of arteries and blood pressure. All these symptoms are caused by persistent incidence of stress, anxiety, and depression.

Dr. David Spiegel, director of Stanford's Psychosocial Treatment Laboratory, conducted a study on psoriasis patients. One group of such patients was given a salve treatment of listening to music, while the other group listened to meditation tapes. It was found that those who learnt meditation healed faster. Jon Kabat-Zinn, who founded the Stress Reduction Clinic at the Umass Medical Center, made research independently on a different group of psoriasis patients and observed similar benefits in meditators compared to others.

Besides, counteracting the harmful biochemistry of stress, meditation has shown beneficial effects on the immune system. In another study by Jon Kabat-Zinn and Wisconsin's Richard Davidson, a group of newly taught meditators and nonmeditators were given flu shots, and the antibody levels in their blood were measured. The meditators were found to have more antibodies during both measurements, after four and eight weeks.

The strengthening effect of meditation on the immune system holds enormous prospects as it protects the body from illnesses. It is therefore not far-fetched to say that meditation would be effective to some extent against all diseases—common or even serious ones that are infectious and not just stress related.

One would wonder how meditation strengthens the immune system. There is nothing supernatural or mysterious about it. The underlying reason is the same, namely the curse of stress. It is proven repeatedly that stress puts strains on immune system and actually undermines it. That is self-evident from the fact that the persons under stress are more vulnerable to diseases. The health problems get exacerbated in the cases of depressed persons. Stress is undeniably the cause of many illnesses, whether stress related or infectious.

Let us look at some more research on the subject. Columbia-Presbyterian Medical Center in New York offers an optional program of Yoga and meditation to every patient coming for a heart surgery. In randomized trials, the patients who opted for Yoga and meditation were discovered to do the best in terms of managing pain and anxiety. This finding is understandable on the following grounds. Human reactions to pain are governed by not only the type of physical injury but also by attitude and approach. The patients coming for heart surgery suffer anxiety and pain more from the psychology of anticipation and uncertainty of what would happen. They are already stressed before the surgery. On the other hand, the patients who learnt meditation were better equipped to cope with the stress and anxieties.

THE NEUROLOGY OF MEDITATION

In the next chapter, we will go into the details of how meditation actually works and accrues extraordinary benefits of stress-reduction. However, let me mention at least one aspect that is quite relevant here.

While scanning the brain at the time of deep meditation, it was observed in several independent studies that the frontal lobe and parietal lobe were deactivated in terms of reduced levels of blood flow. The frontal lobe is the seat of our reasoning power, thoughts, ability of anticipating future, and planning. It also generates some of the secondary emotions peculiar to humans such as guilt, pride, sympathy, wonder, and compassion. On the other hand, the parietal lobe processes the sensory data from the external world and orients us to our surroundings. It is also responsible for our sense of time and space. Under stress, the frontal and parietal lobes operate in frantic pace or fight-or-flight mode.

During meditation, the activities of the frontal lobe and the parietal lobe are practically stopped and the sensory signals from them, which cause anxieties and stress, are not transmitted to other parts of the brain, including those responsible for primary emotions of fear, sadness, anger, and aggressiveness. The deactivation of the parietal lobe detaches the meditators from the sense of time and space or the external world and induces a feeling of timelessness and oneness without any boundaries. The deactivation of frontal lobe results in dissipating worries and anxieties as well as the "me-ness" with its psychological baggage, which is bothersome and nagging. All these factors prevent stress and bring about deep tranquillity of mind.

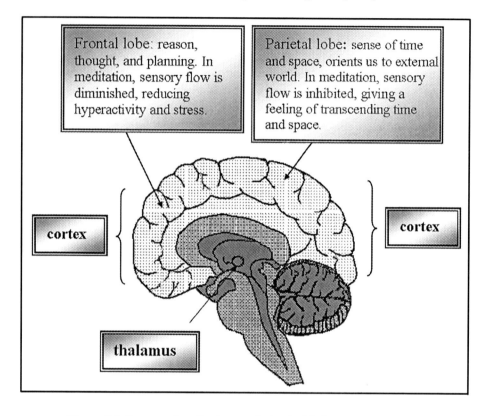

Figure 7.2. Impact of meditation on the brain. Under stress, the frontal lobe and parietal lobe operate in fight-or-flight mode.

This explains why meditation accrues the antistress benefits. A curious question, however, arises: What is the difference between psychological suppression of painful feelings and such reduction of the sensory inputs from those areas of the brain? In my opinion, the difference is quite significant.

The hectic and almost incessant sensory signals from the frontal and parietal lobes provoke the neural assemblies in other parts of the brain to generate the emotions of fear, pain, sorrow, and anxieties that constitute stress and depression. When meditation prevents transmission of the sensory data to these parts of the brain, the phenomenon of stress fails to build up. It means the disturbing thoughts and negative feelings are not generated in the first place and hence the question of suppressing them does not arise.

In contrast, in the act of psychological suppression, the stressful and disturbing thoughts and feelings keep building up in the brain, but the individual simply tries to escape by switching on the television or turning to other avenues of diversion. One tries wilfully to forget and suppress the negative thoughts and feelings, which are then consigned to memories in the deeper corners of the brain. The hidden memories, however, continue to exert pressures in the form of hazy background worries and feelings. They erupt now and then at the conscious level and distort perceptions and behavior.

Here the advantage of the traditional meditation is evident in terms of preventing the sensory data, the causative factors of stress. However, the next question arises about what happens to the bulk of unpleasant or disturbing feelings that are already accumulated in the memory. Moreover, human beings continue this accumulative process as they keep encountering situations that cause negative feelings and anxieties. How is the past and future baggage of negative feelings tackled to prevent them from being the factors of stress?

In this case also, the traditional meditation inhibits the transmission of emotive signals from memory to conscious level or the neocortex. In other words, meditation prevents evocation and replay of such feelings and memories by shutting off the signal processing regions of the brain. This would mean only blocking of the impact of the negative emotions and memories, but still they would continue to throw up disturbing signals and one would be required to keep blocking them off all the time.

THE ADVANTAGES OF AWARENESS MEDITATION

Any peace gained by blocking sensory information can be tentative and short-lived. This is perhaps the reason why many meditators have reported that they need frequent doses of meditation; otherwise, their minds slip back into the old habit of being stressed. Some persons even compare that with the requirement of recharging a battery or regular gas filling of the car.

This is where the awareness meditation has an advantage over the traditional practices. Awareness meditation offers a more lasting solution in terms of making a person face those painful memories directly with the power of inner awareness. The act of facing diffuses the strength of feelings and painful memories. It perhaps undercuts the dispositional patterns of neural firings that are responsible for engendering memories and feelings. Over time, awareness meditation refashions such dispositional tendencies and thus rewires the brain. The net results of this are emotional cleansing and deeper tranquillity of mind.

The traditional meditation suffers from a significant limitation. It fails to tackle the deeper worries, anxieties, and negative emotions that one has accumulated and continues to do so in future, as it is not possible to insulate oneself totally from the harsh realities of life. Although such meditation practices do protect the body from the ravages of stress and depression, their utility is limited. In order to ensure long-term peace and emotional equilibrium, one has to come to terms with oneself by facing the causes of anxieties and worries—both the overt and covert. We need to make sense of our pride and prejudices, our ambitions and our dreams. We cannot afford to remain strangers to ourselves and simply coax our mind to block sensory information from some parts of our brain to avoid tension.

There is no escape from the imperative of facing and understanding our psychic world, even if the task sounds enormously difficult or disturbing. The stakes are indeed too high to be daunted by its apparent enormity. Awareness meditation on a regular basis over time makes it surprisingly easier. It demands an open and alert mind that is not bound in beliefs and borrowed ideas. No short cuts are possible as you have to discover yourself, and no one else can do it for you. One may read books or listen to great scholars, but that knowledge will serve merely as some fuzzy signboards on the road. One has no option but to walk alone on the path and reach the destination—the lasting peace by understanding oneself.

Concerning traditional meditation, there are also open questions about the risks of subjecting the extraordinarily sensitive organ of brain to repetitious practices and coercive concentration on words or images. One cannot rule out a possibility of becoming a bit dull or insensitive. One is also not sure of the long-term impact of the habit of preventing transmission and processing of sensory information in certain parts of the brain. Notwithstanding these concerns, there is no denying the fact that traditional meditation confers the benefits of alleviating stress and improving health.

THE MYTH OF INDIVIDUALISM

There are some other areas of concern regarding traditional meditation. It might foster individualistic preoccupation and mental insulation from the external world of sensory perceptions including interpersonal relations and society. It is perhaps one of the reasons why some persons renounce the worldly life and become monks in an insulated environment. That goes against the imperative that a human being has to relate himself with his fellow beings and the world surrounding him. He has to understand objectively his own feelings, motives, aspirations and actions. Besides, he has to understand others in a similar way and empathize with them in order to strengthen the bonds of humanity. We have to expand the horizons of our consciousness and reach out to other human beings, instead of being confined to our individual concerns only. That would make us share genuinely our joys and sorrows. That alone can build the human societies that are free from divisions, conflicts, and violence.

Awareness meditation leads people in this direction by enabling them to understand self dispassionately and empathize with others. It endows one with a perceptive outlook to discover the subterranean workings of memories and mental conditionings. It gives us insights into not only our emotions, feelings, and anxieties but into the construct of our ambitions, pride, and prejudices. Then the realization dawns upon us that we are essentially not much different from our fellow beings. Behind the apparent and misleading diversity, we are essentially the embodiment of one creative life force. We share the unity and oneness of life as a unique phenomenon on this tiny planet.

Though we tend to take much pride in our individuality, it is a subjective myth created by our apparent differences and idiosyncrasies. Our pride and aspirations might differ in their specifics. Our joys and sorrows may vary in their causes. Yet the essential architecture of our biological and psychic self is the same. All of us are driven by the same biological and mental urges and experience the same feelings of fear, joy, sorrow, wonder, frustration, or elation. Such realization in human beings would bring about a different and enlightened relationship of oneness and liberate them from the narrow confines of myself, my society, my race, and my nation. We would feel the deeper bonds of unity with not only other human beings but also all flora and fauna as parts of a single phenomenon of life. That is the marvellous truth, which, unfortunately, we have lost sight of.

ARISTOTELIAN CATHARSIS

Aristotle in his *Poetics* propounded the theory of catharsis or purging of emotions. While witnessing a Greek tragedy, the spectators identify themselves with the tragic hero and experience his sufferings. In Aristotle's opinion, the evocation of intense fear and pity in the process of watching the drama brings about a catharsis or emotional cleansing in the minds of the spectators. The point to be noted here is that, in catharsis, a spectator goes through the pain and sufferings with an active involvement by identifying himself or herself with the tragic hero.

In my view, awareness meditation offers a different type of catharsis that is more effective and has an amazing practical value to neutralize one's feelings of sorrow, pain, and mental hurts. The meditative catharsis has actually a therapeutic significance for tackling emotions of fear, grief, nervousness, and anxieties. Let us analyse further how Aristotelian catharsis works and then compare it with the emotional cleansing through the awareness meditation.

The Aristotelian catharsis has the following distinct characteristics. First, there is an active mental involvement on the part of the spectators who identify themselves with the tragic hero of the drama, and thus experience his feelings of fear, sorrow, and pity. Secondly, the emotional purification on the part of the spectators is omnibus or general in the sense that it does not transform or dissipate the personal emotions of sorrow, pity, or fear that they have in their lives. It means a spectator would feel a general impact of having been emotionally purified and light, but his own fears or sorrows connected with past and future events remain largely intact and active. Thirdly, the Aristotelian catharsis does not modify significantly the emotional behavior of a spectator in his future life. His emotional reactions remain unchanged in provocative situations later in life.

Fourthly, the memories of intense emotions evoked while witnessing the tragic drama linger on, at least for a few days, in the minds of the spectators. Notwithstanding the emotional purging, the feelings of fear and pity leave behind deep emotional imprints in their minds, which could be disturbing. It would not be surprising if, after watching the Shakespearean tragedy *King Lear* or the film *Gladiator*, you may not be inclined to do serious work in the office as your mind is still under the shadows of the sufferings of the tragic heroes. Though evoked externally by a drama or film, the intense emotions become your own property in memory.

THE FUTILITY OF PUNCHING A PILLOW

The modern methods of psychological treatment owe much to the Aristotelian catharsis. The psychologists normally counsel the patients to express their feelings of sorrow, anger, pity, or fear and not resort to suppression. The patient is supposed to get relief if he expresses his feelings. The pent-up and suppressed feelings prolong the suffering and continue to exert negative impact on one's behavior. A mother numbed with overwhelming shock and sorrow of her child's death would be somewhat relieved if she cries. It is believed that people who vent their feelings do not face psychological complications and recover faster from their emotional turmoil.

By stretching this theory a bit further, people are advised to relieve their anger and aggressiveness by repeatedly punching or kicking a pillow or by shouting in a lone corner. A suppression of feelings is doubtlessly not a healthy behavior, but one is intrigued with such simplistic solutions being fed to the people. One should not forget the fact that each action leaves behind its imprint in memory. A repeated action deepens the memory of the act, and if such a remedy is practiced more frequently, it becomes a habit. Though reversible with hard effort, habit is a persistent fixture manipulating one's conduct.

The emotional ventilation like punching a pillow might give some temporary relief—rather a distraction, but one runs the risk of falling into a habit, and worse, it is hardly a remedy. It should be clearly understood that the expression of feelings is not the act of actually facing the feelings, nor is it a solution of the emotional problem. The symptoms of the affliction can be alleviated temporarily, but the cause persists in its mischief. Like a painkiller, it may provide temporary respite from the pain but does not cure the underlying cause.

The behavioral actions of anger, aggressiveness, mental hurt, or sorrow have to be faced directly in terms of identifying the underlying causes and tackling with intelligence and wisdom. Admittedly, it is not an easy task for all people, but not an impossible one either. It might be harder in the beginning, but the stakes involved are much too high to avoid it.

Of course, one would justifiably argue that intellectual knowledge or identification of underlying cause does not automatically solve the problem, though it is indeed a step forward. In this context, the readers may recall the earlier discussion on the limits of rational decisions and thoughts vis-à-vis the unyielding nature of emotion. Against that backdrop, awareness meditation and meditative catharsis are being explored as a more effective means of dealing with emotive afflictions.

MEDITATIVE CATHARSIS

The catharsis brought about by awareness meditation is different. Its effect is specific, involving a particular feeling or emotion, and not omnibus or general by nature, like the Aristotelian catharsis. It dissipates the intensity and sting of the feeling of sorrow, fear, or pity that has been induced by a specific incident in the life of an individual. It is a method of directly facing the negative feelings that are active in memory and keep disturbing the conscious mind. The net result experienced soon thereafter is that the painful emotion is neutralized as an operating force. The meditative catharsis is also an effective instrument for dealing with worries and anxieties that keep siphoning off our mental energy.

How does one meditate to have such catharsis? How does it work? These questions are addressed in the following way. Since purging of feelings relate to a specific incident, let me explain it with an example. Suppose one is humiliated in some incident. It is our common experience that the feelings of mental hurt and pain overwhelm the mind. The thoughts and memories of the incident keep invading the mind. One is unable to shake off the feelings and memories, which cast dark shadows on one's behavior.

How does one handle this state of mind? One may rationalize the incident, but that does not dissipate the intensity of the feelings. The other way is to allow time to work and bury the experience in memory beyond the reach of the conscious mind. That is, however, an unwise and delusive action as it remains as emotional baggage that continues to operate covertly. The third possibility is to purge the emotion through the power of inner awareness. I call it a *diffusion method*, as narrated below.

The first step of the process in meditation is to be in the state of inner awareness or nonverbal consciousness without any contents of thought, emotion, or memory. This should be possible at least for a few moments for an experienced meditator thought it might pose a problem for the beginners, who are yet to get the knack of being in such awareness.

The second step is to evoke and experience the hurt feeling by consciously reviving the memories of that incident. This has to be done in the shortest possible time (a second or two only) without being drifted away or engulfed in thoughts and memories. The longer one allows the play of thoughts and memory to persist, the more counterproductive it becomes in terms of deepening the hurt feelings. It may be noted that one is supposed to use the thoughts and memories as a spark only to evoke the painful feeling. If the hurt feeling is already present in the conscious mind, one need not use the services of thought and memories. It should be remembered that one could be carried away and drowned in the quicksand of thoughts and memories before one realizes.

In the third step, you experience only the hurt feeling as a pure sensation unadulterated by the intrusion of thought and memory. It means you have quickly discarded the evocative instrument of thought and memory. You should try to stay in that mental state for as many seconds as possible but without regressing to the play of memory and thought.

At this stage, it would appear as if two mental phenomena are operating, namely, inner awareness and the pure feeling. That is not true. As your experience would bear out, the total awareness and pure feeling cannot coexist as two separate entities. Both assume one unified reality. It means awareness merges with the feeling. When you are anchored in the pure feeling, you are just the feeling and nothing else. This will remind the reader of T. S. Eliot's quote, *But you are the music while the music lasts.*

Figure 7.3. Meditative catharsis: In the first stage, only nonverbal awareness prevails. In the second stage, feeling, memories and thought are active. Subsequently, as shown in the figure, the feeling, memories, and thought converge and get transformed into awareness of only the nonverbal feeling. In other words, the memories and thought are deactivated in the final stage. As a result, the negative feeling loses its stronghold and is diffused.

In that stage, you are facing the painful feeling directly without any interference of thought or memory. Such an action of actual facing has an amazing impact in terms of neutralizing or dissolving the pain. However, at the time of meditation one may not perceive any notable difference, but later in the course of the day one would discover that the sting or pain has largely disappeared. The memory of the hurt does not hurt you as much as it did earlier. The past experience does not cast shadows on the state of your mind and you have a remarkable sense of detachment.

THE ILLUSION OF DUALISM

The diffusion method or meditative catharsis is a phenomenon of the observer and the observed becoming one, which was mentioned first by the great Indian philosopher J. Krishnamurti. He was the one who had indicated this possibility of emotional purging, but he vehemently denounced the traditional meditation as a method—a contrived system.

It would be necessary to add a few words on the nature of the observer that operates in the diffusion method described earlier. The observer is nothing but the nonverbal awareness or pure consciousness, which is devoid of thought and memory. It is similar to what Sigmund Freud described as "an evenly hovering attention" and Daniel Golemen as "a neutral mode" of observation. Some psychologists called it even *metacognition*. A beginner in the awareness meditation would need a good effort to distinguish and extricate the neutral observer from thought, memories, and specific feelings. It is, however, not as difficult as it sounds at first.

There is a difference between J. Krishnamurti and the psychologists, like Sigmund Freud and Daniel Golemen, in the way they perceive the "observer" in the act of observation. In the opinion of the psychologists, it remains a neutral observer, while for J. Krishnamurti, it undergoes transformation and becomes one with the pure feeling or sensory experience. This distinction, I believe, is perhaps owing to the confusion about the role of short-term memory.

Krishnamurti extricates nonverbal consciousness or observer from the short-term memory. For him, the nonverbal consciousness is "a movement from moment to moment" without carrying forward the memory of the previous moment. On the other hand, the psychologists take it as a continuum with the ongoing support of short-term memory. Hence, in their perception, the observer is a stream of inner awareness or evenly hovering attention. It may be noted that as pointed out by J. Krishnamurti, pure consciousness or nonverbal awareness is actually distinct from the short-term memory.

PURGATION OF EMOTIVE AFFLICTIONS

When the feeling of mental hurt is neutralized, the memories and thoughts, connected with the incident, lose their obstinate power to haunt the mind. This meditative catharsis or diffusion method can be used to purge any other emotions and feelings such as anger, frustration, bitterness, aggressiveness, and psychological fears. Our anxieties and worries are based largely on psychological fears, which can be diffused with awareness meditation.

This tool of meditative catharsis can be used to dissipate also the deeper layers of background worries and anxieties that make up our moods and manipulate our minds and behavior. I have personally derived benefits of detecting and purging background anxieties and worries. Every day as soon as I wake up, I focus my inner awareness to discover and face the vague layer of feelings that are linked with forthcoming events. Of course, sometimes one is not able to establish their causative links with any specific reasons. These feelings also include anticipatory fears or a sense of deeper insecurity related to the world that is uncertain and unpredictable.

As soon as I feel those vague or clear emotions, I attempt the third stage of diffusion method, namely, applying the power of pure awareness. It quickly cleans up the background worries and anxieties as the sun clears up the clouds. I feel the sunshine of a clear and focused mind. Of course, it is not possible to be completely free from moods or background feelings, but their strength is considerably neutralized, and the moods do not command and distort your behavior as arbitrarily as they normally do. This endows you with a new sense of freedom and space from the despotic governance of emotions and moods. That enables you to experience the innate spontaneity and joy of life that is unfettered by background fears and anxieties. It has immense value in terms of the quality of life one lives. When you have achieved that ability of emotional purging, you will realize what it means to you.

One would wonder why the hazy feelings of worries and anxieties beset us as soon as we wake up every day. Perhaps, it is the conditioning or prewiring of our mind in the course of our evolution, when we lived as animals under constant fears of predators and other dangers. Furthermore, the anticipatory impulse that is located in the frontal lobe of our brain is responsible for this state of affairs. The anticipatory ability is, no doubt, enormously crucial for our survival and welfare, but its ceaseless and arbitrary functioning plays the mischief of inducing stress. It produces and sustains a lingering feeling of deeper insecurity in mind, which is general and vague. All this can be diffused considerably, if not totally, with awareness meditation.

Admittedly, such meditation using the power of inner awareness is easier said than done. But it is not impossible either. When you advance in your practice of awareness meditation, one day you will get the knack of doing it. Let me caution you not to get frustrated, if you cannot succeed as quickly as you wish. If you fail to have requisite strength of pure awareness that can extricate pure feelings from thoughts and memories, you should end the meditation session. If you continue the session with negative feelings entangled in active memories and thoughts, your feelings will be further fuelled and become more painful. In this regard, one should follow the precautions on meditation given in the previous chapter.

In meditation, one should not actively pursue the play of painful memories as that would deepen the emotional scars. Reliving sorrow and fears sustained by thoughts and memories sounds similar to the Aristotelian catharsis, but it is not. It is different in the sense that the spectators identify themselves with the tragic hero of the drama and experience his intense sufferings. But they know that those are not their own sorrows and fears. That is a second-hand experience that does not engulf them so intensely and totally. In contrast, reliving your own sorrows and fears, fuelled by memories and thoughts, burns deeper scars and, in fact, works as an antithesis of catharsis.

One clarification is called for here. It is stated in the third stage of the diffusion method that when awareness (the observer) and the painful feeling (the observed) merge into one, the pain is diffused. How does this differ from our daily experience of emotions and feelings, which constitute the phenomenon of the observer and the observed merging into one? Let us look at that experience more closely. When we are overwhelmed by the surge of any emotion or feeling, the duality of the experiencer and the experienced vanishes totally. For instance, when we are angry, we become anger. Only after a few moments, the pure feeling of anger ebbs and gives way to thought and memory to take over the process. That re-establishes our sense of self or awareness, which was temporarily eclipsed in the wave of anger, and then the thought comes up to tell us that we were angry.

In our daily experience of overwhelming emotions, our nonverbal awareness is washed away in the strong surge of emotions and feelings. In other words, the most dominant force operating at that time in the mind is emotion. Conversely, in meditation, the power of awareness is in command and not the blind emotive force. In the meditative process, our nonverbal awareness absorbs and neutralizes the emotive force. The difference is vast. It is the magic of nonverbal awareness that works and undercuts the force of emotive occurrence. As indicated earlier, the intense focus of nonverbal awareness that is not diluted by thoughts and memory affects the firing patterns of neurons, which are the actual correlates of the emotive occurrence. That is how the meditative catharsis works.

Chapter 8

Rewiring the Brain

Be near me when my light is low,
When the blood creeps, and the nerves prick
And tingle; and the heart is sick,
And all the wheels of Being slow.
—Alfred Tennyson, *In Memoriam*

At the dawn of human history, the life of our ancestors, who spent their days hunting and gathering food, was indeed very simple. Their joys and worries were equally simple and innocent. Their hearts would brim over with joy and laughter when they succeeded in hunting down a deer or found a tree laden with ripe fruits or came across a friendly bushman. Their worries related only to the wild predators lurking in the surrounding forest, a possible attack by other hostile group of tribesmen or a family member falling seriously ill. However, such worries were forgotten soon and they would easily get back to the easy routine of their lives without long bouts of stress or depression.

The progress from the hunter/gatherer era to the agricultural societies was marked also with easy patterns of life. Insecurity of finding food and fears of roaming predators were reduced with group habitation and the growth of stable social structures. However, a few new areas of joys and worries were added concerning good or bad crops, timely rain, social gatherings, festivals, and collective obligations. Humans slowly developed new agricultural implements, domesticated animals for food, travel or hard labour. Gradually, they found more free time, particularly after harvest season, which inspired them to express their creative talents in dance, music, handicrafts and social festivals. The repertoire of cerebral activities began to widen with new joys, dreams, hopes, frustrations as well as pride and prejudices. Yet in all this, the human brain had a routine of predictable and simple tasks to perform.

Until the medieval time, the progress of human societies was, no doubt, remarkable and multifarious, but life continued to move on in an easy and slow lane. Of course, humanity has suffered a lot because of wars, violence, ignorance, epidemics as well as the greed of overlords and kings. All religions preached unity of mankind, love, and sanctity of life, and yet the cruellest irony is that in the entire history of human race, the greatest amount of blood has been shed in the name of God and religion. It is an utter shame that we are yet to outgrow such barbarism. The increasing violence and global terrorism betray that mankind is regressing into the worst levels of barbarism and cruelties that do not spare even small children and women.

The era of industrialism brought in a new paradigm of life—endless quest for luxuries and wealth driven by consumerism, gratifications, and greed, which seem to be insatiable. This paradigm runs on the unsparing principle of cutthroat competition and struggle in every sphere of society. Life and human societies have become immensely complex with dazzling achievements in science and technology. Countless new avenues of entertainment and luxuries are created and the marathon race goes on to add more and more material affluence.

Unfortunately, the unbridled commerce and consumerism seem to mark the direction of our future evolution. These phenomena are driven by the defining property of human desire, which means *more and more* without an end. Given the colossal problems of the environment in the making and the plethora of new illnesses, one earnestly hopes that the human species is not being driven to the dead end of its evolution.

The purpose of depicting this cursory perspective was to underline the fact that the human brain had to handle very simple tasks at a leisurely pace in the prehistoric age, in contrast to the enormously complex demands of the modern age. Actually, the modern era constitutes an unprecedented onslaught on the human brain with constant bombardment of innumerable sensory information that breeds anxieties, psychological fears as well as insatiable cravings for pleasures and luxuries. Consequently, it has to function in the highest gear to cope with the new age of supersonic speed, which has overloaded the brain and created stressful conditions. In order to escape from the mental pressures, we keep seeking opportunities of entertainments and pleasures, but unfortunately, there is always a price. Nothing is free in this universe.

A GATEWAY TO THE UNCONSCIOUS

How do we regulate the hectic inflow of sensory data and stabilize the brain from its hyperactive state? There is an utter need to diminish the constant clattering of the brain machinery and switch it over to an easy and soothing rhythm. It is a sad predicament that our will power is impotent before the might of the subterranean world of our being. The voices of our thoughts and reasoning power never reach there. Even the torchlight of our conscious mind cannot fathom the darkness of the unconscious architecture of our self. The deeper roots of our thoughts, motives, behavior, and autobiographical self are located in the mind that is beyond our conscious reach.

Against this backdrop, expansion of inner awareness through meditation was suggested earlier as a means to convey nonverbal signals and communicate with the subconscious structures of self. An intense application of nonverbal awareness is the only path that can lead our conscious mind to the gateway of the unconscious. That is the only voice, without words, that can be heard there. This is not an attempt to sound poetic. It is factually correct.

In the previous chapter, we discussed the benefits of awareness meditation and briefly touched upon the changes in the electrochemical profile of the brain that were observed by neuroscientists while scanning the brains of the meditators. Still, we have to find a convincing answer to the question about how meditation brings about such impressive benefits covering vast areas. Equally impressive are the positive effects such as behavioral changes, self-detachment, empathetic outlook, emotional equilibrium, and inner joy. The more amazing finding was the way meditation rewired the brain to remain more relaxed, optimistic, and focused without being burdened with anxieties and worries.

The benefits of meditation are quite convincing to the scientists who have carried out research and those who have practiced meditation seriously with an open mind. Conversely, other experts who look at meditation merely with a theoretical interest or intellectual curiosity remain skeptical.

Unfortunately, the effects of meditation fall largely within the subjective domain as they are internal to the mind and body. Before neurologists found the means to peep into the actual processes in the brain of meditators, it was not possible to demonstrate objectively or in a laboratory the evidences supporting the benefits. Hence, some skeptics argued that all this talk of benefits was a belief or self-hypnotism. Others dismissed it as a religious mumbo jumbo.

The neurological findings have made a great contribution in establishing a scientific basis for explaining the benign effects of meditation. There are, however, practical limits to the scientific endeavors. All the benefits cannot be explained objectively, particularly those accruing in the long term, like the changes in attitude and behavioral tendencies for stress, depression, and subjective thinking. For a fair judgment, a serious researcher will have to experiment by practicing meditation himself, while applying his scientific spirit and abandoning both beliefs and disbeliefs.

Fortunately, awareness meditation or any good meditation practice is not conditional upon acceptance of any religious or spiritual beliefs. This should allay any sectarian apprehensions on the part of a researcher. In fact, meditation, essentially, is not a religious practice, though it was evolved originally as a system for religious and spiritual contemplation.

In order to explore the reasons behind the benefits, we need to examine comprehensively the neurological research on the changes that are induced by meditation in different regions of the brain. Therefore, I have given more details of the relevant research and tried to correlate it with awareness meditation. I have also put forward some speculations citing some aspects of the research. These speculations are not wishful guesswork, though further research would be required to fully establish the conclusions.

BLOCKING THE SENSORY TRAFFIC

This part provides details of various studies by neurologists and scientists while the implications of the studies are analyzed in the subsequent part.

Dr. Gregg Jacobs, professor of psychiatry, and Dr. Herbert Benson, professor of medicine, both from Harvard Medical School, studied one group of students that was taught to meditate and another group that was given books and tapes for relaxation. Over the next few months, they found the meditators managed to lower activities of processing sensory information in the parietal lobe of the brain. As mentioned earlier, this region orients us in time and space and processes information from the external world, which is being fed by our sensory receptors. The outpouring of hectic signals from parietal lobe to other regions of the brain often causes anxiety and stress. Obviously, the causes behind most of our worries, stress, and fears emanate from the external world and the way we are able to deal with it.

In comparison to the other students, the meditators also produced notably higher levels of theta waves in their brains, which are produced when the brain is in the state of deep relaxation. This was accompanied by a decrease in beta waves, which are emitted by the brain when it is tense and agitated.

Dr. Benson also studied a group of experienced Sikh meditators. With the help of scanning devices, he observed a decrease in the overall blood flow in their brains, but increase particularly in the limbic system that is evolutionarily an older region. That region is responsible for our primary emotions, memory, and more significantly, consciousness and nonverbal awareness. Since memory, emotions or feelings are not active during deep meditation, it is evident that only consciousness is active predominantly. This is significant in the context of the awareness meditation wherein inner consciousness is supposed to prevail unhindered by thought, feelings, and memory.

Richard Davidson at the University of Wisconsin discovered a different set of evidence to corroborate antistress benefits. He discovered that meditation shifted the activities from the right prefrontal lobe to the left pre-frontal lobe of the brain. The people who increasingly use the pre-frontal cortex in the left hemisphere tend to be more positive, enthusiastic, happy and relaxed. Davidson's research suggested that meditation reoriented the brain from a stressful fight-or-flight mode to a more secure and relaxed attitude toward the realities of life.

In fact, before the brain imaging devices arrived, the contradictory perceptions by the right and left hemispheres of brain were pointed out in 1970s by Stuart Dimond, a psychologist at University College, Cardiff in Wales. In experiments, he used special contact lenses to show films either to the right or left hemisphere only. The participants in the experiments were asked to rate a variety of films in terms of the emotional contents. The results showed a remarkable tendency of the right hemisphere to view the world as more unpleasant, hostile, and even disgusting. In contrast, he found that the left hemisphere was more contented, optimistic, and easygoing.

The research carried out by Dr. Mehmet Oz, director of Columbia-Presbyterian's Heart Institute, also showed results similar to the findings by Richard Davidson. His studies, though focused mainly on the impact of meditation on the immune system, indicated that meditation prevented the fight-or-flight response of our brain, which floods the body with the stress hormone cortisol. Meditation also slowed down the metabolism in red blood cells and suppressed the production of cytokines, proteins associated with the heightened immune response by stressed-out persons such as students taking exams.

In 1997, Dr. Andrew Newberg, a neurologist in the University of Pennsylvania, devised a way to release IVs containing radioactive dye to track down blood flow in the brains of a group of Buddhist meditators when they reached the peak of their meditation—a trance. He discovered that the brain remained alert and did not shut off, but blocked sensory information from the parietal lobe. Since this region of the brain processes information about the external world and orients us to time and space or our surroundings, it explains the reasons why meditators report the experience of being in the mental state transcending time and space.

The nomenclature of transcendental meditation is perhaps linked to this experience of losing self-identity and the sense of boundaries. The great poets William Wordsworth and Walt Whitman went through such trances on their own, without any systemic meditation. Their poetic writings embody their feelings of transcending time and space and being one with the universe.

The deep relaxation and inner joy brought about in the absence of inputs from the parietal lobe and the frontal lobe explain why there is a great deal of fascination among philosophers and spiritual persons for self-transcendence or self-dissolving experiences. That has inspired a great body of writings and philosophic ideologies, which project the ideals of spiritual union with the universe and transcending the realm of time and space. Such philosophy of nondualism is linked with this brain chemistry. The most articulate exponent of the nondualistic philosophy called Advaita in Sanskrit was the great philosopher, Adi Shankara in eight century AD.

Let me briefly summarize the conclusions of the studies mentioned in this section. There was a marked reduction or blocking of hectic outpouring of signals from the frontal lobe and parietal lobe during meditation. Such sensory flow mediated the functioning of the brain and produced stress and depression. Meditation, therefore, caused deep relaxation. As these regions of the neocortex went offline during deep meditation, there were marked changes in the brain wave patterns. The levels of beta brain waves, indicative of excited thoughts and stressful mental activities, declined considerably while an increase of the theta waves was observed. Our brain switches on to the theta wave rhythm in the state of deep relaxation. It changes the fight-or-flight mode of the brain to a more stable and relaxed state of operation.

THE GATEKEEPER

The research cited here indicates that the antistress effects are achieved by reducing or blocking the sensory activities in the parietal lobe and frontal lobe. However, that is a resistive and negative action. Despite reduction of stress and other benefits, one is not absolutely sure of any possible side effects of restricting the sensory activities in these regions of the brain that otherwise perform extremely critical tasks for sustenance and well-being of life. Rather, it would be better to look for a method that is judicious but does not constitute a rigid and arbitrary action. Instead of negating, it should prudently regulate and streamline the inflow and outflow of sensory traffic involving the parietal lobe and frontal lobe.

In order to explore the possibility of such a method, we have to fall back upon the discoveries made by neuroscientists. It is well established in neuroscience that the thalamus acts like a gatekeeper for most of the sensory signals to and from the cerebral cortex and several other parts of the brain. The major bulk of the incoming and outgoing sensory traffic of the brain has to stop and pass through the thalamus. It is also called the relay station of the brain and has connections with most of the regions of the brain, particularly with the neocortex, which is the arena of our conscious experiences and activities like reasoning, thinking, language, planning, and certain emotions.

That would mean that the emotive signals of fear, anger, and sorrow from the limbic region of the brain would be relayed through the thalamus to the neocortex to generate thoughts and other sensory activities there. The signals of the activated memories of good or bad experiences will also pass through the thalamus to activate the neocortex. Conversely, the activities of neocortex will be relayed through the thalamus to other regions of the brain and evoke primary emotions and dormant memories. All these factors indicate the central role of the thalamus in the theatre of brain.

It is also remarkable that the thalamus is divided into about two dozen sections and each one of them is connected with a specific subdivision of the neocortex (Francis Crick, *The Astonishing Hypothesis: the Scientific Search for the Soul* [New York: Simon & Schuster, 1994], 84). Neuroscientists are somewhat surprised about the one-to-one connections and correspondence between each section of the thalamus and its counterpart in the neocortex (see fig. 8.1). That is the reason why Bernard J. Baars has described it as "a mini-brain within the brain" in his book, *In the Theatre of Consciousness: the Workspace of the Mind* (New York: Oxford University Press, 1997), 28.

Why does the sensory traffic from neocortex and other parts of the brain have to stop and pass through the thalamus? Why should it not go directly to its specific destinations, which would be quicker? One of the reasons, according to neurologists, is that the thalamus is responsible for selective attention (Bernard J. Baars, *In the Theatre of Consciousness: the Workspace of the Mind* [New York: Oxford University Press, 1997], 29). It means the thalamus performs the tasks of selecting and directing the sensory traffic in order to meet the urgency of demands of the body or a given external situation. In the absence of such selective control, the sense of priority and urgency would be lost and a general chaos would prevail in attending to myriad sensory inputs from different regions of the brain.

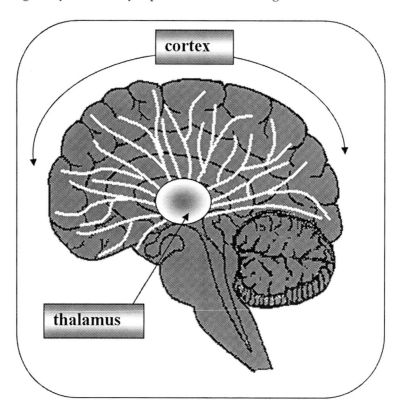

Figure 8.1. The wide network connections of the thalamus with the neocortex. It acts as a gatekeeper of sensory flow from and to the cortex.

Here, it is relevant to recall that attention is one of the qualities associated with consciousness; rather attention is a focused form or a directional application of consciousness. Since attention and awareness are intrinsically the same in nature, this function of the thalamus is quite noteworthy in the context of our discussion on awareness meditation. Later, we will look into this aspect more closely.

Neurologists have discovered the larger and most crucial role of the thalamus as the region that is mainly responsible for sustaining waking consciousness. This was indicated by Wilder Penfield and further corroborated by James Newman, Bernard Baars, and other neuroscientists. There are two thalami, one in each hemisphere of the brain. Each thalamus has an internal section called intralaminar nucleus. In clinical cases, it was found that damage to both intralaminar nuclei resulted in the loss of consciousness and complete coma. Neuroscientists believe that one other part of the brain called the reticular formation also plays a supportive role for the thalamus in sustaining waking consciousness.

Earlier, it was mentioned that the experts were surprised about the one-to-one connections and correspondence between each section of the thalamus and its counterpart in the neocortex. Baars also described the thalamus as "a mini-brain within the brain." Based on this, it would be logical to speculate that the thalamus actually lends the sentient impulse of consciousness or the quality of subjectivity of experience to the mental processes that arise in the neocortex. In the absence of that, thoughts, language, and memories would remain mere verbal and nonverbal images that are mechanical and nonsentient products of electrochemical processes of the body.

The thalamus has connections also with some regions of the limbic system and the brain stem responsible for primary emotions and memory. Hence, it is the thalamus that transforms the electrochemical sensory signals into what we experience as feelings with its dynamic sentience.

Let us revert to the original question of our quest for a prudent method or intelligent arbitrator that can establish a regulated and wise order on the sensory traffic from all directions of the brain. The sensory outpouring is often not just torrential, but becomes chaotic as myriad signals clamour for urgent attention. This is more so in the case of the present human race, which is caught up in the cutthroat competition and endless scrambles of the supersonic age.

Fortunately, we already have a wise arbitrator in the thalamus. Let us sum up its multiple qualities. As mentioned before, waking consciousness is mainly dependent on it. It would be logical to surmise further that the thalamus is the connecting pathway between the unconscious and the conscious mind. In other words, the thalamus has a critically important role in the scheme of the mysterious consciousness, including its unconscious or subconscious segment. That means the thalamus has much to do with the nonverbal awareness.

In sum, the thalamus performs the intelligent and critically significant task of selecting and directing the sensory traffic. Its quality of selective attention further corroborates that it is a site where intelligence originates and operates as a power of perception. This is in consonance with the views held by experts that intelligence, awareness, and understanding are the qualities of consciousness. Finally, all these qualities are predicated on the central fact that the inner parts of the thalami are known to sustain the waking consciousness.

STRENGTHENING THE BRAIN'S RELAY STATION

As we know, stress and anxiety seize the mind when the frantic outpourings of sensory signals are not processed in an orderly fashion and a traffic jam is created. It is logical to assume that the thalamus does not perform its duties with requisite efficiency, particularly in the case of the people suffering from persistent stress. Why does the thalamus, at times, not perform more effectively its duties as the relay station or the gatekeeper? This is a bit intriguing because, given its inherent abilities of selective attention, intelligence, and consciousness; it has the necessary potential to regulate the sensory traffic.

The next question that arises is how one can enhance the performance level of the gatekeeper. How can we further strengthen and activate the thalamus so that it can play a more effective role? Such a role is quite essential for maintaining the emotional equilibrium and a stress-free environment of the brain.

The traditional meditation comes to our rescue in alleviating stress, but most of the traditional practices appear to reduce stress through a different route than activating the gatekeeper, the thalamus. The traditional meditation is found to deactivate the parietal lobe as well as the frontal lobe, and thus diminish or prevent the onslaught of sensory signals. That is accomplished by curbing their activities of thinking, reasoning and anticipatory planning. The curbing of these activities is done by making the brain perform certain fixed drills like repetitive recital of sacred words and fixing the gaze on an image. Basically these practices are coercive and rigid by nature. Therefore, one has to be more cautious, notwithstanding the fact that such meditative practices alleviate stress.

What then is the next alternative? First, it would be advisable to avoid any arbitrary and rigid action of deactivating the parietal lobe and the frontal lobe. Then one should change over to a positive action, which would mean activating the gatekeeper at a higher level of efficiency to select and direct the sensory traffic. Its ability of imposing a prudent control has to be strengthened. How do we do that?

Some experts might argue that the thalamus performs the tasks according to its biological constitution and there is no way to meddle with that. This is an argument of biological predetermination and that should apply similarly to other regions of the brain that perform the tasks of thinking, reasoning, emoting, and planning future. This would imply that we cannot further develop these regions of the brain and their functions. This is not true because all of us have endeavoured and acquired varying levels of abilities to think, reason, and plan.

How do we develop these cerebral parts? The simple answer is to use them more frequently and intensely. The principle of evolution is quite unambiguous concerning our biological abilities, namely, use it or lose it. The possibility of enhancing the capacity of not only any region of the brain but any other part of the body is a fact of life. That is how we develop our bodies and minds at different levels of health and efficiency.

One can easily understand how to increase the use of body parts such as hands or legs. One can also similarly enhance the use of certain regions of the brain like the neocortex in terms of consciously deepening and developing the abilities of thinking, reasoning and language. However, a pertinent question arises as to how one can use the thalamus more. That can be done by extending our attention span and developing our power of inner awareness.

In this context, the readers should remember the statement of William James that spiritual persons have more access to their consciousness. Even if one considers the entity of a spiritual person a debatable point, the possibility of more access to consciousness implied by him does exist. Also, as stated before, the concept of a spiritual person includes the abilities of emotional equilibrium and serenity of mind, which are associated with inner awareness.

In my opinion, awareness meditation holds a reasonable possibility of using and strengthening thalamus. It will expand the attention span, increase access to our consciousness, and promote emotional equilibrium. The benefits of awareness meditation enumerated in the previous chapter further clarify and support this.

REWIRING THE BRAIN

Let us explore the reasons why and how awareness meditation works on the thalamus. The detailed elucidation of awareness meditation in the last two chapters shows that its techniques and guidelines are devised to achieve the central aim of strengthening inner awareness or nonverbal consciousness. The meditator tries to be neutrally aware of the mental processes of thinking, memory, emotions, and feelings. It means the most active region of the brain in that state of meditation would be the one that is responsible for consciousness namely the thalamus in the limbic system.

Let me clarify that in any intense and deep meditation, the mind enters into a state of nonverbal awareness. The distinguishing mark of awareness meditation is that it does not beat about the bush, but directly and consciously leads one into a deep state of inner awareness. In this context, let me remind the readers about the research by Dr. Benson, which was cited earlier. He was able to observe enhanced flow of blood in the limbic area and brain stem while scanning the brains of the experienced Sikh meditators in deep meditation. It indicated activation of the regions in the limbic region, which are responsible for nonverbal consciousness.

It means an awareness meditator, or any experienced meditator, like the subjects of Dr. Benson's observation, uses intensely and purposefully the neural infrastructure of the brain that sustains consciousness. Such meditation practice over a long period would definitely strengthen that part of the brain and enhance the ability of selective attention and intelligent action. That is how the process of rewiring of brain begins and the mind remains stress free, its natural mode. This was substantiated when researchers found higher levels of theta waves in the brains of meditators only after a few weeks. The subject of theta waves, its implications in relaxation, learning, attention span and memory will be dealt with in the last chapter.

The increased and frequent use of the neural structures of the thalamus and the reticular formation would no doubt enhance the power of inner awareness. That would constitute more access to consciousness, which William James mentioned. This was corroborated by experienced meditators who reported improved behavior in terms of developing empathetic attitude, enhanced ability of objective perception, and serenity of mind.

The direct observations by neuroscientists have been corroborated also by external manifestations of the changes induced by meditation. The strongest evidence is in terms of emotional equilibrium and the remarkable reduction of stress reported by meditators. The antistress effects of meditation have been established beyond doubt in several studies. It means the sensory traffic has been well regulated, particularly in the case of an awareness meditator.

Further, practically all experienced meditators have reported in research surveys that they felt more focused in their work, and their mental activities had become more orderly and purposeful. Earlier such mental activities were diffused and unruly. Some other points that serve as external corroborations are mentioned in the previous chapter while describing the benefits of awareness meditation.

One point that is more significant is that an awareness meditator does not make a conscious effort to negate mental processes such as thoughts, memories, and feelings. Hence, he or she does not put any coercive pressure on the parietal lobe, frontal lobe, or the other regions of the brain that evoke memories and emotions. Rather, with the strength of nonverbal awareness, he or she faces the self in its action of thought, emotions, feelings, and desires. This act of facing makes one understand how the self operates in daily life.

A NEW ORDER IN THE BRAIN

Some years ago, it was believed by scientists that brain cells (neurons) did not grow, but remained constant after reaching an optimal plateau. Later, that was proved wrong as growth of new brain cells was detected in new research. This finding is consistent with the evolutionary principle of adaptation and progressive improvement by the organisms through development of new structures. In fact, the present structure and size of the human brain are the result of incremental growth from our reptilian and mammalian past. It suggests that the brain is not a static monolith, but an evolving entity. Of course, evolutionary changes are evident only over many thousands of generations and might be too minute to be detectable in one lifetime, if occurring at all.

Notwithstanding that, some changes do take place in the brain during the lifetime of an individual. For instance, neural changes occur in the brain when one learns a new skill or professional expertise like driving a car or becoming an aircraft pilot. The learning of a new language also brings about neural changes. Such changes are, however, not passed on to the next generations and do not run the evolutionary course of a species.

In research on taxi drivers, it was discovered that the cerebral part responsible for the sense of direction showed noticeable extra growth. In fact, this happened after only a few months when the taxi drivers acquired good familiarity of the streets, road system, and landmarks of the big city. This neural growth, however, vanished a few years after the taxi driver gave up his profession.

Not all changes are detectable in the brain scan. The reason is that the changes occur in two ways: one, as a growth of new neurons, and second, as a reorganization of the firing patterns of the existing neurons. Detection through a brain scan would be possible easily when there is a sizable growth of extra neurons, but the changes in the firing patterns of a group of neurons are difficult with the technology available now. In addition, the growth of a few thousand new neurons here and there would be perhaps indistinguishable for neurologists. The rewiring of the brain or the reprogramming of the firing patterns of the neurons would be, therefore, verifiable only through the difference in the external behavior of an individual.

Now let us see how this is reflected in the case of a meditator. During awareness meditation, the limbic region of the brain engendering consciousness receives increased blood, as observed by Dr. Herbert Benson. It is also a fact that the part of the brain that does not get blood supply consistently over a prolonged period, would remain inactive and lose its optimum potential. For instance, in old age, the hippocampus does not get an adequate blood supply, and consequently its ability of short-term memory declines. That explains why old people have a weak memory and they speak slowly with longer intervals in the flow of their words. Their minds require a longer time to recall words. In extreme cases, when the blood supply is disrupted to any part of the brain for even a short time as in the case of a heart failure, that part gets damaged temporarily or permanently. Many patients have neurological problems subsequent to such illness.

Therefore, it makes sense that regular meditation over the years would definitely result in improving the strength and health of the brain site that is responsible for consciousness. Not only the neural infrastructure of consciousness is being strengthened with long-term enhanced blood flow, but it is also being reprogrammed in favour of the inner consciousness to prevail more often than the emotions.

These factors would definitely bolster up the strength and vitality of inner consciousness, resulting in fortifying its core capability of understanding or intelligence and discretionary control over other mental processes. It would establish a new order in the theatre of the mind assigning a larger role to inner consciousness compared to the other actors like thoughts, emotions, and feelings. The implications of that are obvious in the light of the fact that these actors often tend to play out the melodrama of anxieties, worries, and stress.

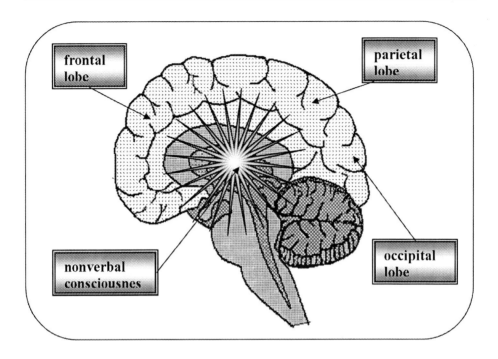

Figure 8.2. New order in the brain, through awareness meditation, with dominant role of nonverbal consciousness—more access to the power of consciousness.

One would wonder whether the prolonged and intense use of the thalamus and reticular formation that are implicated in sustaining consciousness would lead to a detectable neural growth as in the earlier case of the taxi drivers. Such changes have not been reported by the neurologists who scanned the brains of meditators. However, some Yogis and individuals like J. Krishnamurti, who underwent intense experiences of altered consciousness, have reported feelings of physical changes occurring in their brains. Such cases were not scrutinized scientifically, and hence no authentic conclusions can be drawn.

It is, however, reasonable to assume that some minor accretion of neurons might happen, but largely it might be a reprogramming of the neural behavior. The rewiring of the neural activities seems to be the more likely possibility because of the intense activation of inner consciousness in meditation and frequent use of the relevant neural infrastructure.

ENHANCEMENT OF INNATE INTELLIGENCE

It would be logical to assume that the fortification of the neural structure of consciousness would mean a higher manifestation of its inherent properties. As stated before, experts associate the properties of understanding and attention with consciousness. The property of understanding is the product of innate intelligence, and intelligence is the intrinsic quality of consciousness.

The term *intelligence* needs clarification, as it is perceived in different ways. Our reasoning ability, language, analytic power, and planning represent one broad category of intelligence that is manifested through the medium of thought. This type of intelligence that operates in the linear mode is located in the neocortex. The other category of intelligence is the one that is inspirational and brings about an instant insight and understanding. It operates in nonlinear mode transcending the apparatus of thought and deductive or reductionist logic. This insightful intelligence is also called an instinctual perception or emotional intelligence that springs from the nonverbal consciousness. (Emotional intelligence is explained in chapter 4, "Emotions and Feelings.")

In my view, intelligence is only one generic impulse being manifested in both the thoughtful (linear) mode as well as inspirational (nonlinear) mode. It is the integral and indivisible property of consciousness, which originates in the evolutionarily ancient parts of the brain, but pervades the neocortex in the form of our cognitive and thinking abilities. Consciousness, in its implicit (nonverbal) and manifest form, is synonymous with inspirational and thoughtful intelligence, respectively. This is evident in the fact that consciousness and intelligence share the property of global presence in the brain. This property is reflected in all mental processes such as memory, cognition, motor, and sensory operations, which are imbued with intelligence.

It is not possible to measure and quantify the increase of intelligence that is brought about by meditation. This is because what is being discussed is the generic intelligence and not IQ, which is just one manifest aspect of intelligence. However, there are some indicators reported by meditators to suggest enhancement of intelligence, particularly the emotional intelligence. Meditators have reported higher levels of empathetic attitude that enables a person to perceive objectively and appreciate the feelings and actions of others. They have also confirmed that their interpersonal relationships at home and workplace had become more harmonious and the incidence of mental conflict and misunderstanding had decreased.

Feeling more focused in work and perceptive ability is another indicator pointed out by them. Many have confirmed higher levels of attention and mental concentration after a few months of meditation. The more objective and scientific indicator is the increase of theta brain waves in meditators. The last chapter is devoted to theta rhythm of the brain, which is implicated in attention, successful leaning, and memory encoding.

TACKLING EMOTIVE PREPONDERANCE

The question of unyielding power of emotions and feelings has been discussed in the previous chapters. The enormous challenge that we frequently encounter in life is how to rein in negative emotions. Let me dwell upon this in the context of rewiring of the brain through awareness meditation.

We learnt before that in deep meditation, the limbic region was found to be more active, as indicated by an increased flow of blood. The intense operation of inner awareness in meditation was the cause behind the increased activity in the limbic region. Earlier, we also learnt from neurologists that our primary emotions of fear, anger, sorrow, aggressiveness, and love originate in the evolutionarily ancient regions of the brain, namely the brain stem and the limbic region.

This raises a curious question, why do the brain sites known to engender primary emotions fail to evoke emotions when activated in deep meditation? A simple answer might be that only the neural ensembles responsible for consciousness in the limbic region, namely the thalamus and the reticular formation might be activated in deep meditation and not the neural structures that induce emotions. This answer does not seem to be accurate since the scientist Dr. Benson has observed that a larger area of the limbic region is activated in meditation.

This larger coverage of limbic region would perhaps make sense in the context of what the neurologist Dr. Antonio Damasio has observed in his book, *The Feeling of What Happens: Body and Emotion in the Making of Consciousness,* [New York: Harcourt, INC. 1999], *100*. He states, "Emotions and core consciousness require, in part, the same neural substrates." He divides consciousness into core consciousness and extended consciousness. In his definition, core consciousness consists of the unconscious segment, while the *extended* consciousness is represented by its explicit aspects such as conscious experience, thinking, reasoning power, language, and autobiographical self. In other words, the activities of neocortex largely represent the extended consciousness.

Let me clarify that the concept of core consciousness is somewhat similar to the nonverbal or inner consciousness. Also, core consciousness and nonverbal consciousness have the same origin in the brainstem and the limbic region.

I imagine, in many of us, particularly those having emotional problems, the common neural infrastructure is being usurped most of the time by emotions. Consequently, the use of the neural infrastructure by the inner consciousness has been reduced to the minimum. In other words, we have less access to consciousness as William James perhaps would have stated. This brings to my mind an analogy of one house being occupied together by two tenants: a group of rowdy boys and a wise adult. The rowdy boys, with their noisy and aggressive behavior, manage to usurp and occupy the larger part of the house, while the adult is pushed into a corner of the basement. Needless to say that the rowdy boys symbolize emotions, and the wise adult is the inner consciousness. In most of the human beings, the autocratic regime of emotions seems to prevail unchallenged.

Therefore, it is imperative to establish the wise authority of consciousness over emotions and thoughts. Since thoughts and memories are largely driven by emotions in an explicit or implicit manner, it will be easier to allow them their due role under the good governance of consciousness. How do we restore the authority of consciousness? This is possible with an increased use of the common neural infrastructure in the limbic region by the power of consciousness. Awareness meditation is designed to do precisely that, and in fact, if one examines closely, one would find that all the benefits of meditation enumerated in the preceding chapter flow from one source, namely, the power of consciousness.

The prolonged assertion of inner awareness in meditation rewires the brain to bring in an increased element of good governance or a volition power over the inexorable force of emotions and feelings. The enhancement of the governing influence of inner awareness is largely implicit and not openly discernible as an operation of conscious willpower. Such strengthened consciousness works in the background to break the reflex force and habitual obstinacy of emotive occurrences. This is indeed a crucial point, having an amazing practical value in life.

As an aside, let me dwell on one point. Some experts might question the premise that emotions and inner consciousness share the same neural substrates on the ground that the site of consciousness is identified, namely the thalamus. In addition, the sites of primary emotions are different in some cases. For instance, according to experts, the hypothalamus, brain stem, and ventromedial prefrontal cortex are activated during sadness. The brain stem is activated during anger or fear. The activation of amygdala causes intense fear. So how would the seat of consciousness extend control on different parts of the brain responsible for emotions?

The answer lies in the fact that the thalamus acts as the gatekeeper of sensory traffic from and to most of the regions of the brain. It is no exaggeration to say that the seat of consciousness is biologically assigned a central role. It is a question of activating it to play a more effective role, particularly in the situation of hectic and chaotic outpouring of sensory signals.

Secondly, the role of the thalamus is not limited to act just as a mechanical relay station or gatekeeper. Rather, a more significant role played by the thalamus is to provide the impulse of sentience or the vitality of consciousness to all electrochemical sensory signals and in turn, transform them into the subjective experiences of feelings, thoughts, and memories. It is a matter of common experience that consciousness is embedded in all these mental processes. In other words, the core of all mental processes is the nonmaterial impulse of consciousness that makes us what we are—a sentient or living organism. All this suggests that it is not only possible, but also imperative, to establish the enlightened authority of consciousness over all other mental processes and thus eliminate their arbitrary behavior.

THE DANGERS OF MOOD-ENHANCING DRUGS

It would be an omission if the issue of mood enhancing drugs was not examined. Nowadays all over the world, millions and millions of young and old people are being advised by doctors and psychiatrists to use drugs to treat the problems of depression, volatile moods and behavior. The pharmaceutical companies are churning out a variety of such drugs, since it is a market worth billions of dollars. The market has been growing fast every year, given the fact that depression, stress, and anxiety syndromes are the biggest problems of the modern world.

The use of such drugs by adults is already an enormous problem of our time. As if that is not enough, it is being further exacerbated by roping in the young children. The implications of such chemical tinkering with the growing brains are unpredictable and have proved to be devastating in some cases. Even the experts cannot claim to know the long-term impact of such drugs. The different parts of young brain are still in the process of developing and moulding up under a vast array of external influences, and it would be unwise to interfere with that.

Unfortunately, millions of children face the disorders of attention deficit, hyperactivity, generalized anxiety, depression, and compulsive behavior. Of course, parents and doctors are constrained to take risks with the growing brains when they are helpless with the acute and unmanageable problems of behavioral and mood disorders. The drugs being prescribed are often the same for children and adult but in varying doses, although there are some meant only for children. Some of the drugs being used by people are Ritalin, Prozac, Adderall, or Concerta.

The side effects of such drugs are indeed quite serious and diverse, which include insomnia, decreased appetite, weight loss, rapid heart beat, high blood pressure, nausea or fatigue. The side effects differ with each drug depending on the nature of its chemical contents. Some have fewer side effects and others have more. Paradoxically, the intake of some mood-enhancing drugs leads later to nervousness, anxiety, irritability, while others cause seizures, mania, and abnormalities of the liver and white blood cells. There have also been reports of suicidal tendency in a few cases of prolonged use of such drugs.

Such drugs are meant either to supplement or diminish the brain chemicals, which affect the activities of brain cells generating thoughts, emotions, and anxieties. Some drugs like Prozac regulate the level of the brain chemical called serotonin that enhances mood and promotes positive feelings. Ritalin reduces sensory information that accounts for stress and hyperactivity. Similarly, the other drugs affect the parts of the brain like the parietal lobe and frontal lobe to regulate thoughts and hyperactivity. In sum, all these drugs tinker with the electrochemical profiles of several regions of the brain to suppress thoughts, emotions, and memories in order to generate positive moods.

On careful scrutiny, one will be struck by the similarities of workings of these drugs with the impact of meditation on these regions of the brain. The most significant difference in the case of meditation is that it does not have any side effects of the drugs used to cure the mood and behavioral disorders. Conversely, all these drugs have side effects, let alone the high probabilities of affecting the growing process of children's brains and the long-term impact on their lives.

On the basis of their brain imaging studies, scientists tell us that the frontal lobes responsible for the abilities of reasoning, thought, anticipation, and planning do not mature until the age of thirty years. This is the reason why teenagers and young people are often less organized, immature, impulsive, and less bothered about their future. The impatient advice and wise exhortations from parents, teachers, and social leaders asking them to behave differently have less impact and often incite anxieties and emotions of anger, fear, and sadness in the limbic system/brain stem. These emotive sites are relatively more developed in the younger age. That explains proneness of teenagers for emotional reactions instead of thoughtful actions.

The cerebral assets of the young people are not fully developed to enable them to follow the wise exhortations of elders, even if they wish to do so. This makes it incumbent upon the adults to act with more wisdom and sympathy in dealing with the younger generations. That will reduce the universal complaint of generation gap as well the number of angry young people. Empathetic behavior on the part of elders would alleviate the agonies they inflict unawares upon the young and diminish their inclinations for psychotropic drugs.

The serious side effects make it evident that the price we pay for these antidepressants is extremely high, and worse, unknown when it comes to the growth of young brains and the future implications on their lives. Furthermore, in many instances, these drugs do not constitute even lasting remedies. In a majority of cases, depression or psychotic maladies arise out of emotional and other psychological reasons, which have to be identified and tackled properly. Unfortunately, these drugs deal with and alleviate only the symptoms, while the causes of the disorders lie hidden and untreated. That results in recurrence of the problem and prolonged dependence on the drugs.

While resorting to tinkering through external chemicals, it should be borne in mind that the brain is an extraordinarily sensitive system responsible for not only unique mental processes but also for constantly monitoring and governing the growth and health of the body and its vital organs.

In stark contrast to the drugs, the working of meditation stands out as a miraculous remedy and a real benediction. It seems to be a godly gift, and no wonder that it was invented by those noble souls in the ancient days, who roamed around their entire life in search of God and the meaning of human existence. Meditation does not manipulate the brain with external chemicals. Rather, it relies on the inherent potentials of the brain and induces self-discipline on different regions of the brain to regulate sensory inputs. It also brings unique advantages of enhanced attention span, understanding, and above all, emotional equilibrium. These benefits sound too true and magical to be believed and yet these are not the claims touted by magicians and obscurantist gurus. Through brain scan, the scientists have witnessed the miraculous changes taking place in the brain. In research, they have found clear evidence of the beneficial impact of meditation.

CHILDREN AND MEDITATION

Since the use of drugs to correct mood and behavioural disorders has become very widespread, it is quite pertinent to examine the possibility of teaching meditation to children, particularly those who have a short attention span.

I believe that meditation for grown-up children and youth will have very positive impact on moulding their brains and ensuring emotional equilibrium. It will sharpen their intelligence and definitely expand their attention span. They would learn to pause and think before reacting impulsively. I have no doubt that meditation would help also children having disorders of attention deficit and volatile moods. It is a better option than the mood improving drugs having dangerous side effects. It is indeed a wise decision by many schools to have introduced meditation as an additional activity. We should not mix it up with any religion but take it as a mental exercise.

Some extra care is required in introducing children to meditation. We should never compel children to meditate if they are not inclined or not comfortable for any reason. As we know, children are fidgety and have difficulties in remaining seated in a fixed position for even a few minutes. It would be good, if they can be taught the breathing exercise (pranayama) under the guidance of parents or a good teacher. The breathing exercise described in the earlier chapter will definitely boost their health and lengthen their attention span.

Let me narrate my experience concerning my twelve-year-old son, whom my wife and I encouraged to do breathing exercise and meditation. Initially, like any other child, he had difficulty sitting for a few minutes in a fixed posture. We encouraged him to sit down for meditation as long as he liked. Sometimes, we played soothing instrumental music in the background. The instrumental music was selected, because attention to any words in a vocal song would provoke thoughts. He got interested in reciting the word *om* loudly in a prolonged note in which *o* is stretched as much as possible without any break. The note should be a long continuum of *o* and breathing is withheld while doing it, which is akin to a breathing exercise. In fact, we used to have a bit of competition on prolonging the note of *om* as a sort of fun. The word *om* is believed to be sacred in Hindu religion. It attracted my attention because its prolonged recital works as a good breathing exercise, and not because of any religious significance.

As we know, a child's attention is easily engaged if they find the activity funny or interesting. One should keep that in mind while encouraging them to meditate. Let me narrate one humorous analogy which I used for explaining the problem of anxieties to my son. When I reached Vienna for my next diplomatic assignment, my son was admitted to a new school. He was a nine-year-old, and the evening before his first day at the school, he was quite nervous and a bit lost worrying about the next day. I tried to make him happy saying that it was a wonderful school and he would have soon new friends. It is much more likely that the first day would be quite joyful, and he would return with a smile on his face. He would then realize that his worries were pointless.

When I could not succeed in making him relax, I told him, "Listen, my dear boy, your mind is like a beautiful garden, but right now the monkeys of worrisome thoughts have invaded your garden and are spoiling its beauty and peace. The mischievous monkeys are jumping all over and you should drive them away to protect your nice garden!" Next day when he returned from the school, he remembered the story of the monkeys and the garden, and in fact referred to it gleefully in future when he faced some anxieties by saying that the monkeys were jumping in his garden.

My wife and I advised him to meditate for five to ten minutes, but often he felt disinclined and we did not force him. He had some fascination for astronomy, and hence I suggested to him to try imaginary space travel from one planet to the next, cross the solar system, enter the dark intrastellar space, and hop on from one star to the other, and then from one galaxy to the other. Such effort requires mental visualization, which is sustained by inner awareness.

We avoided imposing any method of meditation and persuaded him to sit down and just relax by closing his eyes. Slowly he got interested and on a few occasions, he sat down for ten to fifteen minutes. One day after acting in a drama in his school, he told me with a great joy that he had acted very well because at that time, he had just forgotten himself as I had advised him during one of our meditation sessions. My purpose was served as the seeds were planted, which might make him meditate at the time of any crisis in his life ahead.

ADVERSE EFFECTS OF MEDITATION

Some readers will question whether meditation has any side effects that are negative or unexpected. It was stated earlier that the awareness meditation would lead to enhancement of the role of inner consciousness by rewiring the neural substratum of the brain that is utilized by primary emotions as well. Wouldn't that make a person emotionally deficient or insensitive?

I do not believe that is the case. Rather the enhanced role of inner consciousness leads to preventing the impulsive tendencies of emotional behavior and brings about an emotional stability. Secondly, any emotion is inherently a deep sensory experience of consciousness. Hence, more access to consciousness means more emotional depth. Conversely, an erosion of consciousness, or operating on a narrow band of consciousness, would be erosion of emotional depth and sensitivity. Meditation enables a person to have deeper emotional experience, unadulterated by other mental activities like thought.

Furthermore, meditation accrues the ability of empathetic behavior that enables one to understand feelings of others without being enclosed in one's own emotions and feelings. The strengthening of the neural infrastructure of the limbic area of the brain would certainly enhance the depth of emotions and inner consciousness. Meditation over a long time brings a kind of tenderness and the feeling of bonds with life in all forms. One experiences a positive feeling of closeness and compassion for flora and fauna. It is a new sensitivity one develops as one slowly comes out of the shell of individual self and the horizon of one's consciousness expands.

There can be some other concerns. In research, it was discovered that activities of the neocortex, particularly the parietal lobe and the frontal lobe, are curbed in meditation. Wouldn't that lead to the erosion of our abilities of thinking, reasoning and anticipating the future? Wouldn't it disorient us from the external world and the realities of life? Would meditators become overcomplacent owing to the lack of worries and anxieties?

Such possibilities can exist in the case where a meditator relies for years only on reciting sacred words or concentrating on images. In such instance, a meditator negates other mental processes such as thoughts and memories by locking the mind in a single track of repetitive drill. That could deactivate the parietal lobe and the frontal lobe as observed by neurologists. A coercive activity to suppress thought and emotions without strengthening inner consciousness and understanding of mental processes runs the risk of such negative consequences.

In contrast, awareness meditation does not use rigid and coercive methods to negate mental processes. It is devised to generate understanding of our psychological or autobiographical self and its baggage of self-images, memories, aspirations and mental conditionings. It makes one aware of how our psychic self operates in our daily life in the office or at home. For achieving that deeper understanding, awareness meditation uses the method of applying the power of nonverbal awareness. It uses the properties of consciousness, namely, innate intelligence and understanding.

Second, awareness meditation regulates the hyperactivity of the parietal and frontal lobes and puts in place a healthy and balanced rhythm of processing of sensory data and transmission of signals to other regions of the brain. It is somewhat akin to reducing the high speed of a car from 180 kph to around 100 kph. This is achieved by activating the thalamus, the gatekeeper in the brain, to a higher level of efficiency for streamlining the sensory traffic.

A good meditation makes one more focused in whatever activities are being pursued. It increases the attention span and mental energy, which will make one act more intelligently. It makes a person face the realities of life and not become oblivious to the world or future. Meditation curbs the tendencies for excessive anxieties and worries. It reduces stress, but not the ability to think or reason. In fact, I have found a remarkable enhancement of the ability to visualize things with regular meditation. No doubt that would mean a heightened ability to conceptualize things and visualize the future more clearly.

How about the absence of worries and anxieties making a person complacent? When one is focused and acting intelligently, one does not need anxieties and worries to goad one to action. These psychological phenomena do not lead to a better action; rather they diffuse and divert mental energy that is needed to focus on the tasks ahead. One has to be conscious of the urgency and necessity of attending to one's work or responsibilities, and for that, anxieties and worries are not required. We are used to worries and anxieties so much in our life that we believe them to be essential for action.

One more concern is raised about meditation in general that it encourages the tendency for self-transcendence or negation of self. This needs to be clarified to avoid confusion. Negating self involves two issues: one is a philosophical line of thinking that the psychic self or "me-ness" is an ensemble of subjective images created and accumulated by a person. Since it is a nebulous body of subjectivity, it should be negated to attain nirvana or spiritual liberation. This ideology is associated with some practices of meditation. Instead of getting into more details, I would say that it is an independent ideology or belief, which is not required in awareness meditation.

The second issue is the possibility of using meditation to seek escape from self. It might or might not happen depending on the type of mediation being practiced. I have come across several persons pursuing meditation and spiritual ideas, and they speak eloquently and passionately about their experiences of "the moment when everything, including the self, vanishes, and the inner peace and joy overwhelm them." Some philosophical and spiritual beliefs are built upon such mysterious experience. There is nothing mysterious about that moment of *heavenly bliss*. The psychological fact is that when the self that embodies—inter alia, nagging memories, anxieties, and painful feelings—is eclipsed for a while, one feels unburdened and peaceful.

Neurologists have their own explanation. The experience of self-transcendence is induced when the frontal lobe that is largely responsible for our sense of self is deactivated in meditation. Besides, the deactivation of the parietal lobe disorients one from the sense of time and space. This means one becomes oblivious of the external world and future, which are the sources of innumerable worries and anxieties. These factors would surely bring a temporary feeling of nirvana or freedom from the mundane world and self.

Whether one likes it or not, seeking such experience can be interpreted as a pleasant escape from the harsh realities of self and external world. There would be a temptation to experience that bliss as frequently and as long as possible. The possibility of getting addicted to it knowingly or unknowingly is also strong. One may also use the cover of mysticism and spiritualism so that no rationalist can assail and pick holes in it.

One should be wary of such pitfalls. The meditation that caters to any psychological gratification is not different from suppression of feelings and memories. The original goal of meditation since the ancient days has been to face the self and understand its workings, both covert and overt. That goal was based on the hard and inescapable fact that there can never be a lasting inner peace and emotional stability without actually coming to terms with the realities of self and the world.

EVOLUTIONARY DESTINY

The main thrust of this chapter has been on strengthening the neural infrastructure of inner consciousness and improving the efficiency of the gatekeeper in the brain. If one ponders a bit more, the implications of that are enormous.

The advent of consciousness in evolution bestowed upon the human species the power of conscious behavior and more intelligent action, which meant a large measure of freedom from reflexive and predetermined behavior. It meant a good deal of liberty from the biorobotics that governed life in the earlier phase of our evolution. Unfortunately, there is no room for complacency because there are some factors that might threaten our innate liberty of consciousness.

One factor is the restrictive nature of thought per se that operates in a narrow periphery. The second is the fact that we are increasingly submitting ourselves to habitual and fossilized patterns of mental activities and thus surrendering the precious freedom of enlightened and conscious action. We are under the belief that thought is our free and conscious action—an expression of our intelligent choice. That is true, but not entirely! Unfortunately, our thoughts and emotions have become more habitual and have acquired a greater degree of reflex and autonomic patterns than we realize. It means that the limited periphery of our conscious thought and intelligent willpower is further curtailed.

Our minds are fettered with numerous conditionings that are caused by individual actions, hereditary factors, and the external world, including social and cultural influences. Of course, certain reflexive tendencies are evolved to cope with the circumstances of individual life, while others are passed on genetically as the self-protective adaptations in the course of evolution. One cannot find fault with such self-protective reflexive behavior. For instance, the impulsive fears of reptiles and insects are still useful, though these were prewired in the early evolutionary phase when reptiles ruled the planet.

Many of our social and cultural rituals and beliefs also fall into this category of outdated relics of past, which include our superstitions, hierarchical behavior, aggressive postures, the tendency of domination over others and violence. The feelings of tribalism, racial hatred, and even patriotism are also evolutionary baggage of old herd instincts. Of course, patriotism and nationalism have practical values of governance and social order. Our prejudices and social divisions that cause violent conflicts are nothing but slavery to habitual ideas and emotions.

How do we change and create the human society that is more enlightened, liberal, and not divided? It is the discretionary intelligence of inner consciousness, which can liberate the mind from the autocratic regime of fossilized patterns of thoughts and emotions. Noble ideals and positive feelings do not easily break the old conditionings of the mind. We have to look deeper into ourselves, talk to our neurons, and refashion their old tendencies. Here lies the crucial importance of awareness meditation, which offers a possibility of breaking the old patterns of neural behavior with the power of inner consciousness.

We should not forget that the evolutionary journey of life on this planet has been a movement from the autocratic and brute regime of the unconscious to the enlightened rule of the consciousness. Consciousness was invented by life to maximize the benefits and potential of its biological resources, particularly innate intelligence, so that it can understand better the external world and enhance its adaptive capabilities.

Should we endeavour to accelerate this evolutionary movement toward larger consciousness with its inherent property of understanding? We definitely need to light up our path ahead with the lamp of consciousness that keeps flickering and wavering in the blasts of stressful emotions and thoughts. Do we continue to drift along and leave it to evolution to grind slowly and keep tinkering for eons to seal our fate under the tyranny of chance and chaos? On the other hand, do we as a species that has reached its adulthood, take it upon ourselves to shape our destiny?

As discussed before, our brain is a conglomerate of diverse parts that include evolutionarily older regions like the reptilian complex and limbic system, as well as the modern acquisition, the neocortex. They are still in the process of adjustments and harmonization with each other, yet they often tend to assert themselves as well. The neocortex makes up nearly 80 percent of our brain mass. Yet it is heavily dependent on the ancient parts that are responsible for primary emotions and the major bulk of memories. Above all, the ancient brain is the seat of inner consciousness that is the essence of all mental processes.

The neocortex with its products of thought, reasoning, imagination, and language represents the branches, leaves, flowers, and fruits on the top of the tree of the brain, while the reptilian complex and limbic system are the roots and trunk. On the face of it, this seems to be mere analogical jargon, but if you look more carefully into the symbiosis and mutual dependence of all regions of the brain, the significance of the analogy reveals the depth of the truth it contains. If you cut down the trunk of the tree, the upper structure of branches, leaves, flowers, and fruits fall down. Similarly, when the evolutionarily older regions of the brain are damaged, the functional abilities of the neocortex collapse and the brain goes into coma.

The future evolution of the human brain will be toward better integration and harmonization of its ancient and modern parts. The region supporting the inner consciousness and understanding is required to play a leading role for good governance of divisive and disparate forces of the mind. In order to prevent stress and depression, it is essential to ensure prudent regulation of sensory signals from the cortex. Both these crucial requirements are handled by the thalamus and other parts of the limbic system. Hence, these areas have to be strengthened. In sum, it has to be a consciousness-led evolution of humankind.

At present, the neocortex, our conscious mind, is acutely aware of the problems of stress and anxieties. It is struggling to cope with them by attempting to impose self-discipline that can bring about a functional equilibrium from the fight-or-flight mode. The neocortex is not succeeding on its own because it has to depend largely on its own mechanism of thought and logic. Nobody seems to listen to it in the theatre of mind. Additionally, the cerebral areas engendering memory and emotions are working overtime.

Consciousness, though being the leader, is carrying on listlessly with only the baseline activities. The net result is a chaotic hyperactivity by the elements of thought, emotion, and memory. The immediate need of our times is to impose good governance, which can be done only by the leader namely, the inner consciousness. There is a reasonable possibility of achieving it through awareness meditation by placing it on a more scientific basis. That would mean more access to consciousness, not for being spiritual, but for living life in a more intelligent and enlightened manner.

Chapter 9

A Second Brain and Anxieties

Worry never robs tomorrow of its sorrow, it only saps today of its joy.

—Leo Buscaglia

At one time or another, all of us have experienced butterflies in the stomach while approaching a challenging task like an interview for employment, or when one's name is announced for the stage as the next speaker. Such fluttering sensations of nervousness or sinking feelings of fear are also felt in the stomach when one has to face something ominous. Has it ever surprised us that though our brain is in the head, such feelings are felt in our stomach?

Such immaterial action of the stomach is not limited to sinking or fluttering feelings. It occasionally performs another task of the brain, namely, the intuitive action. We use expressions like "a gut feeling or gut reaction" to indicate an instinctive feeling or action. Such expression is not a cliché, but it describes the actual action performed by the gut. One wonders how the gut possesses the abilities, which normally belong to the dynamic entity of the brain.

Scientists reveal to us an astonishing fact that every human being has two brains: one in the head and other in the gut. Dr. Michael D. Gershon, a professor of anatomy and cell biology at the Columbia-Presbyterian Medical Center in New York, wrote a book in 1998 entitled *The Enteric Nervous System: A Second Brain*. This book attracted worldwide attention and praise. Not only Gershon, but a few other scientists have observed that the fluttering sensations, sinking fears, and the intuitive actions are caused by the second brain. These findings have opened a host of new avenues for research in the vast subject of gastrointestinal problems as well as the emotive interdependence of the two brains.

Scientists theorize that at the dawn of our evolution when we were very tiny creatures stuck to the rocks waiting for food to pass by, we had only this tiny brain. As life evolved with larger biosystems, animals needed a more complex brain for survival. Consequently, a brain inside the skull along with the central nervous system was evolved. However, the ancient brain was preserved as an independent circuit, which is referred to as the enteric nervous system (ENS).

THE SECOND BRAIN

Experts have found that the second brain has about 100 billion neurons, more than the quantity held in the spinal cord. It also contains nearly every chemical substance that helps run and control the brain such as the neurotransmitters: serotonin, dopamine, glutamate, norepinephrine, and nitric oxide. Actually, 95 percent of the serotonin in the body is in the ENS. Two dozen of the brain proteins called neuropeptides that act as neurocommunicators and induce emotions are in the gut's brain. Surprisingly, it also produces benzodiazepine, a drug that relieves anxiety, which shows that the body is producing its own stock of tranquilizers.

Though the second brain has been recently the focus of attention of experts led by Gershon, the two British scientists, William Bayliss and Ernest Starling, discovered it first in the nineteenth century. They established through experiments that the ENS was a self-contained nervous circuit having neural activities independent of the central nervous system. Some years later, the German scientist Paul Trendelenburg confirmed the finding by demonstrating that the peristaltic response could be elicited in the isolated gut of a guinea pig without participation of the brain, the spinal cord and cranial nerves. The functions of the ENS persist even after being disconnected from the central nervous system of the brain.

These research findings at the end of nineteenth century and the beginning of the twentieth century were forgotten in the wave of new discoveries about neurotransmitters. Other scientists have subsequently supported Gershon's rediscovery with a lot more new ideas. Dr. David Wingate, a professor of gastrointestinal science at the University of London, has confirmed the correspondence of the second brain with the central brain. According to him, the gut's brain and the head's brain act the same way in the absence of inputs from the outside world. During sleep, the brain in the head generates alternately the cycles of slow wave sleep and rapid eye movement (REM) sleep. Similarly, during the night when it has no food, the second brain also produces cycles of slow wave muscle contractions punctuated by short bursts of rapid muscle movements. Patients with bowel problem also suffer from abnormal REM sleep. Wingate believes that the two brains influence each other.

These researchers believe that the second brain may save information on physical reactions to mental processes and send signals to influence later decisions. It may also be responsible for causing reactions such as joy and sorrow. Wolfgang Prinz, a professor at the Max Planck Institute for Psychological Research in Munich, stated in the German science magazine *Geo* that this discovery would give a new twist of meaning to the old phrase "gut reaction." He said that people often follow their gut reactions without even knowing why. It is only later that they come up with the logic for acting the way they did. Wolfgang Prinz thinks that the ENS may be the source of some unconscious decisions that the central brain later claims as conscious decisions of its own.

The connection between the two brains cited by Gershon and corroborated by other experts holds a crucial significance for understanding our emotive behavior. Gershon observed that the vagus nerve, which stems from the limbic region of the brain, connects the second brain in the gut. A steady stream of messages flows back and forth between the brain and the ENS. In fact, the messages transmitted by the gut outnumber the opposing traffic by the order of about nine to one. Satiety, nausea, the urge to vomit, and abdominal pain are the gut's way of warning the brain of danger from ingested food or infectious pathogens. The gut's brain can upset the brain just as the brain can upset the gut.

He added that earlier physicians regarded anxiety as the chief cause of peptic ulcer, but now it is firmly established that the bacteria *Helicobacter pylori* is the cause in the majority of cases. It seems that the burning pain in the stomach is responsible for the emotional symptoms, rather than the other way around. Gershon also believes that a balance between the higher brain and the second brain is essential for emotional stability.

A NERVE PLEXUS AND MEDITATION

The readers might wonder at the point of narrating the long story of the second brain. In my opinion, the story of the second brain is quite intertwined with awareness meditation and its antistress impact. Before proceeding to explain that link, it is necessary to clarify that these are my assumptions based on my own experiences of meditation that were quite objective, and I have no doubt that it can be duplicated by any experienced meditator. In other words, the scientists mentioned earlier have nothing to do with the ideas presented in the following part of the chapter and their research does not concern what I now have to say.

In order to support my assumptions, I have utilized some information available from these experts as well as neuroscience. On the other hand, I have also compared the information from the ancient scriptures and knowledge of some well-known Yogis, since they seem to converge and corroborate some aspects of modern neurological findings.

Let me reiterate that my effort of dwelling on these issues concerns the main practical purpose of this book, namely, how to deal with stress and excessive emotional tendencies. A more significant point of interest is that some aspects connected with the second brain provide an easier way of using the power of inner awareness to diffuse negative emotions and background anxieties. Besides, they facilitate the process of awareness meditation.

Even without help from a neurologist, we know by experience that our nervous system is spread out to every minute point of our body. That indicates that the reach of our awareness covers the entire body, and one can selectively focus awareness, or impulse of conscious power, to any point of the body. This can be experienced if you close your eyes and direct your attention like a radar beam to different parts of the body. If your attention is deeper and focused, without interference of any parallel thought or emotion, you will realize that your body has certain areas or points that show more sensitivity and enhanced sensory response.

Experts tell us that the nerve lines that are distributed everywhere in the body have several nervous plexuses or junctions after branching out from their origins in the brain or the spinal cord. A plexus is a closely interwoven nerve circuit from where nerves branch out further to peripheral areas or organs of the body. A plexus seems to heighten and redistribute the sensory impulses and data and thus works like a substation of the main electric power plant. Of course, unlike the electric substation, the plexus carries the sensory traffic both the ways, to and from the brain.

One can actually experience the heightened sensory response of some plexuses by directing the focus of inner awareness. The modern science has not attached any special significance to the role of the nervous plexuses, but the ancient literature of Yoga and the methods of acupuncture assign specific importance to them. In fact, the Yoga scriptures contain several psychological theories and spiritual beliefs concerning the nerve plexuses that are referred to as chakra, meaning "wheel or spherical circuits." I will revert to this subject later, but for the time being, let me add that not much scientific research is done on chakra philosophy and it remains a nebulous subject. Nonetheless, the role of the nerve circuits, at least some of them, needs to be investigated scientifically instead of ignoring them as mere physical junctions of the nerve network.

Let me narrate my one experience of a nervous plexus and its heightened sensory response, which was quite unexpected and self-annihilating. In 1997, while traveling to Berlin from Delhi, I landed at the Frankfurt airport in transit for my onward journey. Since I had still about three hours to while away before catching next flight, I sat down in the lounge of the airline. It was around five o'clock in the morning and I could see outside a couple of aircrafts taxiing around slowly. Inside the lounge, it was utterly quiet with no other passengers. There was no disturbance from any sound or movement outside, thanks to the airtight doors and thick glass walls.

The heavy silence of the early morning slowly crept into my mind. The clattering of the machinery of thought began to die down gradually. I could feel the slowing down of my breathing rhythm. Soon my mind was overwhelmed with the thick silence that descended on me. It was as if my thoughts were immobilized and soon vanished. The aircrafts, the beaming lights in the distance and a few ground staff walking around—all became immaterial, provoking no thought or sensory feeling in my mind. A weighty sway of nonverbal consciousness engulfed not only my mind but also my body and the surroundings. Only the feeling of sole existence and oneness with the universe prevailed in the vast emptiness of silence.

Suddenly, I felt that the anchor of my pure awareness was not in my head but a small area in the middle of the right chest, a couple of inches away from the breast bone (see fig. 9.1). It is not the solar plexus in the upper abdomen. I never experienced before such sensitivity in that area. That day was the beginning of a different phase of meditation for me.

Since then, over the years, I developed the practice of hovering to this area during meditation. That area seemed to be a nervous circuit. I did so because I found amazing advantages of activating this nerve plexus. It established quickly the neutral observer or nonverbal awareness, knocked off the activity of thought, wiped out traces of any anxiety or worry and diffused emotions. I have called it the vagal plexus for which explanation is provided later.

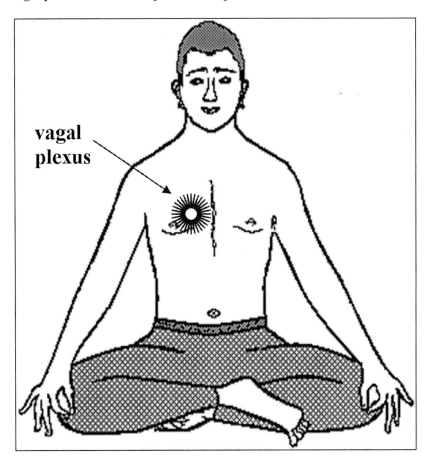

Figure 9.1. A vagal plexus—the nerve circuit having enhanced sensitivity.

It is clarified that there are many plexuses in the network of the vagus nerve covering head, neck, chest, and abdomen. Hence, the term *vagal plexus* used here will be, perhaps, judged by a neurologist as inaccurate. In order to avoid confusion, figure 9.1 indicates the location of the plexus. It is the point of enhanced sensitivity that has impact on the activities of heart, breathing, and the cerebral regions involved in stress phenomena. This explanation may not meet the precision required in neuroscience, but it serves a practical purpose of awareness meditation.

Earlier in chapter 7, we discussed the possibility of diffusing the feelings of mental hurt, nervousness or fear through the technique of "diffusion method"—meditative catharsis. This technique breaks the stronghold of negative feelings on the mind if a person does it correctly by staying with the pure sensory contents of the feeling without any thought or memories. If one meditates by focusing and activating this spot of enhanced sensitivity (designated as vagal plexus), the diffusion technique becomes much easier. The reasons for this are explained in the latter part of this chapter.

DIFFUSING FEAR AND NERVOUSNESS

While discussing the mental process of awareness meditation in the earlier chapter, it was noted that because of the obstinacy of thought, emotion, and memories, a meditator faces an uphill task in establishing nonverbal awareness as the anchor of meditation. This difficulty gets resolved largely when a meditator learns the knack of focusing on and feeling this nervous circuit. Thereafter, more than half of the struggle of a meditator is over, and meditation becomes an easy and joyful affair. This is difficult for the beginner whose neutral observer is still very shaky and transient. It is, however, a matter of more time and mental alertness that will enable one to have that knack.

The most beneficial consequence of activating this vagal plexus in the right chest is that it links up as part of a single stream of nonverbal awareness with the region of the brain responsible for inner consciousness and the second brain in the gut. These three points of the body get immersed in just one stream of inner consciousness. The segment of this stream connecting the vagal plexus with the main brain is experienced more explicitly compared to the other segment connecting the plexus with the second brain. How are we then sure of the linkage of this stream of consciousness with the gut's brain? That is confirmed by the fact that the feeling of butterflies or nervousness in the stomach disappears immediately when such a stream of nonverbal awareness is experienced explicitly.

You can experiment with yourself and find out the truth. The next time you are called upon to come up to speak on the stage or required to face a meeting surrounded by experts, concentrate on that nerve plexus for a few seconds, and you will find the butterflies flying off and the psychological fear getting diffused. You can repeat it now and then each time for two to five minutes during that circumstance and you will find yourself not only more relaxed, but also performing more intelligently. Your performance improves because the nervous feeling, which operates in the background and siphons off mental energy, no longer exists.

For concentrating on the plexus, you do not have to sit down in a meditative posture in front of your boss! With a longer experience of activating this nervous circuit with deep awareness, you will be able to do it anytime almost instantly at will. It will take just a few seconds to command your inner awareness to get anchored at the vagal plexus and establish the stream of consciousness. In fact, it becomes an amazing tool, available any time on demand to wipe out feelings of nervousness, anxiety, or fear.

For the last several years, I have been using this stream of inner consciousness to get rid of negative feelings and anxieties. It may be noted that an intense focus of awareness on the nerve plexus acts as a trigger for bringing into existence such a stream of consciousness. Let me clarify that I happened to read about Dr. Michael Gershon's discovery of the second brain only about two years after my experience at the Frankfurt airport. Before that, I kept wondering why the stream of consciousness linking the brain and the nerve plexus resulted in a diffusion of the sinking feeling in the gut.

Gershon's observations on the relationship between the two brains and the need for harmony between them for emotional balance gave me a lot to think about. In fact, I had no doubt whatsoever about his comments because I had already experienced the truth of his observations even before he published his book on this subject. Of course, Gershon does not talk about the existence of such a vagal plexus and the possibility of establishing a conscious connection between the brain and the gut's brain. The stream of inner awareness is triggered either by activation of the nerve plexus in a meditative state of mind or by an intense focus of nonverbal awareness. Gershon's silence on this might be due to the constraint of the physical science to experience and measure the phenomenon of inner awareness.

SEARCH FOR A NEURAL BASIS

The designation of vagal plexus needs an explanation. A few questions have to be answered to establish clearly what has been theorized in the preceding paragraphs. How is this plexus connected to both brains, in the head and the guts? Why does the intense application of inner awareness on this nerve plexus result in eliminating the nervous feelings in the guts and anxieties in the upper brain? In the opinion of neurologists, the two brains are connected and have two-way traffic of messages between them. Nonetheless, how does the midway substation of the plexus play a dominant role in calming down negative emotions in both the brains?

Let us briefly dwell upon the neurological basis connecting the two brains and the nerve plexus. According to neuroscience, most of the major nerves emerge from the spinal cord and spread out to different parts of the body. However, there are twelve major nerves emerging directly from the brain and hence they are referred to as the cranial nerves. All the cranial nerves are distributed in the head and neck regions of the body, with one conspicuous exception, namely the tenth cranial nerve, called the vagus. The rest of the cranial nerves other than the vagus handle individual tasks of the organs in the head and neck, like vision, smell, hearing, taste, tongue movement, facial expressions, eye movement, and the movement of the back and neck muscles.

The vagus nerve holds a special place among the cranial nerves in terms of its distribution and functions. It is the only one among them that spreads beyond head and neck to the structures in the chest and abdomen. It mediates the functions of the heart rate, constriction of blood vessels, motor functions related to breathing and digestion. On one hand, it connects the brain with the gut's brain, and on the other hand, it links itself with the limbic area and brain stem that affect mood, motivation, sleep, appetite, alertness, and other factors commonly altered by depression (see fig. 9.2).

The vagus nerve is responsible for commanding the neural circuits of the gut's brain. It also commands the microcircuits of the gut to increase serotonin in the event of fear. The experts tell us that the gut's brain has all the qualities similar to those of the head's brain, and therefore it can act on its own when severed from the vagus nerve.

Since the vagus nerve is distributed in the structures of the chest and abdomen, its network includes the nerve plexus in the right chest mentioned earlier. It means the signals, travelling on the vagal nerve route between the upper brain and the second brain, transit through this nerve plexus. That is further confirmed by the fact that an intense focus of awareness on this plexus results in a single stream of consciousness linking the upper brain and the second brain. For easy reference, I call it a *triune stream of consciousness* as it encompasses the two brains and the vagal plexus.

There is even more evidence of the influence and connection of the vagal plexus with the two brains. We learnt earlier that the second brain is also a factor causing emotions. There is a strong correspondence of emotions with heart rate and breathing. When emotions of anger, fear, sorrow, or pleasure are induced, the heart beats faster and the breathing pace accelerates. This acceleration is necessary to pump more blood and more oxygen to meet the heightened state of body in emotions. How does this emotive connection with heart, lungs and the second brain get established?

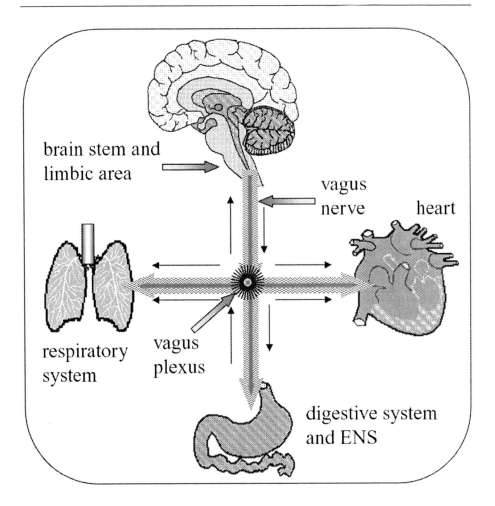

Figure 9.2. The major network connections of the vagus nerve. The diagram shows the origin of the vagus from the limbic region and brain stem and its onward connections with the respiratory apparatus, heart, and digestive system (the second brain). The one-line arrows indicate the movement of the sensory signals. The two-way sensory traffic between the brain and ENS is noteworthy. The second brain (ENS) can also directly deliver sensory signals to the heart and respiratory system, midway before reaching the brain stem and limbic region. Additionally, the vagus network covers the pancreas, spleen, and kidneys (not shown in the diagram). It also connects with the amygdala, hypothalamus, thalamus, frontal cortex, and other limbic regions of the brain linked to mood and anxiety regulation.

The vagus nerve is responsible for establishing this crucial emotive connection. Let us find out how that happens. The vagus nerve originates from the regions of the brain stem and limbic area, which cause the primary emotions of fear, anger, sadness, and love. It means the vagus nerve carries the emotive signals from the brain stem and the limbic region. In addition, the vagus nerve regulates the functional pace of heart, lungs, and even the guts.

Conversely, the stressful signals from the gut's brain are carried by the vagus nerve to the central brain, heart, and lungs. It is quite likely that while carrying the stressful signals from the gut's brain, the vagal nerve accelerates the movements of the heart and lungs before even delivering the signals to the upper brain or before the emotions are recognized by the conscious mind. If so, the vagus nerve is responsible for the synchronization of emotive occurrence and bodily response, particularly the corresponding actions by the heart and the lungs.

In view of this, it would not be illogical to assume that the point of enhanced sensitivity, the vagal plexus, in the network of the vagus nerve plays a more commanding role. That is also corroborated by the actual experience of meditators. An intense focus of inner awareness on the vagal plexus has an impact on the sensory signals (from both brains) that constitute emotions as well as the regulatory commands for the heart and lungs. Any action to regulate emotions also requires simultaneous and corresponding regulation of the functional pace of the heart and the lungs.

TACKLING STRESS AND ANXIETIES

The antistress impact of meditation was corroborated in the extensive research mentioned in the earlier chapters. The activation of the limbic area and the brain stem during meditation results in deep relaxation and emotional equilibrium. The same results are achieved when awareness is strongly focused on the vagal plexus, and the triune stream of consciousness takes place. It slows down and stabilizes the high sensory traffic on the vagus route resulting in a stable heart rate, normal pace of breathing and diffusion of stressful emotions. In fact, I would venture to say that the activation of the vagal plexus through intense awareness can be used as a controlling knob for emotions in the limbic region of the brain. On the other hand, it can also serve as a knob for stabilizing heart rate and breathing pace and for the diffusion of fluttering emotions in the gut's brain.

My years of meditation experience supports these possibilities. In fact, I have found the activation of the vagal plexus to be very useful and handy tool to relax as and when required throughout the day. I would strongly recommend to meditators to aim for reaching that stage, which will amazingly change the quality of their meditation and life.

It seems we have not fully understood and utilized the enormous potentials of the power of inner awareness. Let me mention one amazing instance of how with an intense awareness, one can voluntarily reduce the heart rate. Dr. Deepak Chopra narrates a case proving this in his book, *Ageless Body, Timeless Mind* (New York: Harmony Books, 1993), 36-37. In a series of experiments in the early 1970s at the Menninger Clinic in Houston, a well-known Indian monk, Swami Rama, demonstrated that he could raise his heartbeat at will from seventy to three hundred, a rate far beyond the normal range. His heart did not pump blood in the normal way as it happens in a cardiac flutter. Dr. Chopra adds that in an ordinary person, such cardiac variations can cause heart failure, and many persons do suffer such fatal problems. In contrast, Swami Rama was found to be unaffected and normal during that cardiac event.

This case provides evidence of how a focused stream of consciousness connecting heart and mind can work a miracle. The beneficial impact of inner awareness upon body and mind is also felt in meditation, though on a different scale. This meshes with the scientific research that found reduction of heart rate in meditation.

In my experience, activation of the vagus nerve through the vagal plexus holds a special significance in tackling negative emotions, anxieties and worries. Its crucial advantage lies in the fact that its influence and action are not just limited to the emotive regions of the brain, but reach beyond to cover the body and its vital organs such as the heart, lungs, and guts. These organs and the chemical processes of the body play a critical role in constituting and sustaining emotions.

As neurologists tell us, an emotion takes place first as a complex biochemical response of the body and it is only later that the conscious mind recognizes and experiences it. It means an action to deal with emotions at the conscious level is just a belated action. Worse, it is futile since the conscious mind has hardly any control over the bodily response—emotion—that is involuntary and subconscious. That is why the voice of our thoughts or reason is rarely heard in the realm of emotions (see chapter 4, "Emotions and Feelings").

Hence, activation of the vagus nerve is an answer to subdue the biomechanics of emotions by a direct action in the theatre of the body. That should enable one to tackle anxieties and worries, which are driven by the emotions of fear, nervousness, and insecurity. Of course, anxieties and worries involve additional mental processes of thought, imagination, reasoning that originate from the neocortex. It means not only emotions but other sensory traffic from the neocortex need to be regulated to diminish anxieties. How is it achieved?

As mentioned in the previous chapter, focusing of nonverbal awareness on the limbic area activates the gatekeeper, the thalamus, to streamline the excessive outpouring of sensory signals from the neocortex and other regions of the brain. Further, it is easier to focus and sustain nonverbal awareness in the limbic region through the vagal route or the triune stream of consciousness. Even the background worries and anxieties can be diminished remarkably with the help of that stream of consciousness.

Let me clarify that this method does not amount to suppressing emotions and anxieties. Of course, it is also essential to identify the reasons for persistent emotions and worries and tackle them intelligently with the power of inner awareness.

However, a question does arise: Why should an activation of the vagal plexus make it easier to establish a stream of inner awareness? In other words, why should that make awareness meditation easier?

In the usual way of meditating, the conscious mind tries to disentangle itself from thought, emotions, and memories, but these mental activities often prevail and prevent the conscious mind from assuming the state of nonverbal awareness. The underlying reason for these hurdles is the fact that the neocortex is the common arena of action for the conscious mind as well as thought, reason, working memory, and certain feelings. The conscious mind would, therefore, need to cut through the thick jungle of these psychic forces to arrive at the serene land of nonverbal awareness. Evidently, that is a formidable task. This is further compounded by the fact that the voice of the conscious mind from the neocortex is rarely heard in the parts of the brain that engender primary emotions of fear, anger, or sorrow.

In contrast, meditating by activation of the vagal plexus through nonverbal awareness has some distinct advantages. First, an activation of the vagus nerve represents in itself a pure sensory experience of awareness undiluted by thought, and memory. It constitutes a direct path to pure awareness without having to cut through the dense forest of thoughts, memories, and feelings.

Second, the vagus nerve has direct network connections with the brain stem and limbic regions, which are responsible for primary emotions, dormant memories, nonverbal consciousness, and the unconscious. The activation of the vagus results in easily establishing the neutral observer, or nonverbal stream of consciousness. This, in turn, prevents the neural substrates of the limbic regions from inciting emotions or memories. When memories and emotions are not active, thoughts are denied their major driving force. As we know thought, memories and emotions often act as mutual catalysts and feed on each other. This vicious circle is broken and replaced by a virtuous circle through activation of the vagal plexus.

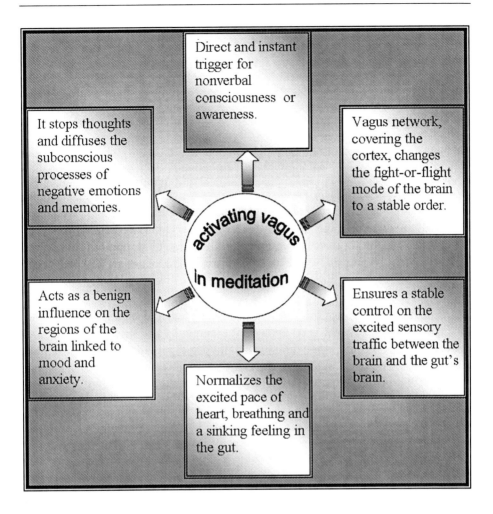

Figure 9.3. Benefits of activation of vagus through focus of nonverbal awareness on the plexus.

The third significant advantage is that the vagal route is a direct action in the theatre of the body to tackle emotions that arise before the conscious mind can recognize them. Nonetheless, the most crucial point is the fact that the vagus has extensive connections with the cortex, thalamus, hypothalamus, amygdale, and other parts of limbic region linked to mood and anxiety. In the previous chapter, we discussed the role of thalamus in sustaining consciousness and as the gatekeeper for sensory traffic. Thus, given its extensive network, the vagus enjoys a unique and critical place in the overall scheme of both the brain and body. In this context, the activation of the vagus through meditation or any other method will entail great benefits in relation to stress, anxieties and other emotional afflictions.

The important conclusion, in my experience, is that it is much easier to have deep meditation via the route of focusing awareness on the vagal plexus compared to the direct effort of the mind to focus on itself. In the direct effort, one ends up provoking thoughts, emotions, and memories quite easily, while in the vagal route these mental processes are not provoked and the neutral observer is established very quickly.

EMPIRICAL CORROBORATIONS

At the beginning, I had stated that these issues would be scrutinized not only from the modern neurological perspective, but also in the light of the experiences of the ancient meditators. The ancient Yoga literature abounds in theories on several nervous plexuses in the human body and mind. This literature refers to the nervous plexus as *chakra*, meaning a "vortex" or "spherical network" of nerves. The philosophy of chakras originally seems to be based on some logic worth investigating.

Unfortunately, no scientific research has been carried out, perhaps because of the obscurantist elements smuggled into later it by the vested interests. The astonishing claims of supernatural powers by some gurus have scared away the scientists interested in investigating the matter. Nowadays, many so-called spiritual gurus and Yoga teachers lure followers by promising psychic powers through their own chakra ideologies, and unfortunately, there is no dearth of followers seeking such illusive powers.

The chakra philosophy needs to be viewed with caution and skepticism till more authentic scrutiny is made. One should avoid being taken in by the lure of supernatural powers. Often people plunge into such obscure pursuits out of motives to escape their nagging self and worldly problems. Meditation and Yoga do not give supernatural powers; they make you live more intelligently and bestow better health of body and mind. Anyway, let me briefly introduce the readers to the chakra philosophy.

The ancient Yogis who practiced the art of awareness through years of meditation described the chakras as nervous circuits or plexuses in various parts of the body. In their opinion, these are the centres of energy or spiritual powers, which could be accessed by awakening the chakras. Normally we are not aware of these chakras, but it is believed that these could be activated or awakened through intense concentration and practice of meditation. The original philosophy of chakras in Hinduism was adopted in Buddhism and the Tibetan philosophy with some modifications.

According to the ancient Yoga scriptures, seven chakras exist in various parts of the body but there is no unanimity of opinion on the exact number of chakras. Some propound four, some more than seven. The Buddhist and Tibetan scriptures mention even larger numbers.

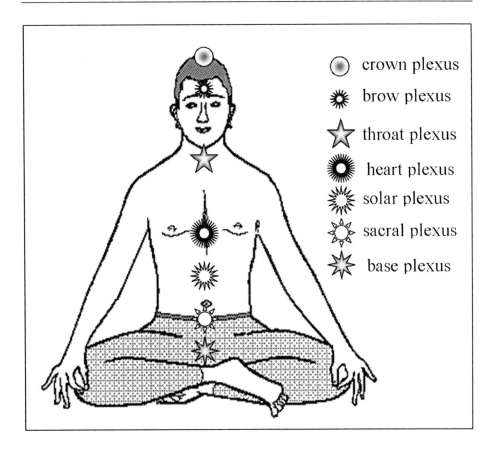

Figure 9.4. The chakra system (nerve plexus) according to the Yoga scriptures.

The major seven chakras along with their functional attributes are mentioned below (see fig. 9.4):

- sahasrara chakra (crown plexus in the brain)—associated with wisdom, spirituality and knowledge of truth.
- ajna chakra (brow plexus)—associated with intuition, perception and vision.
- vishuddha chakra (throat plexus)—governs communication, self-expression and hearing.
- anahata chakra (heart plexus)—concerns emotions, empathy, and relationship.
- manipura chakra (solar plexus)—concerns earthly power, accomplishments, ego, and vigour.
- swadhishthana chakra (sacral plexus below the belly button)—concerns sexuality, creativity, passions.

➢ muladhara or kundalini chakra (base plexus at the tailbone base of spine)—concerns security, survival, and trust.

It is propounded in the ancient Yoga scriptures that the activated chakras give spiritual powers, but their malfunctioning could lead to abnormalities or neurotic problems. In the ancient and recent literature, there is a plethora of theories of spiritual and psychic powers associated with various charkas and I do not see the need to enumerate them. I would rather reiterate advice for caution against that. I have not come across any convincing proof of such claims except some convergence of experience regarding the vagal plexus that seems closer to the heart chakra.

However, in my opinion, there is a difference about the location. The enhanced sensitivity of the vagal plexus experienced by me was in the right chest and not near the heart in the left chest, where the *anahata* or heart chakra is located according to the Yoga literature. Nevertheless, the virtues associated with the heart chakra have some convergence, particularly on the questions of emotional stability, empathy and deep relaxation that I experienced after focused awareness on the vagal plexus.

In Yoga scriptures, the following virtues are attributed to an activated heart chakra. It is considered the site where our *true self* or *spirit* resides that is pure and unaffected by anything. It witnesses all our actions without being affected (neutral observer). It manifests love, empathy, and compassion and destroys fears, anxieties, and mental conditionings. The activation of the heart chakra gives a sense of security and confidence.

The narration of these attributes is couched in a religious idiom. Also, the issues of true self and spirit are matters of beliefs and subjective perceptions. Nevertheless, the qualities associated with them have some convergence with those of the neutral observer or the inner awareness. The other attributes of heart chaka such as empathy, compassion, diminished fear, and anxieties match with the impact of focused awareness on the vagal plexus.

Even besides Yoga literature, other philosophical ideologies of Hinduism have assigned the seat of *soul* to heart, which conceptually transcends passions and emotional vicissitude. The *soul* or *spirit* also symbolizes higher consciousness and enlightenment. By this, I do not try to prove the existence of soul, nor do I suggest that the vagal experience brings enlightenment, whatever it may mean. The significant point being made is that in the ancient time, some people had the experience of an altered consciousness involving the vagal nerve route.

In the same vein, let me add specific instances of Ramana Maharshi and Vivekananda, the two Indian monks well known for their modern attitude and original thinking. Ramana Maharshi spent most of his time in meditation. When a Western scholar inquired about the seat of soul in the body, Raman Maharshi pointed to the right side of his chest. It is not clear whether his response was based on his own sensory experience of the vagal plexus or influenced by the religious beliefs.

The story of Vivekananda is a bit different. In his youth, he was an agnostic looking around for someone who could offer him a proof of the existence of God. One day, he happened to meet the great religious person, Ramakrishna and asked for such a proof. Ramakrishna touched Vivekananda's chest with his finger and looked deep into his eyes. Vivekananda felt a sudden surge of overwhelming sensation like a mild electric shock in his chest, which made him lose his normal orientation of time and the world. It was as if his thoughts and feelings vanished and he remained in a sort of meditative state for quite some time.

Of course, no scientific conclusions can be drawn from this instance as well. It might be a case of some sort of *spiritual* hypnotism or a result of the psychology of expectation. Given the high intellectual integrity of Vivekananda and irrespective of whatever the interpretations of that event, it is reasonable to believe that he underwent an experience that disoriented his normal consciousness for some time. This experience must be connected with the activated awareness of the vagal nerve, which covers heart, lungs and chest area. Later, Vivekananda became a great disciple of Ramakrishna. He earned a great respect and name for his modern and insightful interpretation of the Hindu scriptures such as the Vedanta and Upanishads.

ANTIDEPRESSANT ROLE OF THE VAGUS NERVE

After writing the earlier parts of this chapter, I came across an article entitled "Vagus Nerve Stimulation: A New Tool for Brain Research and Therapy," written by a team of experts from several prestigious universities and medical institutes in USA. The research coordinator of this team was Dr. Mark S. George, Radiology Department, Medical University of South Carolina. That article is about a new therapy called vagus nerve stimulation (VNS) that is being used by doctors in Europe and USA for treating drug-resistant epilepsy. This therapy is also used for chronic and treatment-resistant depression.

Let me summarise the therapy of vagus nerve stimulation mentioned in that article. An electric pulse generator, the size of a pocket watch, is inserted surgically, like the cardiac pacemaker, in the left chest of an epileptic patient and connected with the vagus nerve through a bipolar lead. This implant intermittently stimulates the left vagus nerve with variable electric pulses, which terminates epileptic seizures. As part of the VNS equipment, a programming wand, software, and a personal computer are provided in order to program and monitor the stimulation through telemetric communication. The article mentions that about six thousand people worldwide have had the pulse generator implanted in their bodies (until the year 2000).

During this therapy, doctors happened to notice mood improvement in the epileptic patients, which was later established as independent of the antiepileptic benefits. Subsequently, several other studies have clearly established that VNS induced metabolic and functional changes in the brain stem and limbic system of the brain, which result in significant antidepressant effects. In fact, the first implant for antidepressant effects against treatment resistant depression was done in July 1998 at the Medical University of South Carolina in Charleston.

The brain scan during VNS showed increased blood flow in the right and left thalamus that is implicated in being responsible for waking consciousness and acting as the gatekeeper for the sensory traffic from and to most of the other regions of the brain. In contrast, a decreased blood flow was noticed at that time in the hippocampus, amygdala, and cingulate gyrus.

The activation of the amygdala is known to incite the emotion of strong fear. While in neuroimaging, a decline in the activity of the cingulate gyrus was noticed with antidepressant response in many studies. According to neuroscientists, the hippocampus in the temporal lobe is critical for storage of memory. It appears to be a temporary depository for long-term memories. The hippocampus processes the newly learnt information for some time and then transfers it to the relevant areas of the cerebral cortex (Eric R. Kandel and Robert D. Hawkins, *The Biological Basis of Learning and Individuality*, The Editors of Scientific American, *The Scientific American Book of the Brain*, [The USA: The Lyons Press, 1999], 148).

The implications of these observations are quite significant. Depression, anxieties, and stress are driven by negative emotions particularly fear and insecurity. That explains the connections of the amygdala and cingulate gyrus with depression and severe stress. Memories act as catalysts and driving force for negative emotions that are at the centre of acute anxieties and depression. This accounts for the decrease in the activity of the hippocampus.

It therefore makes sense that the activities of these parts of the brain showed decline during stimulation of the vagus nerve, which causes antidepressant effects.

Similarly, the higher level of blood flow particularly in the right and the left thalamus indicates that the gatekeeper is actively regulating the hectic sensory traffic that is symptomatic of stress and depression and thus ensures emotional balance.

The same article by Dr. Mark S. George and his colleagues also provides evidence of the role of VNS in treating mood disorders with similarities in the results induced by anticonvulsant medications. Further, the neurochemical studies showed changes induced by VNS in the levels of neurotransmitters like serotonin, norepinephrine and glutamate. The currently available mood-enhancing medications contain the same neurotransmitters and cause similar neurochemical effects.

Doubtlessly, the antidepressant effects of VNS have close convergence with the activation of vagus nerve through meditation, which is elucidated earlier in this chapter, particularly in antidepressant results. That also supports the ideas mentioned in the previous chapter concerning the possibility of achieving emotional equilibrium by enhanced activation of the thalamus through awareness meditation. Further, it may be recalled that the vagus nerve is the major route of sensory traffic to the brain and the central nervous system. It is quite logical to assume that regulating the flow of sensory traffic with activation of the vagus nerve would offer possibilities of eliminating stress and anxiety disorders.

It might be still argued that activation of the vagus nerve through awareness meditation cannot be assumed to have the same effect as VNS through the electric pulse generator. That is true, but some similarities in the effects of both methods cannot be denied. Of course, the activation of the vagus nerve through meditation may not be at the level required for therapeutic uses for treating epilepsy. Nevertheless, the antistress and antidepressant effects of meditation have been amply documented in many scientific studies. The activation of the vagus nerve through inner awareness is indeed a more efficacious feature of meditation.

The article also points out studies on VNS indicating benefits in tackling the problems of obesity and sleep disorders. In a study of epileptic patients, improvement in the quality of their sleep was found after high-intensity and high-frequency VNS. Similarly, other research work provided proof of memory enhancement and improved learning.

The medical experts have been now looking for a nonsurgical and noninvasive method of externally stimulating the vagus nerve because both the surgery and an implant in the body entail pain and attendant clinical problems, let alone the high financial costs. They tried magnetic devices, but that did not work, so the search is still continuing. In this context, the method suggested in this book to activate the vagus nerve through application of intense awareness can be a possibility to some extent.

However, some limits have to be overcome. A patient cannot use the awareness route of VNS during the onset of actual epileptic seizure. Though it might not work as an on-the-spot cure, it can certainly be a preventive measure spread over some months or years. Yes, this route would require more time and diligent effort, which might be beyond the capacity of some patients. Nonetheless, it can certainly be used by anyone for benefits like emotional stability, improvement of memory, attention, and quality of sleep. It can help millions of people facing attention deficit disorders (ADD), obesity, chronic depression, and anxiety disorders. Approximately 18 million Americans suffer from depression, about one million of whom have treatment-resistant depression. The numbers of such cases in other countries are equally staggering.

In conclusion, activation of the vagus nerve through meditation is a promising area of further research work to establish it as a noninvasive and more benign way of treating acute cases of depression, stress, and anxiety disorders. That would improve the quality of life of millions of people around the globe, who are otherwise left at the mercy of potent neurochemical drugs with long-term side effects.

THE NEBULOUS MATTER OF HEART

In practically all human societies from the ancient to modern times, the heart is believed to be the undisputed centre of feelings and emotions. The expressions that we hear so commonly are "my heart aches with sorrow," "the love in my heart," "my heart is overwhelmed with pity," "a heart full of compassion," "heart filled with joy," "he broke my heart," "loyalty from the heart," "words of truth from the heart," "cherish memories in my heart," and "he is heartless." All such expressions are meant to convey one feeling or the other. Traditionally, the head stands for reason and thought, while the heart for feelings and emotions. It is head versus heart—sense versus sensibility.

Notwithstanding all that, the fact is that heart is merely a biological organ responsible for pumping of the blood. It is not an emotive apparatus. If one tries to locate the origin of one's feelings, such as sorrow, agony, fear, love, and joy, it would be evident that the heart in the left chest is not the location. Rather with the help of deeper awareness, one would find that the feelings seem to emerge actually from the right chest. Of course, the actual feelings are experienced in the brain, but their clear echoes are felt all the way down the vagus nerve that carries the sensory signals to modulate the functioning of heart and lungs to meet the emotive challenge.

It appears that the heart as a seat of emotions and feelings is a traditional myth, but it is not totally without a basis. Let me try to explain the tenuous basis that, in my opinion, has given rise to this myth. It also needs to be explained why we experience emotional sensitivity in the right chest at the point that I have described as a vagal plexus.

The vagal nerve plexus plays a sensitive role in enabling us to experience feelings. When emotions and feelings are induced in the brain, sensory signals are sent to via the vagal nerve to accelerate the pumping of blood by the heart and the movement of lungs to provide more oxygen. These actions are necessitated to prepare the body for facing the emotional challenge. Actually, the biomechanism of emotion is nothing but an ensemble of strong sensory signals to various organs of the body to react in a particular manner.

Let me reiterate: the vagal nerve holds an exceptional significance as being the only cranial nerve that, unlike all other cranial nerves, extends beyond neck and head to cover the chest, lungs, heart, and brain of the gut. It also originates from the limbic area of the brain responsible for emotions and consciousness. It acts as a high-tension cable connecting more vital organs of the body with the brain, which accounts for its high sensitivity and emotive potentials. In other words, the vagal nerve is the *main highway* of strong sensory or emotive signals for modulating the functioning of the major vital organs. Hence, the impulses of emotions and feelings that originate in the limbic and cortex regions of the brain are experienced more vividly and explicitly on the *vagal nerve route*.

Moreover, the vagal plexus seems to act like a midway substation to boost the sensory signals or impulses. That is perhaps the reason for its extra sensitivity. When this plexus is activated with deeper and steady awareness, it becomes a neutral experience with a stabilizing impact upstream on the mind and downstream on the heart, lungs, and the gut's brain. When the strong sensory inputs of emotions and feelings of fear, sorrow or joy are carried via the vagal plexus, they are experienced as either an aching heart or a cheerful heart.

Despite all that, the tenuous basis of the myth of the heart as a seat of emotions needs further explanation. In my perception, the higher sensitivity of the nervous junction of the vagal plexus with its functional connection with the heart accounts for that. The heart is receiving sensory signals from the brain as well as the gut through the intermediary junction of the vagal plexus. Consequently, the heart does respond in line with the sensory state of the plexus. The actual site where the feelings are experienced is the vagus nerve, particularly its plexus acting as a boost-up circuit. The emotionally live connection of the vagal nerve with the heart makes us misunderstand the heart as the site of actual emotions.

The additional reason for this misunderstanding is the obvious knowledge and visibility of the heart as an organ with its loud voice of palpitation. The accelerated pace of heartbeats during induction of emotion is felt clearly and does not escape attention. In contrast, the story of the vagal plexus and its connection with the second brain remained silent for the ordinary people except some stray experts. The Yogis gave it the garb of a mystic chakra, while the monks turned it into a nebulous entity of soul.

Chapter 10

Sleep, Theta Brain Waves, and Meditation

> *O sleep, O gentle sleep,*
> *Nature's soft nurse, how have I frighted thee,*
> *That thou no more wilt weigh my eyelids down*
> *And steep my senses in forgetfulness?*
> —William Shakespeare, *King Henry IV*

In this chapter, we will deal with the issue of sleep that claims nearly one third of our lives. Sleep mirrors the profile of an individual's life, the way one is able to cope with the world, one's emotions and ambitions. It reflects how intelligently we are able to shape the destiny of the one and only life we have. This chapter deals with one more delicate issue namely, the theta wave activity of the brain, which is closely related to sleep, stress, and meditation.

Sleep deficiency has become a serious and pervasive malady of modern times. There are numerous reasons for that, which are connected with our life style. The abundance of entertainment avenues is one of the causes. Television, movies, computer games, and similar entertainments claim perhaps the major chunk of our time. The technologies and electronic industry ceaselessly churn out innumerable new gadgets to keep people busy with entertainment. That accounts for not only sleep deficiency but also the problems of overweight and obesity that are equally serious and lead to cardiovascular ailments, diabetes, and other illnesses.

The unbridled consumerism itself has become an endless game keeping us on the run. In fact, the way we keep constantly searching for entertainments indicates that the foraging instinct of our itchy ancestors in the wild is still driving us around. Our habit of foraging for entertainment is linked to our highly competitive way of life. In order to free ourselves from the hassle, commotion, and stress of the hectic world, we yearn for relaxation and entertainments, which unfortunately come with a price tag. Insomnia and sleep deficiency are the price we pay for modern luxuries and sedate life.

SLEEP DEFICIENCY AND MORTALITY HAZARD

A great deal of scientific research has been carried out on the consequences of sleep deficiency and its links with aging and health disorders. It was discovered that limiting sleep to four hours a day over a few weeks had a detrimental effect on the immune system. Somehow, sleep deficiency has not attracted as much attention as other modern diseases, despite the fact that it is a potent factor behind many ailments. It might be primarily because of the fact that negative effects of sleep deficiency are slow, long-term, and not easily detected.

How many hours do we need to sleep? Though this is a debatable issue, it has been established through extensive studies that sleep of seven hours a day is essential for adults to maintain a good health. Babies and growing children need more sleep. Among adults, more than one hour beyond or below that sleep limit on a regular habit was found to have negative effect on health, including life span. It is surprising to learn that daily sleep of more than eight hours is detrimental to health and reduces life span. Besides, it contributes to the problems of anxieties, restlessness, and other mental disorders.

Some medical experts from the University of California, San Diego School of Medicine, and the American Cancer Society collaborated on a study on sleep duration and insomnia, which appeared in the *Archives of General Psychiatry*, a journal of the American Medical Association (February 15, 2002). The study involved more than 1.1 million men and women in the age group from 30 to 102 years. The highest survival was found among those who slept seven hours a night. Participants who reported sleeping eight hours or more as a normal habit faced significantly increased mortality hazard, as did those who slept six hours or less. The increased risk exceeded 15 percent for those reporting more than 8.5 hours sleep or less than 3.5 or 4.5 hours.

The study found that sleeping pills significantly increased mortality hazard, while the occasional bouts of insomnia did not increase the mortality rate among the participants. The authors of the study mentioned that insomnia was not synonymous with short sleep. Patients commonly complained of insomnia even though their sleep duration was well within the normal range. In their opinion, often the complaints of insomnia were actually related to depression rather than diagnosis of insomnia.

EVOLUTIONARY PAYOFF

Evolutionists have often wondered why we need to sleep at all. Practically all forms of life need some sleep or hibernation to sustain health and well-being. However, sleep does not make much sense in the evolutionary terms. It amounts to a considerable loss of lifetime, which could have been otherwise available for useful activities. The more worrying reason is that sleep exposes an animal to danger. That is indeed a big stake linked to the very survival of a species. Despite that, nature has retained the need for sleep because it is very essential for sustaining and recuperating the bioprocesses of life. The loss of a few members of a species owing to predatory attacks was definitely a better bargain against the alternative of jeopardizing health of the entire species across the board, let alone the long-term impact on its future evolution.

Yet not all factors involving the case of sleep are negative. There are some safety factors as well in favor of the choice of sleep. Fortunately, the sleep cycles of the predators and the prey generally coincide, reducing the risks to life. Besides, an animal has the possibility to ensure its protection against danger by making a safe burrow, nest, or finding a treetop or a cave for sleep. Sometimes, sleep can also become a factor of protection for animals from predators by reducing the time of their normal active phase that exposes them to dangers. This evolutionary choice by Mother Nature further corroborates the indispensability of adequate sleep, which is unfortunately being undermined in the modern age.

Neuroscientists and biologists have put in great efforts to research the nature of sleep, its likely biological purposes and the neurological processes that take place at the semi-conscious or unconscious levels during sleep. It would be useful to know some aspects of their discoveries before examining the impact of meditation on sleep.

However, let me add a note of caution that science is still struggling to make sense of the phenomenon of sleep and the neurological processes that are associated with it. Scientists continue to encounter mysteries even while discovering some facts. Ironically, discovering certain facts does not mean the end of the road as there is often no convergence among experts in interpreting such facts and in identifying the underlying causes. Nonetheless, there is no denying the fact that the untiring efforts of scientists and their discoveries offer a great deal to enrich our understanding.

THE SLEEP CYCLES

The two American physiologists Eugene Aserinsky and Nathaniel Kleitman were the first to report two cycles of sleep called rapid eye movement (REM) sleep and nonrapid eye movement (NREM) sleep. During REM sleep, eyes move rapidly under closed eyelids, and twitching occurs. Breathing becomes irregular, and heart rate increases during that phase. When awakened from such sleep, people report vivid dreams. The REM sleep is closely akin to wakefulness as it is characterized by short, rapid wave patterns in the brain similar to those occurring in the waking state.

In contrast, NREM sleep is characterized by the absence of dreams, little or no eye movement, and slowdown of breathing and heart rate. Often body temperature and blood pressure also decline. The brain wave activity is marked with waves that are low in frequency and large in amplitude in contrast to short and rapid wave patterns during REM sleep and the waking state. NREM sleep is believed to give deeper relaxation and rest to a person.

Based on electroencephalographic (EEG) recordings, it was discovered that human beings experience a very regular pattern of REM and NREM sleep cycles during night. In adults in the age group of twenty to sixty years, NREM sleep occurs usually in the cycles, each of about 90 minutes followed by a shorter cycle of REM sleep, and then the NREM cycle begins again. The REM sleep in the beginning of the night normally lasts about ten minutes, and then later the cycles grow progressively longer. The last cycle of REM in the early hours of morning lasts up to thirty minutes, and most of the dreams we remember occur during this time. Experts believe that most adults spend about 20 percent of their total sleep time in REM sleep.

Sleep provides much needed rest and relief to animals after their active phase in the day. It also serves the purpose of restoring the wear and tear and energizing the body. Despite these general notions, the functions of sleep remain a mystery to experts. The specific reasons for REM and NREM are not yet clear. The REM and NREM sleep decrease with age. Some research indicates the possibilities of encoding and organization of memory in adults and development of brain of babies and children during REM sleep. The brain development function is assumed from the fact that babies sleep seventeen to eighteen hours a day, spending about half of the time in REM sleep. In addition, those born prematurely continue to have more REM sleep than those born at full term.

The inference about the function of REM sleep, however, does not seem to be entirely true. Experts have observed that animals born in helpless states, like human babies, generally have more REM sleep as newborn than animals that can hunt and defend themselves soon after birth. The size of the animal also seems to have correlation with the length of sleep. The small animals tend to sleep much longer while giraffe and elephant sleep only for two to four hours a day. This might be related to the length of time needed to search for food and the feeling of security. Normally, the bigger and stronger animals would have more sense of security than those which are physically small and weak.

Apart from brain development and memory functions, an inner sense of fear and insecurity might be one of the causes for REM sleep, as it keeps the animal closer to the wakeful state to respond quickly to a sudden danger. The longer REM sleep in small animals and those born in helpless state perhaps accounts for that. The adult humans who are psychologically disturbed or insecure tend to have relatively longer REM sleep and increased incidence of dreams.

SLEEP AND MEDITATION

In the context of sleep deficiency and its negative impact on aging and the immune system, meditation assumes a much greater importance because of its proven beneficial effects on sleep. Most meditators have reported remarkable improvement in the patterns and quality of their sleep after a few weeks of regular meditation. First, they report sound sleep and the feeling of having rested well in the morning, which is much more precious than we normally realize. Apart from the unique experience of deep satisfaction, it keeps a person cheerful and energetic in the course of the day (see fig. 10.2).

Second, the meditators report fewer interruptions of sleep during the night and often not even a single interruption. Third, one does not have to wait long for sleep after getting in the bed. The usual fidgeting and changing sides due to lack of sleep or half sleep becomes a thing of past. I can personally vouch for these benefits from my own experience.

Meditation, of course, cannot override certain negative factors that disturb sleep, such as excessive eating and drinking, late nights, and emotional afflictions during the day. Despite this, meditation works like a boon in the world where sleep has become a scarce commodity for millions and millions of people. The reasons for the miraculous benefits of sleep accruing from meditation are quite convincing and simple.

Stress, depression, and anxiety are the major causes for disturbed sleep or insomnia. Such negative factors are quite pervasive and almost unavoidable, since the world we live in is highly competitive and hectic. The scientific studies have clearly shown the effectiveness of meditation in reducing, or even eliminating, stress and anxiety. The unending outpourings of stressful signals from the neocortex to various regions of our brain are diminished and streamlined through meditation. The fight-or-flight mode of our brain to cope with the challenges of world is turned off through meditation and replaced with a steady mental state.

Emotional crises, challenges, and psychological conflicts are encountered by all of us in the normal course of life and in interpersonal relationships. Losing a friend or a beloved relation can cause trauma, leaving behind emotional scars. Unhappy or bitter memories of the past do keep erupting at times and vitiate the environment of the mind. Often our ambitions, aspirations, desires, and prejudices add to the burden of stress, worries, and anxieties. Our external as well as inner worlds keep bombarding us with all sorts of obstacles and challenges. At times, it is hard to escape the feeling that we are being chased by some hostile existential forces. These factors take their toll in affecting our life and their adverse impact spills over in sleep.

Against all that, meditation offers remarkable benefits such as emotional equilibrium, objective perception, empathetic attitude as well as reduction of psychological fears and worries. Obviously, these benefits would go a long way in improving our interpersonal relationship at home and the workplace, reducing the psychological conflicts and bringing about a healthy and happy environment in our lives and society. It is but natural that this would have corresponding effects on the quality of sleep and dreams. One of the ways to measure the benefits of meditation is to observe and find out whether the quality of sleep has improved or not.

Though a slight digression, let me add one meditative technique to invite quick sleep during the night. In the previous chapter, we discussed extensively the benefits of activating one plexus of the vagus nerve. The vagal plexus can be activated through focused application of nonverbal awareness, which is possible only for an experienced meditator (see fig. 9.1 and 9.2 in the previous chapter).

Those who have the knack of doing that can focus their inner awareness on the vagal plexus, and soon, before they know, they will be fast asleep. The reason is obvious. When awareness is focused pointedly on the plexus, thoughts, emotions and memory cease to operate and the brain slips easily into sleep.

Another beneficial phenomenon that occurs in both sleep and meditation is called *the theta wave activity* of brain. It is also called *theta rhythm* or *theta oscillation*. A great deal of research has been carried out to understand the process and effects of theta rhythm in the brain. Experts have made significant discoveries linking the role of theta activity with the coding and long-term consolidation of memory, cognition, and learning. Besides, as stated before, experts tell us that the theta rhythm is connected with deep relaxation of mind. Further research is still being pursued on these issues, but the results achieved so far by scientists do enrich our understanding of sleep, effects of meditation, and the functioning of our brain.

THETA RHYTHM AND MEMORY

Since the theta rhythm prevails in the brain during meditation, it is necessary to learn more about the studies conducted by the scientists on its role in the functioning of the brain. The following part of this chapter provides some details of the research. One would be struck by the close correspondence of the benefits of meditation mentioned in the earlier chapters with the cerebral processes that are induced by the theta rhythm.

Our brain regulates its activities by means of electric waves emitted at different frequencies that can be recorded in EEG. These brain waves and the activities associated with them are narrated below.

- ➢ Alpha—frequencies ranging from 8 to 13 hertz, during the conscious state of relaxed awareness and attentional activities of learning and performing tasks.

- ➢ Beta—emitted within the frequencies of 18 to 25 hertz, during consciously alert state or when one is tense, anxious or agitated.

- ➢ Delta—frequencies within 0.5 to 3.4 hertz occurring during unconsciousness and deep NREM sleep.

- ➢ Theta—emitted within frequencies of 4 to 7 hertz, during wide variety of behavior in different mammalian species and primates including humans.

Theta rhythm is implicated in memory consolidation, cognition, and contextual representation, and additionally among humans in focused attention, learning, mental imagery, meditation, and deep relaxation.

Experts believe that sleep plays a very significant role in long-term storage of memory. Jonathan Winson, professor emeritus at the Rockefeller University, was among the first few experts who had made commendable research in the 1970s in this area. That was followed by further extensive research in the last few years by several other scientists in various aspects of memory storage and related chemical processes in the brain.

Winson carried out experiments on rats in his laboratory and made valuable discoveries about the role of the theta brain waves in memory processing during REM sleep. The hippocampus is known to provide neural structure for memory along with the neocortex. He found that theta rhythm was produced in two specific sections of the hippocampus. That finding was supplemented by other experts in America who discovered that actually the brain stem activated and controlled the theta rhythm in the hippocampus as well as the neocortex.

Winson established definitive causal links between theta waves and memory. He and his colleagues demonstrated that long-term memory encoding was dependent on the presence of theta rhythm. In further experiment, he observed the specific neurons that were activated during location search by the rat, fired at a significantly higher rate during sleep. It was established that the information gathered by the animal, while being awake and active, was being reprocessed and encoded in the long-term memory during sleep. Many scientists through experiments on animals and humans have since corroborated the connection between theta activity during REM sleep and memory consolidation, also referred by experts as long-term potentiation (LTP).

The connection between REM sleep and memory consolidation was well established. However, the mystery of the role of NREM sleep remained unresolved until Bruce L. McNaughton and his colleagues at the University of Arizona made a new discovery. They developed a technique to identify and record definitive firing patterns of an ensemble of neurons in the hippocampus that map locations. They found that these neurons, which encoded memory in the waking state, reprocessed information during slow-wave or NREM sleep. Their observations suggested that consolidation of memory occurred in two stages—first in slow-wave sleep (NREM) and later in the REM sleep.

Recently research was done on animals and humans to find out how memory is processed during slow wave sleep. There is clear evidence that long-term memory consolidation also occurs during slow wave sleep with activation of the hippocampus and certain areas of the neocortex. This underlines the importance of slow wave sleep and gives a clue as to why we spend a major part of our sleep in the slow wave state. It suggests that sleep deficiency would undermine our ability to remember information gathered earlier in the day and thus affect our ability to learn as well. This would be in addition to the detrimental effects of sleep deficiency on aging and health.

LEARNING AND ATTENTION

Theta waves seem to have their footprints in not only memory consolidation, but also in other important mental activities like learning, cognition, attention, and creativity. That seems logical since memory is closely linked with these activities as a crucial, supportive mechanism. The studies on rats mentioned earlier showed evidences of cognition occurring accompanied by encoding of memory in the presence of theta rhythm.

Laukka and his colleagues (University of Oulu, Finland) found in research a clear link of theta rhythm with successful learning. In this study, subjects were engaged in a simulated driving task of navigating through a series of streets animated on a computer screen. The activities of their brains were monitored through EEG recordings. It was found that theta activity increased in the frontal cortex as the subjects succeeded in making correct decisions. A successful behavior produced more theta waves than the unsuccessful. The experimenters concluded that theta rhythm was linked to the relaxed concentration that was essential for successful learning.

Many other scientists have also observed independently the increased theta activity of the brain during attention and relaxed concentration. It is self-evident that attention is a prerequisite for cognition and learning—the two mental processes that occur in the presence of theta activity of the brain. This may lead to the conclusion that brains of those suffering from attention deficit disorder (ADD) are not capable of producing adequate theta rhythm. It would be also logical to assume that such individuals would suffer from insufficient encoding of long-term memory during the conscious state and thus slow learning as well. The occurrence of ADD is alarmingly pervasive particularly among the growing children. It is also quite common to find many adults who have a short attention span. In fact, most human beings have some degree of ADD, though in many cases that may not be openly discernible.

The situation of growing children and youngsters afflicted by ADD is deeply painful. They go through agonies at school and home because many teachers and parents have an inadequate understanding of this malady. The easy course of action chosen by parents is to put such children on prescription drugs without realizing the serious side effects that have ruined many lives. There have been reports of increased suicidal tendencies and even some actual cases of suicide by youngsters who were on such drugs for long time. To be fair, on the other hand, parents do not find a better alternative. The lack of medical treatment will seriously affect the lives of their children, as they would fail to compete with their peers, lose self-confidence, and face depression. Does it mean that they do not have much hope for respite?

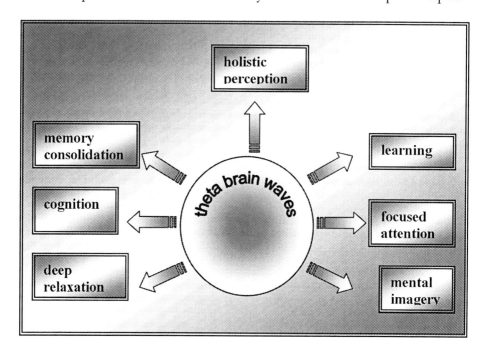

Figure 10.1. Theta waves occur in the brain during the mental activities indicated in the figure. Experts have found enhanced level of theta waves in the brains of meditators, which corroborates similar benefits accruing from meditation.

I am quite convinced that meditation can definitely come to their rescue without any of the nasty side effects. As indicated in the scientific research, meditation induces and enhances the level of theta rhythm of the brain. It was established that theta rhythm prevails in the brain during the relaxed, attentional activities, and successful learning. There is a clear link between the state of attention and theta rhythm of the brain. Therefore, meditation would offer invaluable help in mitigating ADD among not only adults but also children who undergo agonies at home and in the school. In the earlier chapter on "Rewiring the Brain," some advice is offered on how to introduce children to meditation.

THETA RHYTHM AND HOLISTIC PERCEPTION

The virtues of theta rhythm of the brain seem to be surprisingly numerous. The more striking role played by theta wave activity is in bringing about contextual understanding or integral perception. Dr. Robert Miller—at the University of Otago Medical School, New Zealand—in his very interesting book, *Cortico-Hippocampal Interplay and the Representation of Contexts in the Brain* puts forward a theory that the interaction of the hippocampus, neocortex, and theta rhythm results in contextual perception.

A context or associative linkage of apparently diverse elements is at the core in constituting understanding. In other words, representational imagery or correct juxtaposition of images is quite crucial for making it possible to achieve understanding of a complex situation. The human mind is subjected to an infinite amount of information from the external world, and in order to make sense, it has to process it by establishing contexts. In fact, one can go ahead and assert that without contexts, understanding is not possible at all. This would mean that understanding and knowledge are *intrinsically relative* and not absolute.

Let us understand how the theta rhythm works to bring about integral understanding. Neurologists tell us that for encoding memory and processing information, the neurons in the hippocampus and certain parts of the neocortex have to communicate with one another by establishing synaptic connections. Also, for a long-term encoding of memory, the synaptic connections have to be strengthened through repetitive or intensive activities of the neural assemblies. Further, the connectivity of global neural assemblies would be required to facilitate integral processing of inputs from different regions of the brain responsible for visual, motor, olfactory, and emotive actions. All these factors would necessitate extensive physical connections among spatially distant neurons. That would place not only huge burden on the limited neural resources of the brain, but also inject the negative elements of fixity and rigidity in the neural behavior, which is otherwise intrinsically dynamic and plastic.

Here, the theta rhythm, in Robert Miller's opinion, comes into play to mitigate the enormity of the task of physical connections. Without burdening the readers with the technical details, let me convey the thrust of his hypothesis. He observes that the theta rhythm provides interconnectivity between distant neural assemblies in the brain, which is necessary for having contextual representations and inducing understanding and learning. Such global interconnectivity is made possible in the following manner. There are already existing loops between the hippocampus and the cortex. The theta rhythm activates or makes resonant these loops and thus connects the spatially distant neurons to form global assemblies.

This considerably reduces the enormous requirement of physical connections of neurons.

It would be interesting to look into the cerebral interplay that actually causes correlations to support the process of contextual understanding. Such a contextual understanding would require a large bulk of information from memory, *synthetic thinking*, and mental visualization. That, in turn, will require a synchronized global action of widely spread neural assemblies in the neocortex, hippocampus, and limbic system, particularly the thalamus. The role of the thalamus is essential for two reasons: one, it is responsible for waking consciousness, and second, it is a gatekeeper for most of the sensory traffic and has a widespread connectivity with the neocortex and many other regions of the brain. As explained by Robert Miller, the holistic or synthetic perception is possible through synchronized activation of neural assemblies by the theta rhythm. This neural perspective will add further significance to the linkage of theta rhythm with memory and learning. In fact, it would suggest that the presence of theta activity in the brain would enhance the quality of memory and learning.

Though Robert Miller's hypothesis is quite tenable, experts believe that it needs to be corroborated with further research. However, Gyorgi Buzsaki, a well-known neuroscientist at the University of California, San Diego, supports Miller's theory. Despite the debate and the conclusions that might be finally reached, I have no hesitation to confirm that meditation definitely promotes the ability of contextual perception and visualization of abstract ideas. Of course, it would require practice of several months or even a few years. The enhancement of such ability is linked with the higher levels of theta oscillations that were found to prevail in the brain after meditation over a few weeks.

THETA RHYTHM AND MEDITATION

In an earlier chapter, a brief reference was made to theta activity of brain during meditation. However, the connection of theta rhythm with meditation assumes enormous significance in the light of the preceding discussion showing multiple role of theta rhythm in several mental processes. I have, therefore, cited here further research that establishes a connection of theta wave activity of the brain with meditation.

In 1974, Dr. Herbert Benson and Dr. Wallace studied a group of transcendental meditators. The activities in the brains of these meditators were recorded using EEGs. They discovered the typical patterns of alpha rhythm in brain during the early phase of meditation, which moved into theta rhythm as the meditators progressed into deeper meditation. Other scientists working independently on Zen meditation also made similar observations. Such identical neurological phenomena were observed across different meditation traditions.

Later on with further research in 1996, Dr. Benson observed that meditation brought about what he called *relaxation response*, opposite to the brain's behavioral mode of fight-or-flight. A significant increase takes place in the heart rate, blood pressure, and level of adrenaline in the blood during the fight-or-flight behavior. Conversely in meditation, not only the effects of decreased metabolism, but also lower blood lactate levels were observed, which indicated direct correlation between meditation and the relaxation response. This correlation has to be seen in the context of the fact that our brain switches over to the theta rhythm during deep relaxation.

Let me add a useful aside on the blood lactate. In a research carried out by Dr. Jim Holden, a medical physicist at the University of Wisconsin, USA, Quechuas and Sherpas living in high altitudes were found to produce lower levels of lactate in their blood. It suggested that the enzymes that control metabolism in their mitochondria (the *energy battery* in the living cell) had developed a way to use oxygen more efficiently in order to adapt to less oxygen in their environment. Similar results that are even more striking were found among Tibetans. That explained why altitude sickness and high fatigue that can kill even the fittest mountain climbers did not affect Sherpas and Tibetans. This has direct implications on Dr. Benson's research, who found that the meditators consumed 17 percent lower oxygen and had lower levels of blood lactate during meditation.

The more striking discovery made in other research was that not only at the time of meditation, but also after a few weeks of meditation, theta and alpha waves as the percentage of EEG power in the brain were found to have increased quite significantly. The theta and alpha waves showed progressively higher levels as the subjects continued with more meditation sessions. The implications of this are highly significant, given the fact that theta rhythm of the brain activities is associated not only with antistress effects, but also with memory consolidation, successful learning, improved cognition and increased attention span. It would not be far from truth to say that meditators show improvement in all these areas.

This is borne out in ample manner as most people after a few weeks of meditation practice reported being more focused, clear headed, and mentally more energetic. The linkage of theta rhythm with attention, and the fact that meditators have enhanced levels of theta waves as the percentage of EEG power in their brains, would offer greater hope to those suffering from ADD. I am quite convinced that meditation can be a very effective remedy even for ADD, if practiced with patience and care. It will indeed be a boon for millions of children and adults, who otherwise suffer from serious side effects of drugs for volatile moods and ADD.

Further, in this context we should not lose sight of other important facts discussed earlier in this chapter. Meditation also enhances memory power by improving the quality of both the slow wave sleep and REM sleep. It thus plays a twin role of improving memory consolidation with more restful sleep, and increasing theta power of the conscious mind, which accrues additional benefits mentioned earlier.

THE STUFF OF DREAM

We have talked about theta rhythm, meditation and sleep, but not about dream, a closely related subject. The interrelationship of these issues is quite interesting and the scope of this chapter will not be complete without exploring it. However, before doing so, let us look into the eerie reality of dreams—how and why they occur and whether they have any meaning.

Since the dawn of human history, the question of whether dreams hold any meaning has intrigued great thinkers and ordinary men alike. Around the world in all cultures, the phenomenon of dream has been wrapped up in wishful beliefs and myths as a means of foretelling the future or as a medium that gods and spirits choose to communicate with the earthlings. Of course, there can be coincidence of events that have high emotive values. For instance, one might dream about the death of a sick or old relative, who is very dear. It might, by coincidence, turn out to be true in the next few days.

Nonetheless, dreams offer mercifully an alternate world that makes us achieve and experience what we ardently yearn for but fail to do in actual life. Alas, in the elusive reality of dreams, such gratifying fulfillment lasts only for fleeting moments and not as long as we wish. Yet it serves a very useful psychological purpose. Dreams reveal our hidden desires, aspirations, and feelings that often manipulate and shape our external behavior.

This led Sigmund Freud to interpret dreams as the "royal road" to understanding the unconscious. In his opinion, dreams revealed the hidden elements of individual's innermost self. He therefore attached much psychological and therapeutic significance to dreams. Modern psychologists, however, do not attach that much therapeutic value to dreams because most of our dreams are engendered by our ordinary worries, emotions, and memories that get stirred up by the routine incidents in daily life.

Some experts who carried out research on connection of the theta activity of brain with memory believe that dreams play important role in memory processing during the REM stage of sleep. It appears an overlap in assuming that dreams play a role in the encoding of memory. Such an impression is created because both the theta activity that is implicated in memory consolidation as well as dreams occur together in REM sleep. But the connection between memory processing and dreams does not appear to be tenable in the light of the following.

First, on careful scrutiny, dreams appear to be a *spillover* or *replay* of emotions and memories connected with events in the past. As mentioned before, emotions and memories, which were evoked in the recent past, work as the driving force behind dreams. It means memory acts as a stimulating as well as supportive factor for dreams since without the play of memories dreams cannot be sustained. That does not support the view that memories of newly learnt information or skill in the day are encoded through the phenomenon of dreams. Rather, it seems that dreams serve a purpose of purgation or catharsis of emotions and memories, but not of consolidation of new memories.

Secondly, recent studies indicate that REM sleep has different phases with and without dreams. The memory consolidation seems to take place with the theta activity of brain in the dreamless phase of REM sleep. Besides, it is not certain whether the theta rhythm prevails during dreams. If a dream is pleasant or soothing, theta activity, which is associated with relaxation, might take place. Conversely, that may not happen in the case of nightmares or disturbing dreams, which would indicate beta rhythm of the agitated brain. Hence, it appears that further research is necessary to resolve the issue whether dreams actually consolidate memory or merely stir up the images that already exist in memory.

Some neuroscientists consider dreams as meaningless, resulting from random activation of neurons. This theory characterizes dreams as meaningless associations and memories in the forebrain (the neocortex) caused by random signals from the brain stem (responsible, inter alia, for primary emotions and feelings). It suggests that the story lines of the dreams have no realistic meanings. That accounts for the illogical and bizarre story lines of most of our dreams. However, it should not contradict the basic fact that the random activation of neurons is triggered by emotions and memories that are stirred up earlier. It is also true that most of these emotions and memories do not hold any deep psychological significance.

In 1983, Dr. Francis Crick and Graeme Mitchison of the University of Cambridge proposed that dreams represent *reverse learning* or *unlearning* of insignificant and false information. They suggest that the neocortex is overloaded with vast amount of incoming information, which causes spurious associations and false or "parasitic" thoughts. Dreams serve the purpose of erasing such false information. "We dream to forget," according to Crick and Mitchison. This proposition was based on random activation theory. However, they revised their theory to say that the erasure of such overloaded information and thoughts applied to only bizarre dream contents and not to the narrative or emotive aspects.

Though other experts believe that the hypothesis of Dr. Crick and Mitchison falls short of explaining the phenomenon of dreams, I see some convergence with the emotive purgation effected in some instances of dreams. The fantasy and bizarre elements in dream, though provoked by random activation of memory and illogical associations, help in sustaining and fulfilling certain emotions and feelings, which results in emotive purgation or relief. It can be reverse learning in the sense that a person is unburdened of the feelings and associated thoughts that seek expression.

Irrespective of these divergent opinions, the fact that emerges distinctly is that emotions and feelings constitute the central driving force of all dreams. The significance of emotions and feelings as causative factors is not diminished even when they find expressions through bizarre or lucid story lines of dreams. It is also true that most of the emotions that find expressions in dreams are not indicative of psychological problems or scars in the unconscious. Rather these are very common emotions and feelings that constitute routine anxieties and worries concerning one's office, business, family or events. Further, some of them are downright insignificant. For instance, once in my dream I met my childhood friend whom I had not seen for many years. The next day I kept wondering why I had dreamt about him even though I had practically forgotten him. Suddenly, I found out the reason that the previous day I had come across his name in very old list of my contacts for the New Year greetings. Of course, it stirred up the hidden memory of the old friend, but it had hardly any psychological significance.

Fear is, unfortunately, a very wide-based feeling, susceptible to an enormous variety of stimuli—physical, imaginative or psychological. In a survey, a large number of people reported dreams of snakes. Some psychologists have linked that with suppressed sex, which sounds a bit far-fetched. Rather, an explanation offered by evolutionists appears to be more plausible. They believe that the mammals had to wage a long and fearsome battle for survival against reptiles that dominated the planet during an earlier era of evolution. The persistent encroachments of snakes in our dreams are the past remnants carved into our genetic memories. But I would still forsake the lure of such special explanations and prefer to stick to a mundane reason for *reptilian* dreams, namely the fear of death, a devastating factor for anyone, which is strikingly symbolized by these creepy creatures.

MEDITATION AND DREAMS

It is obvious that dreams reflect the quality of one's sleep as well as the profile of the life one leads. Dreams mirror not only the emotions, desires and thoughts experienced in the course of the day, but also how one handles them and reacts to the events in the external world. Furthermore, our joys, sorrows, hurts, and cravings constitute the core of our dreams. These mental processes are ingrained in memory, but the vivacity and intensity of dreams are normally commensurate with the emotive depth of these memories. Nightmares reflect deep fears, emotional scars, and acute anxieties, while bizarre dreams arise from the random associations of memories that are strung together by the underlying emotions and feelings, which may or may not be acute.

It is evident that there are numerous factors behind the construct of dreams, and hence, logically, anything that diminishes the impact of these factors would definitely improve the quality of dreams. Surely, meditation is that instrument, which positively affects all those background factors. It is no wonder that the beneficent effect of meditation on dreams is more spectacular than on sleep.

The benefits of meditation such as emotional equilibrium, tranquility of mind as well as objective and empathetic perception would definitely reduce the multiplicity and severity of the emotional factors that cause dreams. A meditator gets embroiled in relatively much less incidence of intense feelings of fear, sorrow, anger, and bitterness. One normally encounters remarkably less mental conflicts in one's life.

Therefore, it is not surprising that after a few months of practice, meditators report more sound sleep and a marked decrease of dreams. Secondly, the nightmares and bizarre dreams come down gradually to zero. I have personally not experienced a single nightmare or disturbing dream for more than a decade. Thirdly, the story lines of dreams of experienced meditators are relatively more logical and lucid. The conversations and speeches in the dreams are much less weird; rather sometimes as eloquent as in the waking state. The incidents and reactions in the dreams betray milder emotional contents. The melodramatic dreams practically vanish in the life of an experienced meditator.

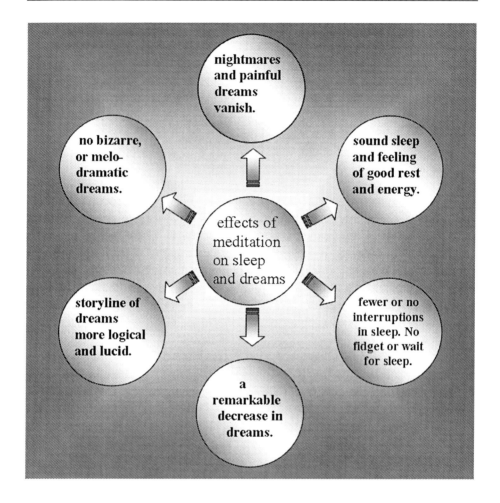

Figure 10.2. Impact of meditation on sleep and dreams.

The bizarre dreams reflect a lesser degree of intelligence and logic, while the melodramatic dreams and nightmares represent the predominance of intense emotions and feelings that have greater power to prevent influence of reason and intelligence.

I have often pondered over the possible reasons for the remarkably higher degree of rationality in the dreams of meditators. In my view, the positive difference is made by the enhanced level of nonverbal awareness in the dreams of an experienced meditator. A mediator's dreams are imbued with a higher degree of intelligence, which is the basic quality of inner awareness. As discussed earlier, meditation increases the percentage of alpha or theta rhythm in the brain, which is indicative of greater depth and prevalence of nonverbal awareness. In my view, that accounts for the relatively more rational quality of the story lines of dreams in the life of an experienced meditator.

What is the impact of meditation on lucid dreaming? Let me first explain what is lucid dreaming. It is a kind of dream when the individual becomes aware that he is dreaming. Such a state would be even more akin to the waking state. Given the fact that awareness percolates at a higher degree in a lucid dream, it has improved level of logical flow, undercutting the bizarre elements. Sometimes, the dreamer can give wishful direction to the story line of the lucid dream in order to have a happy ending or to reduce unpleasant feelings in the dream that may not be lucid to begin with.

Often an emotionally disturbing dream is transformed into a lucid dream by our mind in order to escape the mental pain and conflict. For instance, when a dreamer is about to die or get seriously wounded due to some reason in his dream, the brain gets deeply disturbed and turns the situation in its favor by taking control in the form of a lucid dream.

In my experience, meditation definitely enhances the undercurrent of nonverbal awareness and logic in dreams, which greatly reduces the bizarre elements. However, the random stringing of memories and associations continue to take place in dreams, which corroborates the view that dreams are caused by random evocation of neurons in the brain. However, the notable point in the case of a meditator is that the incidence of illogical bunching of memories gets reduced considerably. The most remarkable benefit of meditation is elimination of painful and fearful dreams because of emotional stability and strengthened undercurrent of inner awareness.

The quality of dreams of experienced meditators is quite similar to lucid dreaming as far as the higher degree of logic is involved, but the incidence of being aware that one is dreaming is absent. I would add that in my case, I have not experienced lucid dreams except on two or three occasions in my life, and that too before I learnt to meditate.

Though, some experts claim creative and even mystical benefits of lucid dreaming, I have no evidence to support it. The business of mystical benefits is often motivated, and one should be wary of that. I have no hesitation to reaffirm that a meditator normally enjoys very sound sleep. His dreams are devoid of melodramatic and bizarre elements and have very mild emotive contents. That is indeed a great boon one can have in the life that is beset with all kinds of challenges and uncertainties.

INDEX

A

adaptation, 53, 73, 83, 100, 149, 191, 205, 243
ADD. *See* attention deficit disorder
Advaita, 184
Ageless Body, Timeless Mind (Chopra), 219
Alzheimer's disease, 30, 31, 116
American Cancer Society. *See under* research institutions
amygdala. *See under* brain
anxiety, 12, 17, 25, 27, 29, 37, 39, 44, 49, 54, 56, 61, 65, 69, 75, 76, 85, 93, 97, 100, 107, 112, 115, 122, 127, 128, 131, 140, 141, 147, 154, 156, 160, 166, 173, 177, 181, 188, 192, 197, 198, 200, 206, 209, 213, 224, 226, 232, 236, 246
Archives of General Psychiatry, 232
Aristotelian catharsis, 32, 171, 178

Aserinsky, Eugene, 234
ashrama, 158
  brahmascharyashram, 158
  gruhasthashram, 158
  sanyasthashram, 159
  vanaprasthashram, 158
Astonishing Hypothesis, The (Crick), 52, 104
attention deficit disorder, 28, 30, 228, 239, 240, 244
autobiographical self, 42, 44, 47, 116, 181, 195, 202
awareness, 25, 86, 89, 105, 106, 108, 109, 113, 116, 124, 127, 129, 130, 175
awareness meditation, 27, 29, 31, 133, 140, 147, 153, 156, 158, 176, 181, 182, 187, 189, 195, 201, 205, 211, 213, 220, 227
  advantages, 169
  adverse effects, 203

251

antistress, 32, 211
instrument of inner inquiry, 156
mental process, 146
practical guidelines, 149
pranayam, 145, 146, 200
safeguards, 151
techniques, 141
awareness meditation postures
padmasan, 142
sukhasan, 142
vajrasan, 142

B

Baars, Bernard, 187
In the Theatre of Consciousness, 185
background feelings, 96, 177
Bayliss, William, 209
Benson, Herbert, 164, 182, 190, 192, 195, 242, 243
benzodiazepine, 209
Bhakti Yoga. *See under* Yoga
biorobotics, 204
Bohm, David, 60, 66
The Limits of Thought: Discussions, 66, 70
brain, 12, 15, 18, 20, 21, 22, 25, 28, 29, 30, 36, 40, 48, 52, 58, 61, 65, 73, 79, 90, 95, 96, 104, 111, 114, 120, 122, 126, 132, 137, 139, 147, 153, 156, 160, 166, 201, 206, 208, 209, 210, 214, 215, 216, 226, 229, 231, 234, 236, 237, 239, 240, 241, 242, 243, 249
amygdala, 85, 196, 217, 226
frontal lobe, 33, 41, 167, 177, 183, 188, 191, 198, 202
growth, 191, 193
hippocampus, 41, 85, 192, 226, 238, 241
hypothalamus, 85, 196, 217

limbic region, 31, 84, 183, 185, 187, 190, 195, 198, 202, 206, 210, 216, 220, 226, 229, 242
neocortex, 21, 25, 61, 63, 84, 85, 115, 169, 184, 189, 194, 202, 206, 219, 220, 236, 238, 241, 245
parietal lobe, 33, 167, 182, 188, 191, 198, 202
reptilian complex, 21, 84, 206
reticular formation, 187
rewiring, 30, 179
thalamus, 85, 105, 185, 193, 203, 217, 219, 221, 226, 227, 242
brain waves
alpha, 237
beta, 184, 237
delta, 237
theta, 151, 164, 195, 237, 238
breathing exercise. *See* awareness meditation:pranayama
Buddha, 157
Buddhism, 119, 123, 141, 157, 222
Buzsaki, Gyorgi, 242

C

Cabalism, 157
chakra philosophy, 212, 222
chakra system, 223
ajna chakra, 223
anahata chakra, 223
manipura chakra, 223
muladhara chakra, 224
sahasrara chakra, 223
swadhishthana chakra, 223
vishuddha chakra, 223
Chopra, Deepak, 164, 219
Ageless Body, Timeless Mind, 219
cognition, 41, 51, 66, 68, 112, 113, 194, 237, 243
cognitive theory, 105

Columbia-Presbyterian Heart Institute.
  See under research institutions
Columbia-Presbyterian Medical Center.
  See under research institutions
commercialism, 16, 29, 36, 77, 101, 126
competition, 15, 16, 83, 101, 149, 180, 187
conditioning, 12, 21, 25, 33, 44, 46, 97, 112, 120, 126, 131, 133, 161, 171, 177, 202, 205, 224
consciousness, 12, 20, 24, 29, 44, 46, 49, 56, 61, 66, 68, 69, 72, 80, 83, 89, 92, 96, 100, 103, 113, 120, 141, 147, 150, 159, 171, 174, 176, 183, 187, 212, 216, 224, 229, 242
  access, 12, 24, 25, 44, 95, 116, 124, 130, 133, 154, 189, 193, 196, 201
  and short-term momeory, 116
  global quality, 105, 114, 121, 123
  power of, 23, 95
  question of, 104
conscious experience, 81, 89, 120, 195
Cortico-Hippocampal Interplay and the Representation of Contexts in the Brain (Miller), 241
cortisol, 165, 184
counseling, 18, 132
Creation of Matter, The: The Universe from the Beginning to End (Fritzsch), 73
creative intelligence, 66, 67
Crick, Francis, 120, 121, 246
  The Astonishing Hypothesis, 52, 104
cytokines, 166, 184

D

Damasio, Antonio, 88, 90, 91
  The Feeling of What Happens: Body and the Making of Consciousness, 44, 79, 85, 195

Darwin, Charles
  The Origin of the Species, 83
Davidson, Richard, 166, 183
Davis, Adelle, 162
  Let's Eat Right to Keep Fit, 163
  Let's Get Well, 163
Dawkins, Richard
  The Selfish Gene, 52
depression, 16, 25, 27, 29, 39, 53, 56, 70, 76, 79, 81, 91, 93, 98, 103, 115, 117, 122, 124, 134, 139, 141, 149, 154, 160, 162, 166, 168, 179, 182, 184, 197, 206, 216, 226, 233, 236, 240
  treatment-resistant, 31, 225, 228
Descartes, Rene, 55
Desert Fathers, 157
DHEA (Dehydroepiandrosterone), 164
Dhyan, 158
Dimond, Stuart, 183
dispositional automation, 66
dispositional representation, 43, 66
Dragons of Eden, The: Speculations on the Evolution of Human Intelligence (Sagan), 21, 67, 83, 91
dreams
  lucid dreaming, 249
  and meditation, 249
drug-resistant epilepsy, 31
dualism, 176

E

Einstein, Albert, 16, 46, 60, 67, 71, 119
  "Truth and the Nature of Reality", 72
Eliot, T. S., 19
emotional equilibrium, 13, 24, 25, 29, 30, 164, 170, 181, 188, 189, 190, 199, 218, 227, 236, 247
emotions, 12, 18, 29, 32, 36, 44, 47, 54, 56, 60, 61, 74, 78, 86, 105, 109,

111, 121, 129, 134, 139, 147, 161, 167, 172, 177, 183, 187, 190, 202, 205, 211, 215, 228, 245
   as defense mechanisms, 88, 91
   fear, 16, 20, 32, 76, 80, 85, 86, 91, 93, 97, 113, 126, 144, 150, 160, 167, 168, 177, 183, 185, 195, 198, 205, 208, 214, 216, 219, 224, 235, 246
   versus thought, 82
emotive afflictions, 95, 173, 176
emotive preponderance, 195
ENS. *See* enteric nervous system
enteric nervous system, 32, 214, 217, 230
Enteric Nervous System, The
   A Second Brain (Gershon), 32, 209
EQ. *See under* intelligence
evolution, 12, 15, 16, 21, 32, 37, 46, 52, 58, 64, 67, 73, 76, 80, 83, 86, 99, 112, 126, 133, 149, 177, 180, 189, 191, 204, 205, 209, 233, 246
existential claustrophobia, 73

F

fatalism, 100
fear. *See under* emotions
feelings, 18, 23, 29, 33, 35, 41, 44, 45, 47, 59, 61, 63, 73, 85, 93, 103, 113, 119, 130, 139, 147, 158, 168, 183, 193, 194, 196, 202, 203, 214, 220, 228, 245
Feeling of What Happens, The
   Body and the Making of Consciousness (Damasio), 44, 79, 85, 195
fight-or-flight mode, 166, 167, 168, 183, 184, 206, 236, 243
Four Quartets (Eliot), 130
Freud, Sigmund, 24, 36, 111, 176, 244
"fringe", 121
Fritzsch, Harald
   The Creation of Matter: The Universe from the Beginning to End, 73
frontal lobe. *See under* brain

G

gatekeeper. *See* brain:thalamus
Geo, 210
George, Mark, 31, 225, 227
Gershon, Michael, 209, 215
   The Enteric Nervous System: A Second Brain, 32, 209
Glaser, Jay, 164
Goswami, Amit, 106
gut feeling. *See* intuitive action
gut's brain. *See* enteric nervous system

H

Harvard Medical School. *See under* research institutions
heart, 228
   myth, 229
Heisenberg, Harper
   Physics and Beyond: Encounters and Conversations, 73
Helicobacter pylori, 210
Hinduism, 119, 141, 156, 222, 224
hippocampus. *See under* brian
Holden, Jim, 243
hypothalamus. *See under* brain

I

individualism, 170
inner awareness, 25, 26, 32, 44, 46, 54, 90, 128, 130, 145, 146, 153, 169, 174, 181, 189, 190, 195, 201, 211, 215, 218, 224, 227, 248
inner consciousness, 25, 27, 44, 92, 95, 183, 192, 196, 201, 202, 204, 207, 214

inner peace, 140, 150, 160, 203
insomnia, 198, 232, 236
instant intelligent perception, 67
Institute of Theoretical Sciences. *See under* research institutions
intelligence, 24, 26, 27, 33, 38, 45, 51, 60, 61, 73, 77, 89, 90, 91, 100, 105, 110, 111, 117, 122, 134, 149, 173, 188, 192, 202, 205, 248
  and emotions, 90
  EQ (emotional intelligence), 91
  IQ (intelligence quotient), 91, 92, 194
intuitive action, 68, 69, 208
In the Theatre of Consciousness (Baars), 185
IQ. *See under* intelligence
irreducible subjectivity, 106

J

Jacobs, Gregg, 182
James, William, 103, 121, 124, 125, 189, 190, 196
  The Varieties of Religious Experience, 24
Jnana Yoga. *See under* Yoga
Jung, Carl, 24, 111

K

Kabat-Zinn, Jon, 166
Kleitman, Nathaniel, 234
Krishnamurti, Jiduu, 66, 70, 129, 133, 176, 193
  The Limits of Thought: Discussions, 66, 70
kundalini chakra. *See* chakra system: muladhara chakra
kundalini chakra. *See* chakra system: muladhara chakra
Kundalini Yoga. *See under* Yoga

L

Laukka (scientist), 239
Let's Eat Right to Keep Fit (Davis), 163
Let's Get Well (Davis), 163
limbic structure. *See* brain:limbic region
limbic system. *See* brain:limbic region
Limits of Thought, The: Discussions (Bohm, Krishnamurti), 66, 70
linguistic ability, 23, 37, 47, 57, 79, 91, 122
long-term potentiation (LTP), 238
lucid dreaming. *See under* dreams

M

mantra, 32
Max Planck Institute for Psychological Research. *See under* research institutions
McGinn, Colin
  The Problems of Consciousness, 106
McNaughton, Bruce, 238
Medical University of South Carolina. *See under* research institutions
meditation
  adverse effects, 202
  and children, 199
  antidepressant, 227
  antistress, 28, 156, 168, 183, 185, 190, 218, 227, 243
  effect on brain, 192
  impact on illness, 166
  neurology of, 167
  other benefits, 155, 160
  precautions, 139
  relaxation, 28, 151, 164, 184, 243
  scientific research, 28, 29, 133, 137, 139, 144, 146, 155, 158, 163, 165, 166, 167, 181, 183, 190, 199, 202, 219, 237, 240, 242, 243, *See also* research institutions

skepticism on, 29, 156, 181
meditative catharsis, 32, 171, 173, 214
memory, 13, 15, 19, 22, 23, 26, 27, 30, 35, 36, 37, 46, 55, 58, 69, 75, 76, 79, 84, 88, 93, 99, 103, 105, 112, 121, 122, 123, 127, 129, 131, 134, 147, 155, 169, 172, 183, 187, 190, 194, 195, 206, 226, 227, 235, 237, 242
associative nature, 47
catalyst of stress, 49, 226
long-term, 21, 28, 37, 38, 45, 48, 226, 238, 241
short-term, 38, 45, 109, 113, 116, 122, 176, 192
memory loss, 40, 45, 116
Menninger Clinic. *See under* research institutions
metacognition, 176
Miller, Robert, 241
Cortico-Hippocampal Interplay and the Representation of Contexts in the Brain, 241
Mitchison, Graeme, 246
mood-enhancing drugs, 227
dangers, 197
Muslim Sufis, 157

N

neocortex. *See under* brain
nervous plexus. *See* chakra system
neuroimaging, 41, 226
neurons, 36, 43, 52, 101, 104, 106, 117, 122, 147, 191, 193, 205, 209, 238, 241, 245, 249
neuropeptides, 209
neuroscience, 30, 105, 185, 211, 213, 215
Newberg, Andrew, 184
Newman, James, 187
nirvana, 119, 203
nondualism, 184

nonrapid eye movement (NREM), 234, 237, 238
nonverbal consciousness. *See* inner awareness

O

om, 200
Order out of Chaos (Prigogine, Stengers), 73
Origin of the Species, The (Darwin), 83
Oz, Mehmet, 166, 183

P

padmasan. *See under* awareness meditation
Para-Brahman. *See* Supreme Being
parietal lobe. *See under* brain
Penfield, Wilder, 187
Physics and Beyond: Encounters and Conversations (Heisenberg), 73
Prigogine, Ilya
Order out of Chaos, 73
pranayama. *See under* awareness meditation
Prinz, Wolfgang, 210
Problems of Consciousness, The (McGinn), 106
psychic predators, 21
psychological baggage, 33, 161, 168

Q

quantum self, 18, 132
Quechuas, 243

R

Raja Yoga. *See under* Yoga
Rama, Swami, 219
Ramdev, Swami, 146

Ramakrishna, 225
Ramana Maharsi, 225
rapid eye movement (REM), 151, 210, 234, 238, 244
reality, 56, 70
  perceptions of, 71
reality-out-there, 71, 72
reflex thoughts, 65, 126, 131
relaxation response, 243
replicators, 52, 83
research institutions
  American Cancer Society, 232
  Columbia-Presbyterian Heart Institute, 166, 183
  Columbia-Presbyterian Medical Center, 32, 167, 209
  Harvard Medical School, 164, 182
  Institute of Theoretical Sciences, 106
  Max Planck Institute for Psychological Research, 210
  Medical University of South Carolina, 31, 225
  Menninger Clinic, 219
  Rockefeller University, 238
  Rutgers University, 106
  San Diego School of Medicine, 232
  Stanford Psychosocial Treatment Laboratory, 166
  Umass Medical Center Stress Reduction Clinic, 166
  University of Arizona, 238
  University of California, Los Angeles, 164, 232
  University of California, San Diego, 242
  University of Cambridge, 246
  University of London, 210
  University of Otago Medical School, 241
  University of Oulu, 239
  University of Pennsylvania, 184
  University of Wisconsin, 183, 243
reticular formation. *See under* brain
Rigveda, 159
Rockefeller University. *See under* research institutions
Rutgers University. *See under* research institutions

S

Sagan, Carl
  The Dragons of Eden: Speculations on the Evolution of Human Intelligence, 21, 67, 83, 91
San Diego School of Medicine. *See under* research institutions
Sanskrit, 119, 158, 184
sarvangasan, 137
Schrödinger, Erwin, 119
second brain. *See* enteric nervous system
self, 12, 18, 19, 23, 26, 29, 36, 44, 46, 52, 54, 56, 106, 117, 119, 130, 140, 147, 150, 157, 159, 171, 181, 191, 202, 203, 204, 222
  architecture of, 118, 171, 181
  biological, 44, 45, 52, 117, 119
  psychological, 44, 45, 117, 132
  viewed as illusion, 52, 119, 123
self-hypnosis, 29, 140, 152
self-observation, 53
self-transcendence, 184, 203
Selfish Gene, The (Dawkins), 52
sensory traffic, 26, 32, 185, 186, 187, 190, 197, 203, 211, 217, 221
  regulation, 182, 218, 226, 227, 242
Sherpas, 243
Sikh meditators, 183, 190
silence of thought, 68
sirshasan, 137
sleep, 31, 50, 55, 81, 99, 107, 144, 152, 156, 164, 210, 228, 244, 248

sleeping pills, 233
Spiegel, David, 166
Stanford Psychosocial Treatment Laboratory. *See under* research institutions
Starling, Ernest, 209
Stengers, Isabelle
   Order out of Chaos, 73
stress, 12, 16, 23, 37, 44, 47, 49, 53, 56, 61, 65, 69, 70, 73, 76, 79, 81, 84, 91, 103, 107, 112, 115, 122, 124, 127, 133, 139, 140, 141, 144, 149, 154, 156, 160, 161, 162, 163, 165, 177, 179, 188, 190, 192, 197, 203, 206, 211, 213, 218, 221, 226, 231, 236
   aging, 163
   anatomy of, 94
   defined, 16
   management, 18, 37
subjective experience, 36, 46, 106, 118, 121, 124
subjectivity, 41, 45, 61, 74, 105, 113, 117, 187
supernatural powers, 29, 138, 140, 152, 166, 222
Supreme Being, 73, 119, 136, 159

T

Tagore, Rabindranath
   "Truth and the Nature of Reality", 72
thalamus. *See under* brain
theta wave activity. *See* theta wave rhythm
theta wave rhythm, 184, 195, 238, 240, 248
   and holistic perception, 241
   and meditation, 28, 242
thinking machine, 66
thought, 19, 22, 25, 33, 37, 41, 53
   as errand boy, 55
   characteristics, 61
   limits, 70
   thought-based solutions, 20
Time, 28, 134
traditional meditation, 28
   limits, 32
transcendental meditators, 164, 184, 242
Trendelenburg, Paul, 209
true self, 224
"Truth and the Nature of Reality" (Eisntein, Tagore), 72

U

Ultimate Being. *See* Supreme Being
Umass Medical Center Stress Reduction Clinic. *See under* research institutions
unconscious, 24, 45, 80, 95, 109, 126, 181, 187, 205, 220, 244, 246
unconscious mind. *See* unconscious
University of Arizona. *See under* research institutions
University of California, Los Angeles. *See under* research institutions
University of California, San Diego. *See under* research institutions
University of Cambridge. *See under* research institutions
University of London. *See under* research institutions
University of Otago Medical School. *See under* research institutions
University of Oulu. *See under* research institutions
University of Pennsylvania. *See under* research institutions
University of Wisconsin. *See under* research institutions, *See under* research institutions

V

vagal plexus, 213, 214, 215, 216, 218, 219, 220, 222, 224, 229, 230, 237
vagus nerve, 30, 210, 213, 216, 217, 226, 236
vagus nerve stimulation, 31, 225
"Vagus Nerve Stimulation: A New Tool for Brain Research and Therapy", 31, 225
vajrasan. *See under* awareness meditation
Varieties of Religious Experience, The (James), 24
Vedanta, 73, 141, 159, 225
Vedas, 159
vitamin B6, 162
vitamin B complex, 162
vitamin deficiencies
  and stress, 162
Vivekananda, Swami, 82, 133, 141, 225
VNS. *See* vagus nerve stimulation

W

Wallace, R. Keith, 164, 242
Whitman, Walt, 184
Wingate, David, 210
Winson, Jonathan, 238
Wordsworth, William, 129, 184
working memory. *See* memory:short-term
worry, 85, 97, 213

Y

Yoga, 157
  benefits, 135, 167
  Bhakti Yoga, 135
  commercialism of, 29
  Jnana Yoga, 135
  Kundalini Yoga, 135
  pitfalls, 135, 137, 138, 222
  Raja Yoga, 133, 135
Yoga-nindra, 152

Z

Zen meditation, 243

CPSIA information can be obtained at www.ICGtesting.com
Printed in the USA
LVOW102203270112

265901LV00002B/125/A